James A Wade, Adam Milne

History of St. Mary's Abbey, Melrose

James A Wade, Adam Milne

History of St. Mary's Abbey, Melrose

ISBN/EAN: 9783744689861

Printed in Europe, USA, Canada, Australia, Japan

Cover: Foto ©ninafisch / pixelio.de

More available books at **www.hansebooks.com**

HISTORY

OF

ST. MARY'S ABBEY, MELROSE,

THE MONASTERY OF OLD MELROSE,

AND

THE TOWN AND PARISH OF MELROSE.

BY

JAMES A. WADE.

WITH NUMEROUS ILLUSTRATIONS BY THE AUTHOR.

EDINBURGH:

THOMAS C. JACK, 92, PRINCES STREET,

LONDON: HAMILTON, ADAMS, AND CO.

MDCCCLXI.

PREFACE.

NOTHING seems more difficult to write than a Preface. But we shall be brief and explicit. We have studied to produce a work accessible to all classes of readers, as there appeared to us no royal road to direct the historian, antiquary, or tourist, through the endless mazes of enchantment, that lie deeply embosomed in every nook and corner of this classic land. Our aim has been to give increased information, in less than the accustomed space, and at a minimum cost; and to preserve dates of remarkable historical events and circumstances, in correctly classified and methodical order. It would be invidious to render thanks to some, where gratitude is due to all who have given us their kind assistance and valuable co-operation. We have laboriously consulted contemporaneous history, and endeavoured to build our structure upon the simple narration of facts, evidenced to us by truthful and impartial witnesses. There may be faults of omission and commission, perhaps, but these we shall only be too glad to correct in a future issue of this work. To float with the stream of time for upwards of a thousand years, and take up and set down those we chose to travel with, each at the proper offing and the right time, is a voyage of greater magnitude than some may contemplate. We have made free use of the writings and opinions of others, our end and aim being to conduct those who trust us by the best and easiest route, whether by the highway of those who have preceded us, or the byway of our own choosing.

If the footfalls of the following unassuming pages, leave just impressions on the minds of those who read them, and truth and goodness seem the lovelier in their historic robes, our wish and purpose will be magnanimously and happily accomplished.

It may interest some to know that the illustrations are all from drawings taken from the ruins.   No effort has been spared to make them accurate as well as artistically elaborate.

Ivy Cottage, Darnick, by Melrose,
August, 1861.

CONTENTS.

CONTENTS.

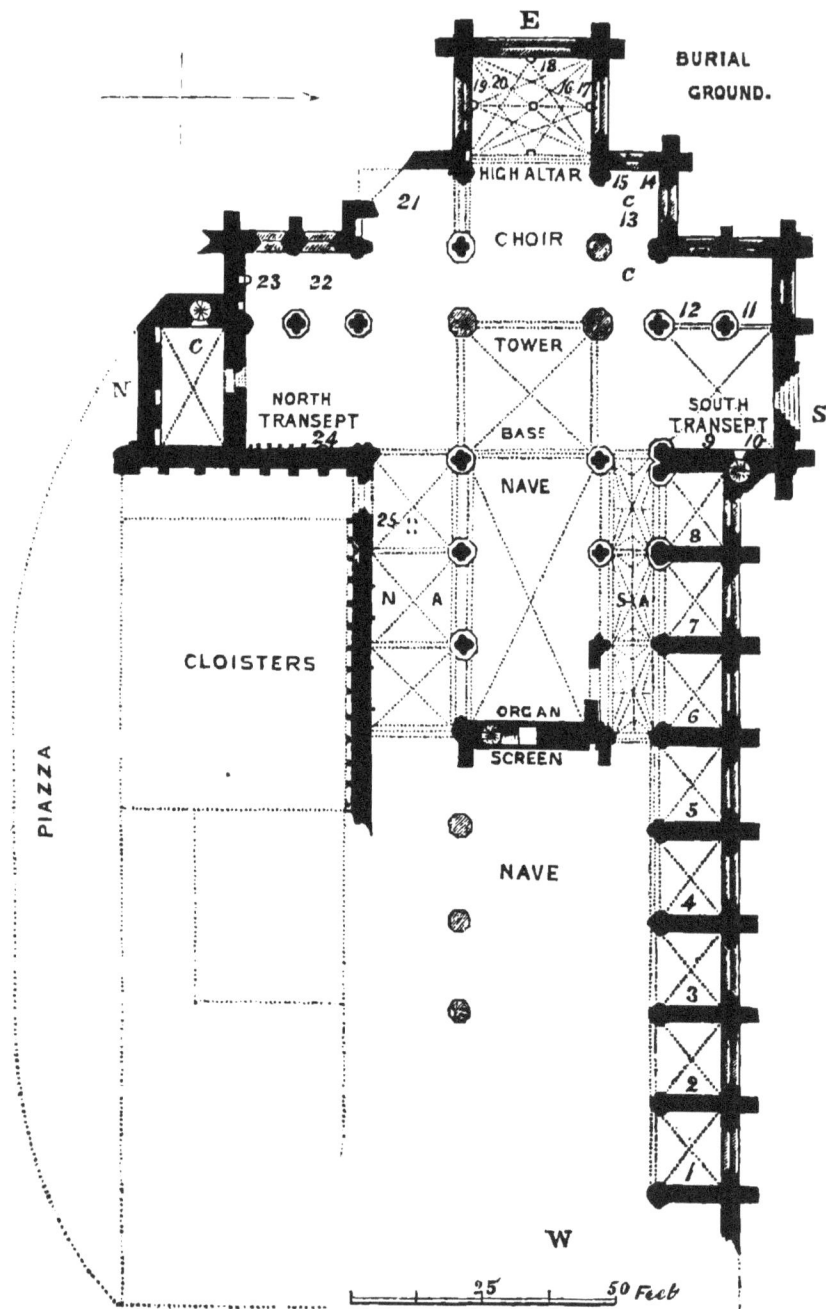

GROUND PLAN OF THE ABBEY.

Melrose Abbey.

ILLUSTRATION OF THE GROUND PLAN,

ENTERING ST. MARY'S ON THE WEST, AND CONTINUING TO THE RIGHT HAND.

W.   West or public entrance to the Abbey.

S.   South door, with its glorious window. What is now the churchyard was once the garden of of the Monastery.

E.   East window, called also "The 'Prentice Window."

N.   Entrance to Cloisters and religious houses.

C.   Eight Chapels facing south aisle, dedicated to saints in the Roman Calendar, also signifying Chapels in Transepts and Choir.

C.   Cellary, where the Sacramental Vessels were kept, and the Wax Tapers for lighting the Shrines of the Saints. The Cellarist was an important personage. It is now called the Wax Cellar.

S. A.   South Aisle of Nave.

N. A.   North Aisle of do.

DIMENSIONS.

Nave, due east and west, in its present condition.

258 feet long by 79 feet broad : height, east end, 50 feet.

Transept, due north and south, 130 feet long by 44 feet broad.

High Altar and Choir to line of Transept, 50 feet from the great east window.

Grand South Window, 24 feet by 16 broad.

East or 'Prentice Window, 36 feet by 16 broad.

Tower rising centrally between the Transepts, 84 feet high, west side only standing.

Chapel Windows, 16 feet by 8 broad.

—   Tombs partly concealed, inscribed with Saxon characters.

✚   Pillars still standing, supporting roof.

●   The pillars gone, indications where they stood.

.....   The dotted lines within the figure of the building show where the roof is still there, and the vacant spaces where it is gone.

Cloisters. These lay on the north side, of a quadrangular form also several other religious houses and offices, the whole surrounded by an arcade or piazza, all of which have disappeared.

No. 1. to 8. Chapels south side of Nave. See "Tombs."

9.   Door leading to the clock and on to the roof,

10.   John Mordo's inscription. See History of the Abbey.

11.   St. Bridget's Chapel and Statue still standing.

12.   Chapel.

13.   Chapel. 14. Tomb of Sir Brian Latoun rather than Michael Scott the Wizard. 15. Tomb of Sir Ralph Evers, " orate : : anima ivoors de corbirccg." Evers and Latoun fell at the battle of Ancrum Moor, 1545, and were buried at Melrose.

16.   Grave of Alexander II—curiously petrified gravestone.

17.   No memorial, but most probably the Tomb of some sainted personage.

18.   Rest of the heart of Robert the Bruce.

19, 20.   Wm. Douglas, "The Dark Knight of Liddesdale;" Douglas, hero of Otterbourne, or Chevy Chase, and an illustrious line of this heroic name, were interred on the north side of the Chancel.

21—23.   Chapels. 21. North-east end of chapel destroyed.

24.   Font at foot of Refectory or Abbot's Staircase.

25.   Inscription : " Here lyis the race of the house of Zair," (Yair). Opposite are the graves of this ancient family, Karr, Kar, Carre, Ker, Kerr, &c. of Kippelaw.

N.B.—Many of the numbers in the plan are referred to in the description of the abbey. The exterior of the abbey is illustrated, commencing at the extreme west end, near the entrance to the churchyard.

ORDER OF THE ILLUSTRATIONS.

Introduction.

——

S a suitable introduction to the following pages, some historical account of the Borders and Borderers will be interesting to the reader. The divisional line, between the south of Scotland and the north of England, was in ancient times an ideal one. The inhabitants of both sides were much alike, in manners and occupation. They spoke the same language, the Anglo-Danish dialect of the people who lived north and south of them. They were neither Scotch nor English, properly speaking, and the only name by whic they were known, was that of Borderers. After the Romans had left this part of Britain, the Borders became a sort of settlement and refuge for adventurers from many parts. Both English and Scotch, who could re-

B

main no longer in their own countries, on account of either treason or crime, occasionally cast in their lot among them. The Border population was an aggregate of all the races of men that had come into Britain ;— of Britons expelled by Anglo-Saxons ; of Saxons expelled by Normans ; and of Anglo-Normans or Scots, banished for theft and other crimes. The Scots were the men of the hills, and the Picts those of the plains, and were both united into one monarchy in the ninth century, by Kenneth II., when the country became known by the name of Scotland.

The Borderers divided themselves into families or clans, like the Celtic clans; the names of their clans, being for the most part English or French. Chief and vassal lived familiarly together; the one in his stronghold or tower, surrounded by a moat or pallisades, and the other in huts erected round about the former. The occupations of both were the same, all being thieves and marauders. They subsisted on mutton and beef, and stole with impunity sheep and cattle from the neighbouring plains. They armed with a long lance or spear, somewhat after the fashion of the Romans; their defensive armour consisting of a quilted doublet, to which were fastened plates of brass or iron. Their expeditions were frequently conducted on horseback. They owned no authority beyond the will of their chief. The kings, whether of England or Scotland, were simply regarded as foreigners. All were by turns Scots, when incursions were to be made into England for forage and plunder; and, in like manner, all were English, when a descent was to be made upon Scotland for the same object. They seldom quarrelled amongst themselves. Where they had power, they showed no mercy, either in robbery or violence. They sometimes, however, committed robberies professionally, observing some rules of honour, such as leaving their victims a portion of their food, furniture, clothing, and money. Following the fashion introduced by the Normans, the more rich and powerful assumed armorial bearings. Their arms denoted their manner of life and predatory habits. Those still worn by some families admit of easy interpretation. The field of the escutcheon is generally the sky, with stars and different phases of the moon upon it. And the mottoes, whether in English or Latin, are none the less significant. For example—"Sleep not, for I watch"—"Watch weel"—"Ye shall want ere I want," and such like. They dressed in brown heath-coloured clothes,

the more effectually to screen themselves from obser-
vation during their nocturnal visitations.

> " Right ready were they aye to aid
>   Their arming lords, when to the field
> They started on the moonlight raid,
>   To take what Border pastures yield ;
> And if they fell, as fall might they,
>   There always came a reck'ning day."

Thus, the ancient Borderers held an important intermediate position, as it were, between England and Scotland; and, in the several invasions of either, played
a selfish and mercenary part. The monarch who had
the largest force, and where probability of circumstances foreshadowed victory, where plunder and spoil
was to be the order of the day without reserve—to
his standards they flocked in vast numbers, became
the spies of the land they would desolate, and the
guides of invaders on their relentless mission. Nor
were they always faithful to the chief they thus allied
themselves to; treason sometimes oozed out in the
camp, often in the field, and still more frequently in
defeat or the apprehension of it.

Happily hostilities on both sides of the Borders
have now ceased, and the inhabitants dwell peacefully

united under the same crown   Places once the theatre
of war and conflagration, of deadly strife and murderous
forage, are now the scenes of peace and security, of
hospitality and common brotherhood.   The strongholds
of Border chiefs, and the massive castles of feudal
barons, lie in ruins on every hand.   The scenes of
carnage and misery are now redolent of pastoral wealth
and contentment.   The county of Roxburgh suffered
more severely than any other during the Border wars,
and the district of Melrose particularly so, being the
highway to the rich and fertile provinces of the kingdom.   The religious edifices were of great celebrity,
those of Melrose and Dryburgh being famed throughout
Europe.   The former surpassed in wealth and splendour all similar establishments then existing.   Its
domains equalled in extent the possessions of the most
powerful barons, and were by far the richest and best
cultivated in the kingdom.   Its occupants were not
only the instructors, but the spiritual guides of the
people, and the people almost to idolatry esteemed
them as such.   They were the indulgent masters of
numerous vassals, and the liberal and generous benefactors of the wayfaring stranger and the neighbouring poor.   Their monastic buildings were raised with

consummate skill, and became the chief architectural ornaments of the country. Their domestic offices combined all the requisites of civilized life, and every economic contrivance, with the greatest convenience. Their halls were the seats of splendid hospitality and great magnificence. Princes and nobles were their patrons and guests alternately, and the philosophers and minstrels of the age their favoured and welcome visitors. History presents no such reverse of fortune as that which befel the monasteries and their communities at the Reformation. In a few years, their wealth, their honours, their holy and beautiful houses, in which they and their fathers praised, were a wreck, a ruin, and a thing of the past.

The scenery of Melrose and the neighbourhood, with all the grandeur of monastic antiquity which it presents, is not less charming than instructive. We have said in the following chapters, that it is truly classic ground, for we know of none equally rich with the spoils of time, the gifts of the muses, and the glorious footprints of antiquity. Men of letters have long shown a remarkable predilection for this beautiful region. Here the amiable James Thomson, the expressive poet of the *Seasons*, drew his natal breath.

Thomson was born at Ednam, by the lovely river Eden,
and educated at Jedburgh. The historian of Queen
Anne, Dr Somerville, was for more than half a century
minister of Jedburgh, which was the birth-place of the
amiable and celebrated Mrs Mary Somerville. Near
Melrose, the late Sir Walter Scott erected the house
of his heart, and the chief romance of his ambition ;
here, too, his genius reached the highest pinnacle of
fame. In times more remote, the beautiful ballads
of Thomas the Rhymer, the laureate of his age, and
the prophet of the district, owed their magical influence and chief interest to the Eildon tree, Huntley-
burn, and the elfin spirits of the mountains and the
streams.

The immortal Burns sang to the "braw lads o' Gala
Water," and poured his seraphic minstrelsy to the shade
of "Thomson;" the pastoral poet. Hoy was a native
of Gattonside; and the rural lanes and winding woodland paths of both Gattonside and Abbotsford were
familiar to the steps of Miss Edgeworth and of Words-
worth. Sir David Brewster, who has reached a green
and honourable age, found a soothing retirement on
the murmuring banks of the Tweed, and pursued for
many long and arduous years a course of philosophical

study, attended by results so splendid, as to render
him one of the brightest ornaments of the age. This
distinguished philosopher is also a native of Jedburgh,
and a constant summer resident at his sylvan seat of
Allerly, near Melrose.

One of the galaxy of Border literati was Thomas
Pringle. Who has not read, with hallowed pensive-
ness of soul, "The Emigrant's Farewell?"

> " Our native land—our native vale,
>   A long and last adieu !
>   Farewell to bonny Teviotdale,
>   And Cheviot mountains blue."

The astronomer Veitch, whom to name is to eulogise,
was a resident at Inchbonny for several years. Captain Hamilton, the talented author of *Cyril Thorn-
ton*, occupied for many years Chiefswood Cottage, the
present residence of John Broad, Esq., which is a snug,
romantic, woodland spot, within fifteen minutes' walk
of Melrose. J. G. Lockhart, son-in-law of Scott, and
the brilliant editor of the *Quarterly Review*, passed
the summer months for several years at this delightful
place, previous to the death of Sir Walter Scott. Thomas Hannah, the astronomer, was born at Dryburgh ;

and Chaucer, the father of English poetry, spent some time at its famed monastery, in company with Ralph Strode, the Welsh savant, philosopher, preaching friar, and poet-laureate of Oxford.* It was also at Dryburgh that Thomson composed the first poem, "Winter," of his classical *Seasons.* Gower the poet was a monk of Dryburgh. G. P. R. James, the accomplished author of *Richelieu,* and other inimitable fictions, was for two years tenant of Maxpoffle, the present residence of John Boyd, Esq., and once the seat of John Ainslie, a gentleman of considerable literary acquirements.

William Laidlaw, the secretary and friend of Sir Walter Scott, lived for many years at Kaeside, close by Abbotsford. Thomas Aird, author of *Religious Characteristics,* and the writer of some admirable pieces of poetry, was a native of Bowden. Sir William Jardine, the gifted author of the *Naturalist's Library,* lived at Holmes, a few miles further down the Tweed than Melrose. The adventurous African traveller, Mungo Park, was a native of Foulshiels, whose dilapidated homestead stands almost fronting Newark Castle. Beneath the classic shades of Dryburgh, Sir David Erskine wooed well and long the lyric muse.

* Fabricius.

Truly was it said,—

> " Then haste with me where sweets combine
>   To form in sooth a scene divine,
>   And while away a summer hour
>   In Dryburgh's mild and classic bower."

James Hogg, the Ettrick shepherd, was familiarly known to many of the people of Melrose. He attended their fairs and markets during many long and pleasant years. Sir Walter Scott, Bart., was sheriff of Ettrick Forest. James Renwick, the last of Scottish martyrs, preached his final sermon on the banks of Yarrow. Thomas Boston was minister of Ettrick.* In the Forest Kirk, Sir William Wallace was chosen guardian of Scotland. Professor John Wilson drew the inspiring draughts which made magical his *Noctes Ambrosianæ*, from the vales of Yarrow, Ettrick, and Tweed. Dr John Leyden, the friend of Scott, the distinguished

---

* This good man says of his last communion, " There were nearly eight hundred communicants, great numbers of them from a considerable distance. The hospitality of the farmers, and all those who had it in their power to accommodate and support them, during the preaching days, was beyond all praise. At one farm-place they accommodated nine score, at another they had half a boll of meal baken, besides a quantity of loaf bread; they killed three lambs, and made up thirty beds." These were certainly the " times of refreshing," and we should rejoice to witness a revival of the same spirit that seemed in those days to animate both preachers and hearers.

scholar, poet, and linguist, wrote his touching and impassioned *Scenes of Infancy* from the bosom of the people and country we are writing about. Dr Leyden was a native of Denholm, and a public testimonial to his memory is now in course of erection upon his native village green. Dr Chalmers was once assistant minister of Cavers. The Rev. James Morton, author of the *Monastic Annals of Teviotdale*, was born at Kelso. We shall, for the present, content ourselves by maintaining that Melrose and its vicinity is classic ground. The entire district, for some miles around, is truly fascinating in its fine diversity of form and character, its heath-crowned summits, and its sheltered vales. It is transcendently famous in song and fiction, unequalled in its historical associations and traditions. To heroic patriotism and heaven-born piety it has been ever, and is still held, truly sacred. Its sons wear the mantle of an enlightened and universal emancipation, adorned by friendship, love, and truth. Correctly, then, do we call Melrose and the district classic ground.

Chapter First.

HE following description or account of the parish of Melrose was written by the Rev. Adam Milne, minister of the Established Church of Scotland. He settled at Melrose in 1711, and officiated until 1747, when he died. His only child was a daughter, who married Mr Hunter of Linthill. His history of Melrose was first printed in 1743, by T. W. and T. Ruddimans, Edinburgh, and passed through two or three editions. It is given verbatim, and *in extenso*, without the least alteration, in the following pages, which commend themselves as being at once truthful, carefully collated, and accurately described:—

A DESCRIPTION OF THE PARISH OF MELROSE,

IN ANSWER TO

MR MAITLAND'S QUERIES TO EACH PARISH OF THE KINGDOM.

The Parish of Melrose, in the Shire of Roxburgh and

Presbytery of Selkirk, is in breadth from South to North, about eight or nine miles, in length from East to West in some places about four. It is divided by the river Tweed: it is bounded by the Parish of Galashiels on the West, on this side of Tweed, and on the other side of Tweed by the Water of Galla, which falls into Tweed a little below Westerlonglee; on the North-west by the Parish of Stow, on the North by Lawder; on the East by the Water of Lawder or Leeder, which falls into Tweed a little below Dry-grange; and by the River of Tweed on the East and South-east; and on the South by the Parish of Les-suden, or rather Lesaidan, and the Parish of Bowdean or rather Bethendean.   •

About a mile and a half from the Town of Melrose to the east, stands Old Melrose, or Mailross, or rather Mulross, signifying a bare Promontory;* for Ross, in the ancient Language, signifieth a Peninsula, and Mul, bare. It is almost encompassed with Tweed, famous for its ancient Monastery as one among the first seats of the Kingdom, of the Religious Keledei, or Culdei, or as Fordun explains the name, Cultores Dei, Wor-shippers of God, though Toland says they were so named from the original Irish, or ancient Scottish Word Ceilede, signifying separated or espoused to God; and Nicholson, Bishop of Derry says, they were so named

---

* IRVINE'S *Nom.*, p. 161.

from the Black Habit, for Culdee, says he, signifies a black Monk.* But whatever this signifies, they were religious persons who admitted of nothing but what is contained in the Scriptures, the Writings of the Prophets, Apostles and Evangelists, and as Bede observes of them, were diligent observers of the Works of Piety and Charity, which they had learned out of the Prophetick and Apostolick Writings, wherein they maintained themselves a long time against the Canons and Ordinances of the Romish Councils, so much pressed upon them by the Disciples and Proselytes of that See.

We have no account by whom this Monastery was founded, it is likely by Columbus or by Aidan, who are said to have built so many Monasteries in other Places. It is probable it was founded about the End of the sixth Century; Bede gives us an account of its Situation on the Bank of the river Tweed† and likewise of its Abbots. 1st, Eata. Boisil succeeded him; Dempster says he died anno 643, and to him St Cuthbert (who afterwards quitted the Monastery and went to Lindisfarne, now called the Holy Island), and to him Ethelwold. This place was a famous Nursery for learned and religious Men, who were filled with zeal for propagating the Christian Religion, particularly among their Neighbours the Pagan Saxons.

* Preface to the *Irish Historical Library*, p. 30.
† BEDE, lib. 4, cap. 27.

Nennius, a British Historian, who lived, as some, in the year 620, or rather, as the Bishop of Carlisle places him, anno 853.* He speaks of the noble and great Monastery of Melrose, cap. 63, which was ruined likely then after the destruction of the Churches and Monasteries by the Pagan Danes,† who burnt the Churches and Houses wherever they came. 'Tis probable this Monastery was repaired and continued till the other was founded by King David.

This Convent has been inclosed with a stone wall reaching from the South Corner of the Tweed to the West Corner of it, where the Neck of Land is narrow, the Foundations of the Wall are yet still to be seen. At the entrance to the Convent about the Middle of this Wall, there has been an House built, likely for their Porters, called yet the Redhouse. The place where the Chapel stood is still called the Chapel-know, and Places on Tweed at this Place still retain their names from the Monks there, as the Haly-wheel and the Monk-ford. I do not think there has been any great building about it, for, as Bede acquaints us, their Churches then were all of Oak and thatched with Reeds. The Situation of the Place is most pleasant and agreeable, being almost surrounded with Tweed and having a fine Prospect towards Gladswood.

* *Eng. Histor. Libr.*, folio, p. 33.
† DALRYMPLE'S *Collections*, p. 57.

About a mile to the West on the Tweed, stands Newstead, a Place noted for an ancient Lodge of Masons, but more remarkable for another Abbacy on the East-side of it, called Red Abbey-stead. Whether it got this name from the colour of the stones wherewith it was built; or because it was an House belonging to the Templars, they wearing a red Cross for their distinguishing Badge, I cannot determine; but it is certain, when the Ground here is plowed or ditched, the foundations of several Houses are discovered, a great deal of Lead got, and some curious Seals.

At this Place likewise there has been a famous Bridge over Tweed; the Entrance to it on the Southside is very evident, and a great deal of fine stones are dug out of the Arches of the Bridge when the water is low. About half a mile fron Newstead on the South side of Tweed, stands the present Melrose. There was a great Wood betwixt these foresaid places, planted with Oaks, beginning at Ekidean, or rather Oakdean, and is still called the Prior-wood; and on the Highroad to Melrose, there was a famous Cross, called the Prior-wood cross.

It is surrounded with Mountains, as Jerusalem of old; it is about four miles distant from Selkirk to the West, eight from Jedburgh to the South, and eight from Kelso to the East. It is famous for its Monastery, the Fabrick of which was very large and spacious, as

C

appears from the Ruins of it yet remaining, and one of the most magnificent and stately in the Kingdom, and continues still to be the admiration of Strangers, who for the Height and embellishing of its Pillars with all kind of Sculpture, the Beauty of its Stones, and Symmetry of its Parts, do reckon it one of the best of the Gothick kind they have seen.

There was a new erection of an Abbacy at this Place, and not a reviving of the ancient Monastery of Old Melrose. It was founded by King David anno 1136, according to these Monkish Verses:—

> Anno milleno centeno, ter quoque deno,
> Et sexto Christi, Melrose, fundata fuisti.

It was dedicate to the Virgin Mary, as appears by the original Charter of Foundation, bearing the Grant to be, " Deo and Sanctæ Mariæ de Mailross and Monachis, ibidem Deo servientibus de Rievallis," &c., and so of the Cistertian Order.* The Chronicle of Mailross acquaints us, that it was dedicate anno 1146, ten years after its Foundation. The Church is built in the Form of St. John's Cross; the Chancel, which is a very stately building, is still standing, its Roof is very curious, and has much of the Scripture History upon it, and its Window a fine piece of Architecture, wherein has been a great Variety of baken Glass and painted Glass, which sometimes have been dug out of

* DALRYMP., *Coll.*, p. 257.

the Ground.   Our History bears, that King Alexander
II. was buried here at the High Altar, with this Inscription on his Tomb:—

> Ecclesiæ clypeus, pax plebis, dux miserorum,
> Rex rectus, rigidus, sapiens, consultus, honestus;
> Rex pius, rex fortis, rex optimus, rex opulentus,
>   Nominis istius ipse secundus erat.
> Annis ter denis et quintis rex fuit ipse,
> Insula quæ Carneri dicitur hunc rapuit,
> Spiritus alta petit, cœlestibus associatus,
>   Sed Melrossensis ossa sepulta tenet.

But there appears no such Tomb or Inscription here:
There is indeed a fine Marble Stone in the Form of a
Coffin, without any Inscription, which I think has been
laid on Waldevus, the second Abbot, who was canoni-
zed; for the Chronicle of Melrosse acquaints us, that
Ingeram Bishop of Glasgow and four Abbots came to
Melrose, and opened his grave twelve Years after his
Death, and found not the least Corruption about his
holy Body, upon which they laid a fine new polished
Marble stone, and this was done with great Joy, all
crying out, " Vere hic homo Dei est."

Many of the Earls of Douglas were likewise buried
here, as Earl William and his heroick Son James, who
was killed at the Battle of Otterburn, August 5, anno
1388, fought betwixt him and Sir Henry Percy, surnamed Hotspur, afterwards Earl of Northumberland.
He was interr'd with a military Pomp of the whole

Army, and all the Honour that could be devised for him besides, by the Abbot and Monks of that Convent, after the most solemn Manners of these Times.* As also the Lord of Liddisdale, called the Flower of Chivalry, and many others of great Note, such as the De Valoniis, Vausses of Dirlton, Somervils, Balfours, and others; some of them are said by the Book of Melrose to be buried in " capitulo ecclesiæ," *i. e.*, in the Chapter-house. This is all the Account I can give, the Obituary of this Monastery being destroyed.

Within, on the North side of the Cross, there are beautiful Pillars, and the Sculpture as fresh as if it had been but newly cut. Here is a Place called the Wax-Cellar; where they kept their Tapers and Candles for burning at the Altars and Shrines of their Saints, especially at the Altar of St. Mary and St. Waldave. Above this Wax-Cellar there was lately discovered a curious Vault; there was no Entry into it but by lifting up the first Step of the Turnpike, which certainly had been contrived for concealing their valuable things, in case of an invasion by the English, which they frequently felt and were threatened with: It had no Light but at this Entry. This famous Turnpike was only demolished about six Years ago. The Abbot had a fine House, adjoining to the Church here, with an Entry to the Church by a Stair, the Remains of

* HUME's *Hist. of Douglasses*, p. 105.

which are to be seen, with a Font at the Foot of it. On the West side of the Cross there is the Statue of Peter with a Book open, his Right Hand on it, and two Keys hanging on the Left; and then to the South side of this Statue is that of Paul with a sword. In the middle of the Cross stood the Steeple, a Piece of notable Architecture; a Quarter of it is yet standing, but the Spire is gone. The Bells here could not but have a fine and melodious Sound from the Hills and Water.

The Roof of the South-side of the Cross is still standing, one of the Key Stones has on it I. H. S. *i.e.*, Jesus Hominum Salvator. There is a beautiful Turnpike here, which is much admired by Strangers, the Roof of it winding like a Snail Cap. Above the Door of this, there is a Compass with this Inscription:—

Sa gayes the Compass ev'n about,
So Truth and Laute do but doubt,
Behald to the End. JOHN MURDO.

On the South-side of this Door there is another:—

JOHN MURDO sum tym callit was I,
And born in Parysse certainly;
And had in kepying all Mason Werk,
Of Santandroys the hye Kyrk,
Of Glasgu, Melros and Paslay,
Of Nyddysdayl and of Galway,
Pray to God, and Mari baith,
And sweet St. John keep this haly Kirk frae Skaith.

There are within the Church a vast Number of

Fonts curiously carved, where they had their Altars dedicate to such and such a Saint, and several Gentlemen mortified a certain Annuity, called Altarage Money, for the maintenance of a fit and qualified Person to say so many Masses at such an Altar, for their own Souls, and the Souls of their Ancestors and Successors. I have observed above some of these Altars a Pulley, on which there was a little Bell, to be rung at the Elevation of the Host, or for hanging Lamps.

In the Place where the Congregation meets for divine Worship, there are two Rows of Pillars of excellent Workmanship, especially that to the South-east, which for the Fineness of it looks like Flanders Lace. The Roof of this Place of the Church was put on anno 1618, by the Masons of Newstead, a Place famous for several Centuries for Masonry, though this Roof bears no Resemblance to the former.

On the South-side of the Church there is a fine Monument, erected for Mr David Fletcher, who had been Minister of this Congregation for several Years, and after King Charles II. his Restoration, was made Bishop of Argyle. This Monument was erected by his Son Mr William Fletcher, an eminent Lawyer.

On the West-side of this, within the Church, is the Burial place of the Pringles of Galashiels, where the Portraiture of Sir James Pringle is to be seen as big as the life.

On the West-side of this is the Burial place of the Pringles of Whitebank, the undoubted Male Representatives of the ancient Family of Galashiels. It appears by the Gravestones here, that they have matched with very honourable Families, as with the Lundins of that Ilk, with the Homes of Wedderburn, and one of them with Sophia Shoner, a Dane, Maid of Honour to Queen Anne of Denmark.

On the North-side of the Church within, at the Entry called the Valley-gate, is the Burial-place of the Kers of Yair, since of Sutherland-hall, where their Arms are to be seen on the Wall, viz., A Stag's Head raised on a Cheveron, three Stars, with this Inscription below,

Here lies the Race of the House of Zair.

Having given a lame Description of what is remarkable within the Church, we shall take notice of what is observable without. And to begin with the East Window, which is the Head of the Cross, where the High Altar was: This is a beautiful Structure. consisting of four Pillars or Bars, with a great deal of curious Work betwixt the Pillars for the Support of them. On each side of the Window, there are a great Number of Niches for Statues, and on the Head of it an old Man with a Globe in his Left Hand resting on his knee, and a young Man on his Right, both in a sitting Posture, with an open Crown over their Heads.

It has been a current Tradition in this Place, that it has been a Representation of the Trinity, and that there had been betwixt them the shape of a Dove, as an Emblem of the Holy Ghost; but I see not any Foundation for this Conjecture, for there is not the least Vestige of a Dove here: it appears rather to be a Statue of King David, the Founder of this Church, and his Queen, or his Son Prince Henry. On the North-side of this Window and South, there are two great Windows, with three Bars almost as high as the former, but not so broad.

The Niches are curiously carved, both the Pedestals and Canopies, and on the Canopies are to be observed several Creatures, cut curiously in Miniature, and under some of the Statues and Pillars, are the Figures of Men cut, some with their Legs cross, and others leaning on one Knee, putting back one of their hands to support their Burdens, the Muscles of their Neck standing out as crushed with the Pressure, and gaping with their Mouths.

On the South-east of this Church are a great many Musicians admirably cut, with much Pleasantness and Gaiety in their Countenance, with their Instruments in their hands, such as the Bag-pipe, after the Highland Fashion, Fiddles, Dulcimers, Organs, and the like; as also several Nuns with their Vails, and others richly dress'd.

On the South Entry there is a Window very much admired for its Height and curious Workmanship; there are Niches on each side of it and above, where have been the Statues of our Saviour and the Apostles. On the Head of the Door is a Lion rampant, within a double Tressure, and above this John the Baptist, looking up with one eye, with this Inscription, "Ecce filius Dei." Below John are the Statues of his Disciples, which are now sadly defaced.

On the East of this Window there is a Niche, having a Monk for the Supporter of the Statue, holding a Bend with each Hand about his Breast; on the Bend is written, "Passus, e. q. ipse voluit," *i.e.* Passus est quia ipse voluit. The Monks are curiously cut, with their Beards and Cowls, some of them holding a String of Beads in their hands.

On the West side of this Window, there is another Monk with a Bend about his Breast, on which is written, "Cu. venit Jes. seq. cessabit umbra," *i.e.* Cum venit Jesus, sequitur, cessabit umbra. To the West of this there is a Cripple, on the back of one that is Blind; this is very much admired by the curious: on one side of the blind's Beard is Uncte, and on the other Dei, by way of Petition, that Christ might have Mercy on them. There are a great many Niches in this Place, and several Creatures cut very nicely, as Boars, Greyhounds, Lions, Monkies, and others.

To the West of this Window there are eight still remaining entire, with the Face of a Man or Woman on
each side, some of them in a very antick Figure, after
the Gothick Way. Above is the Statue of St. Andrew
to be seen with a Piece of his Cross, and to the West
of this the Statue of the Virgin Mary, holding the Babe
in her Left Arm: this Niche excells all for its fine
Sculpture and Drapery. Below, at one of the Windows
are the Arms of the Hunters, there being several of
that name Abbots here, namely, Two hunting Horns
string'd, two Crosiers, as the Badge of his Office, crossing other in Saltier, or in the Form of a St. Andrew's
Cross, and a Rose at the Top betwixt the Crosiers; the
Arms supported by two Mermaids, and below R. H.
On the West of these are the Arms of the Abbacy,
namely, a Mail and a Rose, a perfect pun, it having no
Relation to the antient Name Mul-ross. To the West
of these are the Scots Arms which have been set up
there in King James IV.'s Time, for on the one side
above is an I, and on the other side a Q, and below
Anno. Dom. 1505, two Years after his Marriage, which
was concerted here betwixt the said King and Richard
Fox, Bishop of Durham, and eight before the fatal
Battle of Flouden. Above the Arms are I.H.S. *i.e.*
Jesus hominum salvator.

There are about sixty-eight Niches standing, the
Statues were only demolished about the year 1649, by

whose authority I know not. There is a traditional
Story here, that the Person that was employed to de-
molish them, while he was striking at the Babe in the
Virgin Mary's Arms, a Piece of that stone fell on his
Arm, which he never had the use of afterwards.

The Cloyster has been on the North-side of the
Church, a Part of the Wall is still remaining, where
may be observed their pleasant Walks and Seats, and a
great deal of fine Flowers nicely cut, as Lilies, Ferns,
Grapes, House Leeks, and the like, as also Escalops,
and Fir-seed and others. There is a Font at the North
Entry to the Church, and the Door curiously embossed,
and the Foliage here, and in several Places of the Church
very curious.

There has been a Gallery through the whole Church,
with Ballisters before, where one may walk safely.
The ingenious Mr Slezer gives us a good Draught of
this Church in his Theatre of Scotland. I have taken
the Measure of what is standing, though much of the
West Part is so entirely demolished, that we cannot
know how far it has reached that Way, and the principal Entry has been to the West. Its just Length is
258 feet, its Breadth 137 feet and an half, its circumference round about is 943; the Day-light of the South
Window, or its Height, 24, the Breadth with four Bars
16; the Day-light of the East Window, its Height, 36
feet, with four Bars; the Breadth of the East Window

16 feet; the Height of the Steeple from its Foundation 75 feet, the Spire being gone.

I am now to give an account at what Time, and by whom much of it has been laid in Ruins. It was several Times defaced by the English, lying near the Borders, particularly by Edward II., anno 1322. This was in his second Attempt in Scotland, when, after he had come the Length of Edinburgh, he was forced to return, to his great Dishonour, without having effectuated any thing, but only the spoiling and burning the Abbeys of Melrose and Dryburgh, and killing many of the Monks;* for the repairing of which, King Robert the Bruce makes a Grant to the Abbot and Religious of Melrose of two thousand Pounds Sterling, for building of new the Fabrick of their Church of St. Mary, to be paid out of all Wards, Relieves, Marriages, Escheats, Fines, Amerciaments, Exits, and Perquisites, belonging and falling to the Crown out of the Shire of Roxburgh; The Date is at Scone, on the 29th of March, anno 1326.† This was a great Sum in these Times, but we are to observe, that there were some forfaulted who had large Possessions about this Place, such as Sir John Sowles, to whom belonged the Lands of Nisbet, the Baronies of Langnewton, Maxton and Caverton, as also Sir Richard Moubray, to whom belonged the

---

* BUCHANAN, lib. 8, p. 265.
† SYMSON's *Hist. of Stuarts,* p. 151.

Lands of Eckford. John Major in his sixth Book
acquaints us, that Richard II., King of England, burnt
this Monastery, and at the same time Edinburgh, Newbottle, and Dryburgh. It was likewise demolished,
a great Part of it, after K. James the Fifth's Death,
during the Regency of the Earl of Arran, when Sir
Ralph Ivers and Sir Bryan Laton, under Henry VIII.
of England, had taken Charter of the Merse and Teviotdale to be holden of the King of England, and came to
take Sasine and Possession, which when Archibald the
seventh Earl of Angus heard, he vowed that he should
write the Instrument with sharp Pens and red Ink
upon their own Skins, because they had defaced the
Tombs of his Ancestors at Melrose,* which he performed at Ancrum Muir, about five Miles South from
Melrose, or Lilliard's Edge, as it is commonly called,
from a Woman that fought with great Bravery there,
to whose Memory there was a Monument erected in the
Field of Battle, with this Inscription, as the traditional
Report goes:—

> Fair Maiden LILLIARD lies under this Stane,
> Little was her Stature, but great her Fame,
> On the English Lads she laid many Thumps,
> And when her Legs were off, she fought upon her Stumps.

I have seen the Monument, which is now all broken
in Pieces, but the Place of Battle not being within the

---

* HUME'S *Hist. Doug.*, p. 269. CRAWF. *Notes on Buchanan*, p. 144.

Parish of Melrose, I forbear to give any further account about it; a Battle, says Mr Crawford, for the valour of so few against so many, the Wisdom in taking the Advantages, and a most noble Victory, worthy to be more famous than it is. After the Reformation, anno 1569, it was fully defaced, as Lesly acquaints us, lib. 10, p. 527, says he, "Monasteria Dumfermlingense, Melrossense, Kelsoum, miseris modis sectarii vestabant." And it seems probable, that many of the Houses within the Convent have been ruined by Fire, from the Lead and burnt Timber that is to be found in several places.

After the Reformation, James Douglas, Commendator, did take down a great Part of it, for the building of a fine House for himself, which is still standing, and his Name and his Lady's on one of the Windows, anno 1590. As much of it has been demolished lately for building a Tolbooth, for the repairing their Mills and helping their Sluices; the People here have a superstitious Conceit, that the Baillies who give Orders for the pulling down of any Part of it do not long continue in their Office; and of this they give many Instances, as in the Commendator and others, though the same that make this remark have no Scruple to take these Stones for their own Houses.

I am now to give an account of some of the Abbots and Monks of this Place, that were distinguished for their Piety, Learning, and Offices. I have not seen the Chartulary. The Monks here were Cistertians, so named from their chief House and first Monasteries, Citeaux or Cistertium in Burgundy. They were brought here from Rievalle, an Abbey in Yorkshire; Richard the first Abbot was install'd in the year 1136, being the same year on which it was founded by King David. To him succeeded Walterus or Waldevus, Son to King David; for besides Prince Henry, by most authors mentioned as the only child of King David, we have good authority to believe that he had a second Son, named Waldevus, whom the Chronicle of Melrose calls Uncle to King Malcome IV.* This person was elected Bishop of St. Andrew's, but declin'd that Honour, saying that he had washed his Feet, and could not contaminate them again with the Dust of earthly Cares.† He is said by Fordun to have wrought many Miracles, and is now ranked among the Saints of the Roman Church. Many Offerings were made at the Tomb of the said Waldeve, as appears by Sir John Stuart of Bonkyll his Charter granted to the said Abbacy.‡ Joceline, a Man of considerable Learning, was Abbot here, and afterwards Bishop of Glasgow; he was buried here, and a great Benefactor to the Abbey.

* ABERCROMBY's *Martial Achievements*, p. 404, vol. i.
† SPOTISWOOD's *Hist.*, p. 36.
‡ SYMSON's *Hist. of Stuarts*, p. 61.

Laurentius is said to have been a Person of great Meekness, and a learned Divine.

Another was Rodulph, anno 1194, a Person of great Learning, whom Pope Innocent III.'s Legate, had such a Regard for, that he took him along with him to Ireland and made him Bishop of Down.* This Legate staid in Melrose fifty days, and was honourably entertained by the Convent, as Mr Hay acquaints us in his Scotia Sacra. He came to make up a Difference betwixt the Monks of Calchow and the Monks of Melrose; he took their Money and Gold, and left the Plea undetermined. I find in the year 1268, that the Abbot and a great Part of the Convent were excommunicated in a Council at Perth, for breaking the Peace with the Men of Wedale, for killing a Clergyman there, and leaving several wounded. I find this Convent has had a great many Debates with those of Wedale about their Marches. Wedale is Stow, and the Places about called Vallis Doloris. This belonged to the Bishop of St. Andrews.

I find one Patrick Abbe de Meaross, as it is exprest in the Ragman Roll, swearing Fealty to Edward I., anno 1206.†

Robert of Kildalach, formerly a Monk and Abbot of Dunfermline, Chancellor of Scotland, was made Abbot

* Spotis. *Hist.*, lib. ii., p. 41.
† Prynne, p. 653.

of this Place. John Fogo, Abbot also of this Monastery, was Confessor to King James I., and much taken notice of for his Learning. Boethius and Lesly say he was a Professor of Divinity, and Spotiswood, that he disputed with great Force against Friar Harding.* And the same Historians acquaint us, that he was the principal Man that confuted Paul Craw the Bohemian. Andrew Hunter, Abbot of this Place, was Confessor to King James II., and Lord High Treasurer, anno 1449. Mr Crawford, in his Lives and Characters of the Officers of the Crown and of the State, thinks he was either of the House of Powmood or Hunterstone; but I think he was of the Hunters of Hag-burn in this Parish, a Family of a very long standing; for besides him, there were some others of that Name Abbots here.

After him were some of the Name of Dury and Fogo's. Lesley says, lib. 10, that James Stuart, eldest natural Son to King James V., was Abbot of Kelso and Melrose; he died in the year 1559.† After him Cardinal de Guise was named Abbot by Mary of Lorrain, Queen Dowager, but never got Possession thereof. I find some of them have been employed in several

---

* SPOTIS., p. 56.

† It may be a doubt, whether this Abbot of Melrose, or his other natural Son of the same Name, were eldest, since by the Order in which Dr Mackenzie has placed them, in his Lives and Characters of the Scottish Writers, vol. ii., p. 595, it would seem the Earl of Murray was the eldest.

D

honourable Embassies to the Pope and Kings of England, and Members at their General Councils.

The Monastery of Melrose was a Mother Church or Nursery to all the Order of Cistertians in Scotland, such as Glenluce or Vallis Lucis in Galloway: the Monks of that Monastery were brought from Melrose, and kept a close correspondence with the Abbots and Monks here, as appears by that famous letter William Abbot of Glenluce writes to the Abbot of Melrose about an appearance in the Heavens;* Newbottle in Mid-lothian, Kinloss in Murray, Coupar in Angus, Balmerinoch in Fife, and others. It would appear that the Abbot of Melrose had a vote in the Election of the Abbots of these Monasteries; for Ferrerius, a Native of Piedmont, the Continuer of Boethius's History, and Author of the Register of Kinloss, in the History of the Abbots of that Place, acquaints us that the Abbots of that Place, " Canonicè eligebantur per Monachorum suffragia, et patris Abbatis a Melross electionem, simul et confirmationem." Machline in Kyle, a District in the Shire of Air, was a Cell of Melrose, founded as some say, by King David I., but it rather appears, that it was the Stuarts who founded Machline, and bestowed it on Melrose.

The Monks of this Abbacy wrote a Chronicle, called the Chronicle of Melrose, of which we have several

---

* Vid. *Chron. de Mailross*, p. 192.

Manuscript Copies, both in Scotland and England.
It begins anno 735, and is continued by several
Hands down to the Year 1270. The Bishop of Carlisle hath placed this Chronicle in his English as
well as in the Scottish Historical Library, the Subjects of both having had a hand in the composure of
it: And since, in the first Part, it chiefly insists
upon the Affairs of that Kingdom, and is a Continu-
ation of Bede's History, these Collections must be supposed to have been made when Melrose was in the
Hands of the English. The second Part appears to
have been written by the Abbot or Prior of Dundrennan in Galloway, a Nursery under Melrose, a great
Favourite of Walter Great Steward of Scotland. The
learned Dr Gale published this Chronicle at the Theatre
of Oxford in the Year 1684. It is observed by some
that this printed Chronicle is not so full and exact as
to our Scots affairs as the Manuscript Copies we have
of it; and Dr Jamieson has observed, that if any of
these Manuscripts were to be published, it should be
with three different Sorts of Notes and Observations.*

This famous Abbacy was endued with large Revenues and many immunities, as appears by the Charters
granted to the Abbot and Convent by our Kings. It
was the favourite Abbacy of David I., the Founder of

---

* See the Appendix to Dr NICOLSON's *Scots Historical Library*,
Num. iii.

it, as Mr Innes observes in a Manuscript he had seen in the Colbertine Library, giving an Account of the several religious Houses built by the said David; it is added, " Sed Melrossensem præcipue inter omnes ecclesias et fideliter defensabat, et dulciter diligebat, et suis opibus exornabat." Mr Hay says, 'tis recorded in the Book of Taxes of the Apostolic Chamber, that King David bestowed on this Abbacy 1880 Florins. The original Charter of Foundation is confirmed by his Son Prince Henry, and bears that he gave to this Abbacy the whole Lands of Melrose, Eldun of Dernewie,* Galtownside, Galtownside-haugh, and Galtownside-wood, and many Privileges in the Forests of Selkirk and Traquair, particularly betwixt Galla and Leeder. The Charter also bears, that these Lands had been perambulate by the King himself and the Prince, with Richard the first Abbot. The Date of this Charter is the second Year after Stephen of Boloign, King of England, was taken Prisoner, which must be in the Year 1143. The Witnesses are Hugo de Moreville, William de Somerville, Gervasius Riddel, and others.

And it is said that King William, sirnamed the Lyon, after his Return from England, "abbatiam magnifice datavit." Alexander II., though the Dominicans were his favourite Order, he gives to this Abbacy the Forest of Ettrick. Robert the Bruce did enrich it with many

* Eildon and Darnick.

Donations. The Stuarts, both before their Accession to the Throne and afterwards, have been the greatest Benefactors to it, as appears from Mr Symson's Genealogical and Historical Account of the illustrious Name of Stuart.

There were likewise many Donations granted to it by our Nobles, Gentlemen, and Bishops of Glasgow. I find from the Chronicle of Mailross, that Richardus de Moreville, High Constable of Scotland, gives Park to to this Abbey; Dunbar, Earl of March, gives a Grant also of many lands in the Merse and East Lothian; Hugh Gifford, Lord Yester, grants the Monklands of Yester; and William, first Earl of Douglas, grants likewise the Patronage of the Church of Cavers to this Abbacy; Riddel of Riddel, Haig of Bemerside, and many others. I have had no access to see the Chartulary: those Accounts I have glean'd from some of our Historians, which are well attested.

From the Rent of the whole great Church Benefices within the Kingdom, as they were given up at the general Assumption, 1561: ABBACY OF MELROSE:—

In Money, 1758 L.
    Wheat, 14 Chalders, 9 Bolls.
    Bear, 56 Chalders, 5 Bolls.
    Meal, 78 Chalders, 13 Bolls, 1 Firlot.
    Aittes, 44 Chalders, 10 Bolls.
    Capons, 84.
    Poultry, 620.

Butter, 105 Stone.

Salt, paid out of Prestonpans, 8 Chalders.

Peats, 340 Loads.

Carriages, 500.

The temporal Lands thereof; the Lands of Melrosland, Kyllesmuir, and Barmuir; for they had a great many Lands in Kyle and Carrick, the Monkland in Cliddesdale, and the Monkland in Niddisdale, called Dunscoir.

Kirks belonging thereto; the Kirk of Cavers, the Right of the Patronage of this was granted by James Douglas, Commendator, to the Family of Cavers; the Kirks of Hassendean, of Wester-Ker, Dunscoir, Ochiltree, and Machline.

This account differs from what Mr Keith gives us in his Collections. It is said, out of this Rent, assignation is made to eleven Monks and three Portioners, it is likely to those who had renounced Popery, 20 Merks to each, item Wheat 4 Bolls, Bear 1 Chalder, Meal 2 Chalders. The Dean of the Chapter, called John Watson, comply'd with the Reformation. Mr Kay, in his Scotia Sacra,* gives us a further account of the rich allowances that were granted to this Abbey. I shall give it in his own Words:

"In charta visitationis 1542 invenio, monachos ibi fuisse 100; anno 1520, 80; anno 1540, 70. et 60 conversos, quibus dabantur modia frumenti, annuatim 60.

_____
* _Scotia Sacra_, p. 542, in Bibl. I Ct., Edinb.

cervisiæ dolia 300, ad missaram solemnia vini dolia 18,
ad hospites suspiciendos dolia vini 20; cervisiae 40,
frumenti modia 30, infirmis nutriendis 4000 Lib. Tu-
ron tonsori Lib. 400." He adds, " Porro Monasterium
omnium erat in Scotia pulcherrimum atque opulentissi-
mum."

After the Reformation, I find by the bounding
Charter of Newstead, one Michael Commendator, anno
1564. After this a Grant was made of this Abbey
with all the Lands and Tythes thereto belonging, by
Queen Mary, to James Earl of Bothwel and Duke of
Orkney, who was forfeited for Treason. James Douglas, second Son of William Douglas of Lochleven, afterwards Earl of Morton, was advanced to be Commendator of Melrose, by whose Care and Industry all the
original Evidences were preserved, and are still extant
in the Custody, as I am inform'd, of the Earl of Morton.
After this, a Grant was made of it to Sir John Ramsay,
in consideration of his good Services in rescuing King
James VI. from the attempt of the Earl of Gowry and
his Brother at Perth, who was created Viscount of
Haddington, and afterwards was made a Peer of England
by the Title of Earl of Hulderness. In the Preamble of
this Grant, and ratified by Parliament anno 1609, we
have a full account of Gowry's Conspiracy, and it
appears by it, that James Douglas the former Commendator, had a handsome allowance during his Life, which

'tis probable he disponed to Mr John Hamilton ; for I find by the Grant afterwards made to Thomas, Earl of Melrose, he purchases a Demission from Mr John Hamilton, Commendator of Melrose, for demitting the said Abbey.

When this Abbacy was erected in a temporal Lordship, in favour of Ramsay, Viscount of Haddington, a great many Lands that belonged to the Abbacy are excepted and given to others; such as the Tenantry of Dumfidling, Wester-Ker or Wester-Kirk to the Earl of Morton; to the Lord Lowdon, the Lands and Barony of Kylesmure and Barmure, and the Parish-kirk of Mauchline ; to Sir James Hay of Fingask, Comptroller, Grange and Grangemure in the Constabulary of Haddington ; to the Lord Ochiltree, the Kirk of Ochiltree, and the Tiends of the Parish thereof.

It was afterwards acquired by Sir Thomas Hamilton, employ'd by King James VI., in several honourable Offices, or, as others, that he got a gift of it, as he did likewise of the rich Nunnery of Coldstream in favour of his third Son, Sir John Hamilton of Trabrown, by the Influence of his Brother-in-law, the Earl of Somerset, the great but unfortunate Favourite of King James VI., and he was dignified with the Title of the Earl of Melrose anno 1619, upon which he assumed three Roses into his Arms. This he exchanged afterwards for the Title of Haddington. 'Tis storied that he was a little hard

and severe on his vassals and Feuars here, which gave
occasion to that Epitaph made by Mr Thomas Forrester,
Minister here:

> Here lies one, who, while he stood,
> Was matchless if he had been ———.
> This Epitaph's a Syllable short,
> Which if you please you may add to't ;
> But what that syllable doth import,
> That noble Peer could never do't.

But whatever he was to his vassals, it must be
owned that all his successors were extremely kind to
them, of which they still retain a grateful sense. In
the Grant that is made to the Earl of Melrose, a great
many Lands are likewise excepted and given to others,
or their holding altered. To Walter, Earl of Buccleugh,
the Kirk of Hassendean, Hassendean Tower, alias
Monks Tower; many of the Monks, besides those who
attended on the Kirks of Cavers and Hassendean, residing there; Ringwood, with its Steadings, Cauld-
cleugh, Northhouse, Braidhaugh, Cralleshope, Cortburgh,
Sudanrig, Westcortrig, Priesthaugh, Eskdale-muir, and
others. To the Earl of Wigton, Kingildores: and
granted to Sir Gideon Murray of Elibank, that the
Barony of Longshaw shall hold of the King; as also to
William Douglas Feuar of Cavers, that the Five Merk
Lands, called the Kirklands of Cavers, shall hold of the
King, and the Kirk of Ettrick to Sir Walter Scott of

Thirlestain. To whom the Monk-lands of Nithisdale, called Dunscoir was given, I can have no information.

It has lately been purchased by the Duchess of Buccleugh, whose Predecessors were heritable bailies, before the Reformation, of this Burgh of Regality, for which they had several Lands in the Parish, as the Superiority of Appletreeleaves, the lands in Darnick, called since the Laird's lands, and, while designed of Murdiston and Ranelburn, were very kind to the Abbacy.*

There were several Lands depending on this Abbacy, lately sold off to Mr Baillie of Jerviswood, such as the Barony of Longshaw and Blainslies in this Parish, that belonged to the Regality, & Redpath and Park in the Parish of Earlstone. The several Places that hold on it at this time, paying a certain Feu-duty, are the whole Parish of Melrose, the Barony of Longshaw and Blainslies excepted; the whole Parish of Lessuden, and,

Belonging to the Duke of Roxburgh, the Lands of Salfat, Tron, Cocklaw, Capelrodick, Evenshaw, Brossness, Sourhope, Rashaw, Gateshaw, Hownamgrange, Southcote, Cliftone-cote, Mill of Hownamgrange.

The Marquis of Tweeddale for Monkland at Yester.

To Lord Belhaven, the Lands of Easter, Wester, and Middle Hartsides, Milnhaugh of Newgrange.

* CRAWFORD'S *Peerage*, p. 52.

To Lord David Hay, Penshiels, Priesthall, Kingside.

To the Laird of Roughlie, Frierdykes, Wintershiels.

To the Laird of Drumelzier, Littlehope, Micklehope, Langhope, Hope Cartone, Whitehope, Chapelhope.

To Sir Walter Riddel, Cringils.

To Sir William Scot of Thirlestain, Ramseycleugh, Scabbiecleugh, Kirkhope, Craigie, Craigiehill.

To Archibald Douglas of Cavers, a Five Merk Land called the Kirk-land of Cavers, viz., the Three Merk Land of Crook, a Merk Land in Whitrig called the Hussie, and a Merk Land in Cavers called the Boag.

To Mr Ker of Littledean, Plewland.

To Mr Ker, Morrieston.

To the Laird of Whitslaid, Ettrickhouse, Shorthope.

To Sir William Menzies of Gladstanes, Wolfclyde.

To Sir William Purves, Pittlesheugh.

To Alexander Pringle of Whitebank, Friarscroft.

To Charles Balfour of Broadmeadows, Glenkerrie, Midgehope.

To George Douglas, Friarshaw.

To George Mason, Clerklees.

To Walter Williamson of Cardrona, Espinghope, Brockhope, Landhope.

To John Haliburton, Muirhouselaw.

To Robert Scott of Horsliehill, Monkscroft in Hassendean.

To the Laird of Hairhope, Hairhope.

To Mr Francis Scott, Phaup.

To Mr Scott of Burnhead, a Merk land in Hassendean, half Merk Land in Clarilaw.

To Mr Ogilvie of Hartwoodmires, Hornhole, Calford.

To Mr John Watson, Overmains.

To Mr John Scot, a Merk Land in Hassendean.

To the Laird of Stonefauld, Harelaw, East End of Hassendean.

To George Rutherford of Fairnington, Monksclose and Meadow.

To Thomas Inglis, a Tenement of Land and half Croft in Selkirk.

To George Fairbairn, a Tenement and half Croft in Selkirk.

To William Turnbul, the Clerk Croft in Hassendean.

To Alexander Hume, an acre in Hassendean.

James Corsar, for his lands in Hessington.

I am now to give an account of the Ministers that have been here since the Reformation anno 1560. I find by the Acts of our first assemblies, that Mr Pont was appointed to preach here, how long he continued, and whether he was settled in the place, I cannot determine. The next was Mr John Knox, a Nephew of Mr Knox the Reformer. He continued here for a considerable Time, and died only anno 1623, as appears by his Gravestone.

To him succeeded Mr Thomas Forrester, one that

was taken notice of for his facetious Poetry and satyrick
Verses. He was deposed by the assembly at Glasgow
anno 1638, and, as Honorius Regius acquaints us,
" classe Mulrossiana accusante, probatum fuit," that he
had publickly declared, that any servile Work might
be done on the Lord's Day, and as an Example to the
People, he brought home his Corn out of the Fields to
his Barn-yard on that Day, as also that he had said,
that the Publick and ordinary Preaching of the Word
was no necessary Part of Divine Worship, that the
reading of the Liturgy was to be preferr'd to it; that
Pastors and private Christians should use no other
Prayers but what were prescrib'd in the Liturgy.
They charge him likewise with Arminianism and
Popery; and that he said publickly, that the Reformers
had done more harm to the Christian Churches, than
the Popes of Rome had done for ten Ages. I am
surprized that no Notice is taken of his Litany, which
made a great Noise in these Times: Bishop Guthry in
his Memoirs only mentions it;

> " From Dickson, Henderson and Cant,
>   Th' Apostles of the Covenant,
>   Good Lord deliver us."

I hae been at great Pains to find out this Litany in
the Libraries of the curious, but in vain. There was
an old gentlewoman here, who remembered some Parts
of it, such as,

> " From the Jesuit Knave in grain,
> And from the She Priest crack'd in Brain,
> From her and a' such bad Lasses,
> And a' bald ignorant asses,
> Such as John Ross, that donnard Goose,
> And Dan Duncanson that duncy Ghost,
>   Good Lord deliver us."

For the understanding of this Part of the Litany, we are to observe that there was one Abernethy, who from a Jesuite Priest turn'd a zealous Presbyterian, and was settled Minister at Hownam in Teviotdale; he said the Liturgy of Scotland was sent to Rome to some Cardinals, to be revised by them, and that Signior Con had shewed it to himself there: He is the Jesuite. And as to the She Priest, this was one Mrs Mitchelson, who was look'd upon as a Person inspir'd of God, and her Words were recited as Oracles, not a few taking them from her Mouth in Characters. Most of her Speeches were about the Covenant:*

> " From Lay Lads in Pulpit prattling,
> Twice a Day rambling and rattling,"

And concludes his Litany—

> " From all the knock-down Race of Knoxes,
>   Good Lord deliver us."

'Tis said that he made that Epitaph on the Earl of Strafford, which is in Cleveland's Poems, and that Mr Cleveland acknowledged that he was the Author of it.

* Burnet's *Mem. of the Dukes of Hamilton*, p. 83.

The witty Turns in it are much of a piece with other Performances of his which I have heard of. The Epitaph is,—

> " Here lies wise and valiant Dust,
> Huddled up 'twixt fit and just;
> Strafford, who was hurried hence,
> 'Twixt Reason and Convenience.
> He spent his Time here in a Mist,
> A Papist, yet a Calvinist;
> His Prince's nearest Joy and Grief,
> He had, yet wanted all Relief,
> The Prop and Ruin of the State,
> The People's violent Love and Hate,
> One in Extremes, lov'd and abhorr'd,
> Riddles lie here, and in a Word,
> Here lies Blood, and let it lie.
> Speechless still, and never cry. "

To Mr Forrester succeeded Mr Alexander Scot, who was admitted Minister here, anno 1640, and died the same Year. To him succeeded Mr David Fletcher. Before the Year 1638 he had been second Minister at St. Cuthbert's or the West-kirk at Edinburgh; he was then zealous for Episcopacy, as appears by the Information that he and others sent by one Learmonth to the Archbishop of St. Andrews, then at London.* When he came to Melrose he was as zealous for Presbytery, and after the Restoration of King Charles II. anno 1662 he was made Bishop of Argyle by the Influence of his Brother Sir John Fletcher the King's

* BURNET'S *Mem.*, p. 41.

Advocate. It was in his Time that the Statues were demolished: He died anno 1665 as appears by his Tomb. To him succeeded Mr Alexander Bisset, who had been transported from Tyningham to this Place, and died anno 1689. To him succeeded Mr Robert Wilson, who was settled here anno 1690, and died anno 1713. He was succeeded by Mr Adam Milne, who was admitted anno 1711, and died June 8, 1747.

There were also here a vast many fine Buildings within the Convent, for the Residence and Service of the Abbot and Monks, with Gardens and other Conveniences, all this inclosed within an high Wall about a Mile in Circuit. Besides the High Church, there has been a large fine Chapel, where the Manse now is, and another House adjoining to it, where the Foundations of the Pillars are still to be seen. On the North side of this House, there has been a curious Oratory or private Chapel, the foundations of which have been discovered this Year, and a large Cistern of one Stone, with a leaden Pipe conveying the Water to it.

To the North of this there have been several Bridges over the Dam, which runs from Tweed this way, the Foundations of which are yet to be seen, and two of them entire, many of their Houses being built on the North-side of the Dam.

At a Place called the Bakehouse Yard, near the Mill, was an Oven of excellent Architecture, with several Stories of Ovens above others, as high as the Steeple in the Church, and built with as fine hewn Stone; this was taken down about 36 Years ago. In ditching this Bakehouse-yard about six years ago, there was found a large Kettle for brewing, sold at L.5 Sterling. From the Bakehouse there was a common Sewer or Drain, to several Places of the Convent, so high and large that two or three may walk easily abreast under it. In ditching any Place within the Convent, particularly near the Church, the Foundations of Houses have been discovered. Not only the Monks had their Houses here, but several Gentlemen that retir'd from the World built for themselves convenient Lodgings; the Ruins of one of these is only to be seen, called Chisholm's Tower.

The Town without the Convent, named now Melrose, was anciently called Little Fordell. It has the Privilege of a Burgh of Regality, a weekly Market on Saturday, not much frequented, four Fairs in the Year, one on Martinmas, another on Lammas, one on the last Wednesday of May, another on the Thursday before Easter. This, in the Time of Popery, was their great Fair, called Skeir Thursday, or Schier, pure, holy. There is a Corporation of the Weavers here within the Regality, established by a Charter, which they call the Seal of Cause, granted by John Earl of Haddington anno 1668, containing many Privileges,

E

Freedoms, and Immunities. They choose their Deacon and Boxmaster annually at Michaelmas. This Corporation have a fine Seat in the Church, with their Arms and Motto, viz., " Non vi, sed virtute conamur."

Several Roman Medals or Coins have been found about this Place, some of Gold, some of Silver, and some of Brass, as of Vespasian, Trajan, Hadrian, Antoninus Pius, M. Aurelius and Constantine; as also several of the old English Coins in Silver, particularly of the Edwards, and on the Reverse the Names of several Cities in England and Ireland, as, Civitas London, Lincoln, Dublin, Waterford, &c., and likewise several of our own Coins, as of Robert Bruce and his Son David, &c.

There have been several consecrated Wells about this Place; whether they have been frequented as Medicinal, I know not, such as St. Helen's, St. Robert's, Duddingston or rather St. Dunstan's. Dunstan's and Eldun Wells are still made use of by the Country People as a sovereign Remedy against Cholicks.

A little to the South of Melrose, there is a small Village, called Dingleton, or Daniels-town; there is a Place here called the Locked Well, and several Springs about it, from whence Water was brought into the Monastery by Leaden Pipes. A little to the South-west of Dingleton there was a famous Cross, yet called the Crosshillhead, but anciently the Halesing of St.

Wada; for these that came from the South had first a
View of the Church here and of the Tomb of St.
Waldave, and bowed and said their Ave.

To the South of Daniel-town there are three remarkable Hills, called Eldon or Hildon Hills, *i. e.*, high
Hills, which afford a fine Prospect to all the Country
about, Merse, Northumberland, Teviotdale, and For-
rest. The Root of these Hills will be in Compass six
or seven Miles, the Height of two of them to the North
about a Mile and an half. On the Top of the North-
east Hill are plain vestiges of a Roman Camp, being
well fortified with two Fosses and Dikes of Earth,
more than a Mile and a-half in Circuit, with a large
Plain near the Top of the Hill called the Floors. On
the Head of the Hill may be seen the Prætorium, or
the General's Quarter, surrounded with many Huts.
There are Ports from this Camp to the East, the West
to the North, from a Place called the Haxrecrag a
plain Way to Melrose, called the Stile-Dyke. The
principal Entry to the Camp has been from the South
towards Bethendean, where the Ground slopeth more
easily, from a Place near the South Hill called the
Castlesteed.

It has all the Properties of a well-chosen Camp,
according to the Rules Vegetius has given for a Camp.
It has a large Prospect of all the Countries lying upon
each Side of it. It hath many Springs of good Water

near it; the Sides of the Hill have been covered with
Wood, and the Camp is of that Extent, that neither
Man, Beasts, nor Baggage, could be pinched for want
of Room.

On the North-side of the middle Hill, near the Foot
of it, there is a Place called Bourjo, where I think the
Druids have offered their Sacrifices, and performed
their superstitious Rites in this Grove to Jupiter, it
being all planted with Oak. The Bower has been surrounded with a deep Trench, and a plain Way made to
it from the East and to the West. From this Camp
there is a large Ditch, or Rampier for two Miles to the
West, reaching to another Camp on the Top of Cald-
shiel Hill. This Camp has been strongly fortified,
with a double Trench, and the Circumvallations of it
continue for a good Way.

This Camp, with that in Darnwick Ground, called
Castlesteed, make almost a Triangle, with the large
Camp on Eldonhill, and I think these two have been
castra exploratorum, or the Out-guards.

To the South-east of Eldonhills, are two Villages,
Newtown and Hildon. There are several Feuers in the
Newtown of an old Standing, such as the Milns, Veres
and Stenhouses; the Writs of the latter I have seen
of ancient Date. There has been a military Way
here, which may be traced a great way to the South
and to the North.

To the South-west of these Hills there has been a beautiful Military Way, raised in some Places high above the
Ground, and of a considerable Breadth, in some Places
military Stations upon it, as at Kippilaw. It runs
through Halidun Park, and in some Places is carried
through Lakes and Marshes. It has had a Communication with the Camp in Caldshiels, and likewise with
another Camp on the other Side of Tweed called the
Rink.

About a Mile to the West of Melrose, on the South
of Tweed, is Darnwick or Dernewie. In the High road
to this Place there has been another remarkable Cross,
called the High Cross. In this Place there are two old
Towers, belonging to the Fishers and Hytons, Names
of an old standing, and a Place there called the Skinner
Hill, but properly the Skirmishhill, from the Battle
that was fought there July 18th, anno 1526, the occasion of which was that King James V. frequently com-
plaining to his Friends, particularly to the Earl of Lennox, of the Restraint he was under while he was in the
Earl of Angus's Hands, Lennox advised him to employ the Laird of Buccleugh to relieve him, for he was
a most powerful Man upon the Borders, and had an
inveterate Hatred against the Earl of Angus. Buccleugh being advertised of this privately, encourages
the Borderers to commit great Disorders, on purpose
to bring the King in Person there to rectify them.

The Design took, and the King, to do Justice, accompanied with the Earls of Angus and Lennox, Lords Hutñe, Fleming, and Erskine, with Cessford, Farniehirst and others, came to Jedburgh.

It was concerted that Buccleugh, who dwelt within a little of Jedburgh, should invite the King to his House, and·retain him there till more were come to his assistance; but that Plot fail'd, and the King was brought back to Melrose, as Buchanan expresses it. However, Buccleugh resolved to prosecute what he intended. He assembled about 1000 Horse of his Friends and Dependents, and as the King was on his Way to pass the Bridge on Tweed, about half a mile from the Field of Battle, they perceived a Body of armed Men coming down Halidon Hill, which being come within Distance of discerning, were known to be commanded by the Laird of Buccleugh. The Earl of Angus immediately dispatches an Herald, to know what their Intentions were, and commanding them to withdraw out of the Way. The Laird of Buccleugh's answer was, that he came to do the King Service, to invite him to his House, or, as others say, that he knew the King's mind as well as he, and would not go away till he saw him, nor obey any but his Prince. Upon this the Earl of Angus presently alighted from his Horse, and gave Orders that those that were with him should do so and fight on foot. The first onset was given by Buccleugh and his Men with mighty Fury, and a great Shout, and the Battle for a while was very fierce, as being in the Presence of the King, who was a Beholder, and was to be the Rewarder of the Victor. At last Buccleugh being wounded, his whole Company turned their Backs, there being fourscore of them slain; and a great many were kill'd upon the Earl of Angus's Side, particularly Andrew Ker of Cessford. Hereupon began deadly Feuds betwixt the Kers and Scots, and continued divers Years after, and several Murders and Slaughters followed upon it, amongst which was the Slaughter of Sir Walter Scot himself in Edinburgh.

There is extant an Indenture betwixt the Kers and Scots, made at Ancrum 16th March, 1529, which, for the Curiosity of it, I have thought fit here to insert.

"Thir Indentures, made at Ancrum the 16th March, 1529 Years, contains, proports, and bears liel and suithfast Witnessing, That it is appointed, agreed and finally accorded betwixt honourable Men, that is to say, Walter Ker of Cessford, Andrew Ker of Fairniehirst, Mark Ker of Dolphinston, George Ker, Tutor of Cessford, and Andrew Ker of Primesideloch, for themselves, Kin, Friends, Mentennants, Assisters, Allies, Adherents, and Partakers, on the one Part; and Walter Scot of Branxholm, Knight, Robert Scot of Allanhaugh, Robert Scot, Tutor of Howpaisly, John Scot of Roberton, and Walter Scot of Stirkshaws, for themselves, their

Kin, Friends, Mentennants, Servants, Assisters, and
Adherents, on the other Part, in manner, Form and
Effect as after follows, For staunching of all Discord
and Variance betwixt them, and for furthbearing of the
King's Authority, and punishing Trespasses, and for
amending all Slaughters, Heritages and Steedings, and
all other Pleas concerning thereto, either of these
Parties to others, and for Unite Friendship and Concord to be had in Time coming 'twixt them, of our
Sovereign Lord's special Command: That is to say,
Either of the said Parties, by the Tenor hereof, remits
and forgives to others the Rancour, Hatred and Malice
of their Hearts; and the said Walter Scot of Branxholm shall gang, or cause gang, at the Will of the
Party, to the four Head pilgrimages of Scotland, and
shall say a Mass for the Souls of umquhile Andrew
Ker of Cessford, and them that were slain in his Company in the Field of Melrose, and upon his Expence
shall cause a Chaplain say a Mass daily, when he is
disposed, in what Place the said Walter Ker and his
Friends pleases, for the Weil of the said Souls, for the
Space of five Years next to come: Mark Ker of Dolphinston, Andrew Ker of Graden, shall gang at the
Will of the Party to the four Head pilgrimages of
Scotland, and shall gar say a Mass for the Souls of
umquhile James Scot of Eskirk, and other Scots their
Friends slain in the Field of Melrose, and upon their

Expence shall gar a Chaplain say a Mass daily, when
he is disposed, for the Heal of their Souls, where the
said Walter Scot and his Friends pleases, for the Space
of three Years next to come: And the said Walter Scot
of Branxholm shall marry his Son and Heir upon one
of the said Walter Ker his Sisters; he paying therefore
a competent Portion to the said Walter Ker and his
Heir, at the Sight of the Friends of baith Parties. And
also, baith the said Parties bind and oblige them, be
the Faith and Truth of their Bodies, that they abide at
the Decree and Deliverance of the six Men chosen
Arbiters, anent all other Matters, Quarrels, Actions and
Debates, whilk either of them likes to propone against
others betwixt the said Parties: And also the six
Arbiters are bound and obliged to decreet and deliver
and give forth their Deliverance thereuntil, within
Year and Day after the Date hereof. And attour either
of the said Parties binds and obliges them, be the
Faith and Truth of their Bodies, ilk ane to others, that
they shall be leil and true to others, and neither of
them will another's Skaith, but they shall lett it at their
Power, and give to others their best Counsel, and it be
asked; and shall take leil and affald Part ilk ane with
others, with their Kin, Friends, Servants, Allies, and
Partakers, in all and sundry their Actions, Quarrels
and Debates against all that live and die (may the
Allegiance to our Sovereign Lord the King allenarly

be excepted). And for the obliging and keeping all
thir Premises above written, baith the said Parties are
bound and obliged, ilk ane to others, be the Faith and
Truth of their Bodies, but Fraud or Guile, under the
Pain of Perjury, Men swearing, Defalcation, and breaking of the Bond of deadly. And in Witness of the whilk,
ilk ane to the Procuratory of this Indenture remain with
the said Walter Scot and his Friends, the said Walter
Ker of Cessford has affixed his proper Seal, with his
Subscription manual, and with the Subscription of the
said Andrew Ker of Fairniehirst, Mark Ker of Dolphin-
ston, George Ker, Tutor of Cessford, and Andrew Ker
of Primesideloch, before these Witnesses, Mr Andrew
Durie Abbot of Melrose, and George Douglas of Boon-
jedward, John Riddel of that ilk, and William Stewart,
　　　　　　Sic subscribitur
　　　　　　　　"WALTER KER of Cessford.
　　　　　　　　"ANDREW KER of Fairniehirst.
　　　　　　　　"MARK KER.
　　　　　　　　"GEORGE KER.
　　　　　　　　"ANDREW KER of Primesideloch.

"N.B.—The four Pilgrimages are, Scoon, Dundee,
Paislaw and Melross."

I do not think that ever this Indenture took place,
for both Lesly and Crawford, in his Notes on Buchanan's
History, acquaints us, that the Kers slew the Laird of

Buccleugh in Edinburgh, anno 1552, three and twenty Years after this Indenture.

A little to the South of Darnick is a Place called the Tile-house, where they made their Tile for the Service of the Monastery, and a great deal of it is sometimes found there finely glazed.

About half a Mile above Darnick to the West, on the South-side of Tweed, stands Bridgend, called so from the Bridge there, three Pillars of which are still standing. It has been a Timber Bridge; in the middle Pillar there has been a Chain for a Drawbridge, with a little House for the Conveniency of those that kept the Bridge and received the Custom.

On this same Pillar are the Arms of the Pringles of Galashiels; it is likely that Family has contributed largely for the building of it.

I am surprised that Mr Gordon in his Journey over Scotland, could receive such a lame account, from any, namely, That he was informed, that long ago a Country Man and his Family liv'd in this Tower, and got his Livelihood by laying out Planks from Pillar to Pillar, and conveying Passengers over the River; whereas 'tis plain and obvious to any, that it has been a very considerable Drawbridge, and very necessary to this Place.

There has been a plain Way from this Bridge through the Muirs to Sautrahill, called yet the Girthgate; for

Sautra was an Hospital founded by Malcolm IV. for the Relief of Pilgrims, for poor and sickly People, and had the Privilege of a Sanctuary, as Girth signifieth. The Way is so good and easy, that it may put one in Mind of the Roads that led to the Cities of Refuge.

On the South-west from Bridgend, on the North-side of the Highway to Selkirk, there are the Vestiges of a considerable Camp to be seen, called yet the Castle-steed. It is surrounded with a deep Ditch, in some Places with two Fosses, more than a Mile and an-half in Compass, called the Kae-side, or rather the Kid-side.' Some part of the Ditch is about ten Feet high. The Place where the Camp has been, there are two very deep Fosses to the North, but to the South the Ram-pires are broke down, and the Ditches filled up by labouring and tilling the Ground. From the Camp there is a plain military Way leading to Tweed at the Nether-Barnford. and a deep Ditch on each Side, in some Places about twenty Feet broad. From this Camp there is a large Prospect to the North. They were supplied with Water from Tweed, and two Wells near the Camp, Whitehill Well and St. John's Well. About a Mile to the South of this Camp, near Huntlie-wood, there has been another large Camp, called by the People the Roundabout, but the greatest Part of it is levelled by Tillage.

This Part of the Parish that lies on the South of

Tweed is fruitful in Corn and Pasturage, but the Inhabitants very much straitned for Fuel, having no Coals,
but what they get from England or the Lothians, and
being at a great Distance from any Moss.

In the Description of this Parish on the North-side
of Tweed, I begin with Drygrange on the East, standing
near the Confluence of Tweed and Leeder. In King
James V's Time, David Lithgow of Drygrange gets a
Charter from the Abbot and Convent of Melrose of the
Lands of Drygrange, for his special Service in resisting
to the Hazard of his Life, Depredators and Robbers of
the Dominion of Melrose. That Family was forfeited,
and one of that Name and Family purchased these
Lands from John Earl of Haddington, as they were
lately acquired by Robert Paterson, and are now the
Heritage of Mr Colin Maclaurin, Professor of Mathe-
maticks in the University of Edinburgh. Fordun gives
us an Account of two Granges in this Parish,* one
called Heldwii, or perhaps Hardwii, from whence the
Place has taken its Name Drygrange, and the other at
Gattonside: and he acquaints us, that in a great
Famine, about four thousand Poor came to the Convent
of Melrose for Relief, whom Waldeve the Abbot pity-
ing, he went with his Cellarer or Butler Tyna to his
Grange at Haldwii and then to Gattonside, and having
put in the Staff which he carried in his Hand among

* THOMAS HEARNE'S Edition, p. 572.

the Corn, it was multiplied by the Sign of the Cross, both for the Supply of the Convent, and all these numerous Poor. I observe this Office of the Cellarer has been very considerable, having many Lands assigned them, particularly at Darnick, called yet Cellary Lands.

There is a Ferry-boat on Tweed here, and good Fishing for Salmon.

To the West of Drygrange near Tweed, on the Head of a Hill, there has been a Camp; it bears no resemblance of a Roman Camp. If I may be allow'd my Conjecture, I think it has been made by the Governor and Earl of Angus before the Battle of Ancrum Muir, or Lilliard's Edge; for, as Buchanan acquaints us,* the Governor and Earl of Angus came with their Men to Melrose upon Tweed, where they intended to stay and wait for the rest that were coming. The English were come to Jedburgh before, and being advertised of the small Number of the Scottish Army, they marched towards Melrose, having 5000 Men in their Army, in great Confidence to defeat so small a Number as was with the Governor. The Scots had notice of their coming, and thereupon retired to the next Hills, where they might with safety espy what Course the Enemy would take, and it is likely made some Encampment there. From this Hill they had a

* BUCHAN., lib. 15, p. 515.

clear View of the March of the Enemy from Jedburgh.
The Trench is pretty deep, but of no great Compass.

To the West of Drygrange, on the North-side of
Tweed, is Gattonside, pleasantly situated on the Side of
an Hill, from whence it has its Name. The Inhabitants
here, and these on the South-side of Tweed, are generally Feuers to the Right Honourable Lady Isabella
Scot, Daughter to the late Duchess of Buccleugh, and
Charles Lord Cornwallis. There has been a fine
Chapel in this Place, all built of hewn Stone, near the
Vicar's House. This Person is called so because some
of his Predecessors feu'd the small Vicarage Tithes of
this Town from the Commendator, though others say
they had a Gift of them before the Reformation from
Abbot Durie, one of that Family having married his
natural Daughter. Many of the Stones of the Chapel
are to be seen in his House, and some of them curiously
carved. The People here in digging and ditching
their Yards, particularly near where the Chapel has
stood, find several Vaults, and a great many hewn
Stones, by which it appears, that in the time of Popery
there have been several good Buildings here.

The Inhabitants of this Parish, particularly on Tweed,
used to reap great Benefit from their Linen Manufacture, they being very expert in Spinning, weaving and
whitening both fine and coarse Linen; Melroseland
Linen being famous throughout the Kingdom. Some of

them carry on a profitable Trade by their Cabbage
Plants in the Season, which are very good here, by
taking them to Dumfries, Carnwath, and other Places;
and others receive great Benefit from their Fruit-yards,
one in Gattonside tells me, that some Years he has received three hundred Merks for the Fruit of his
Garden. On the South Part of this Town, was the
Grange Fordun speaks of, which at this Time is called
the Grange-gate.

To the West of Gattonside there is a Place called the
Tiend or Tythe-yard. Above this there was a fine Orchard belonging to the Convent, it still retains the Name,
consisting of above five acres of Ground. There is a Meadow here, called the Cellary Meadow, belonging to the
Cellarist of the Abbey, as on the East side of the Town
the Abbot had a Meadow called the Abbot's Meadow.

On the Head of the Hill, on the side of which Gattonside is founded, there has been a large Camp. It
has a Rampier or Wall about it of Stone, about half
a Mile in Compass. There is a plain Entry to it from
the West and to the East. Near to the West Entry,
called the Closses, there are a great many fine Springs.
Near to this Camp there is a Place called the Round-
abouts, of a circular Figure; whether it has been a
kind of Roman Temple, I leave it to others to determine.

About half a Mile from this Camp to the East, on
the Head of the Hill, opposite to Newstead, there has

been a large Camp, with a deep Ditch, a great Part of
the South side being levelled by Tillage. It seems to
have been about three Quarters of a Mile in Circumference; the People call it the Chester-know or knoll,
and it is to be observed, that usually there were Roman
Camps where the Places carry the Name of Chesters.

To the North of these Camps, at some Distance from
them, there appears to have been a Village, with two
Rows of Houses, the People do not remember the Name
of it, but call it the Weather-coat-ridges.

To the West from Gattonside about half a Mile, there
is a good Ferry-boat on Tweed, called the Westhouses
Boathouse. This Boat having a good Pool, and being
the ordinary Passage from the South to Edinburgh, is
very much frequented. They have likewise here a good
Fishing for Salmon. Above the Boat is Westhouses,
the old Possession of the Ormistons for many Years;
they have had a good House here, with many Vaults
and Gun-holes on every side, after the old Form. I see
their Names on the principal Gate, anno 1581. They
had the Custom of the Bridge while it was standing,
and a considerable Interest about this Place, and in Old
Melrose. It is said that George Ormiston, late Hang-
man in Edinburgh, was a Cadet of this Family, if not
the Representative of it; a Memorandum to old Families not to be puff'd up with Pride on account of
their Antiquity, for they know not what mean Offices

F

they or theirs may be obliged to stoop to. This Place
was in the Possession of Pringles of Blindlee for some
Time, and now belongs to Mr Scott of Galashiels.

There is a little Water that runs into Tweed at this
Place, with a Stone Bridge of one Arch over it; the
People call it Ellwand Water, but it rather should be
Allan, having its Source from Allanshaws about four
Miles to the North. The Trouts in this Water are
observed to be very good, being fed from the Mosses.
About half a Mile to the North of this little Water,
near Easter-Longlee, there is a Place called the Name-
less Dean, where, on the Side of the Brae, are to be
found divers curious formed Stones, some of them in
Shape resembling Guns, Butter-caps, Cradles, Buttons,
and that like. There is an high Bank above the Water
here, where they are found, and after great Rains are
washed into the Water. The Matter of these Stones
seem to be fine Marle; whether they are so formed
in the Bowels of the Earth, or petrified by the Springs
in the Side of the Brae and the Heat of the Sun, I
leave to others to determine.

About a Mile to the West of this, on the East-side
of Galla, is Wester-Longlee, called also Galla Bridge,
from a Bridge that had been here over Galla; it is
now the Possession of Mr Tait of Pirn. It belonged
anciently to the Cairncrosses, and here there is a
pleasant Haugh on Tweed, called the Cellary-haugh.

To the North of this on the same Side of Galla, is Long-haugh, a small Village pleasantly situated, and on an eminence Apple-tree-leaves. The Darlings have been long Feuars here; and, next to the Pringles, is a Name of the oldest standing on this Water. Near to this Place is an high Hill of a large Compass, all green, which affords good Pasture for Sheep, called Buckholmhill, and not far from it the House of Buckholm, of considerable Strength, which is now ruinous. It and Williamlaw, lying contiguous to it, belonged for several ages to the Pringles, descended of Galashiels, and was lately purchased by Mr Rutherford of Fairnielee. There has been a beautiful Wood here on the Water of Galla, but much of it now destroyed, and the Ground turned to Arable Land. It would appear from its Name, and a pleasant Place on the Water of Galla, called the Isle of Roe, that there have been many Deer in this Place.

Williamlaw is a very high Hill, and on the Top of it a Cairn of Stones, called Bellscairn, from which there is a fine Prospect to all the Country about.

Near to Williamlaw on the Water of Galla, is Whitelaw and Hagburn, the Possession anciently of the Hunters, afterwards of the Wallaces and Macdougals. It was lately acquired by Mr Andrew Fisher, Wright in Edinburgh, and is now in Possession of his Brother-german, the Laird of Housebyres.

I find from the Chronicle of Mailrose, that the Marches betwixt the Convent and those of Weddal or Stow were early fixed, namely, Crosselete, and a little Water called Fasseburn, the Inhabitants here have entirely forgot the Name of it. To the East of this is Allanshaws, where the Water of Allan has its Rise, from a Place called Allanhead. This Water divides the Parish on the North-side of Tweed; it runs by Threepwood, where there have been many Feuars for a long Time of the Name of Moffat; and then by Colmsliehill, the old Possession of the Hogs, it directs its Course to Colmsly. There has been a Chapel here, the Ruins of which are yet to be seen: It has been dedicate to Columbo Abbot of Hii, from whence the Place seems to take its Name, as it is likewise called Cellmuir, from the Chapel in the Muir. On the West-side of the Rivulet stands Colmsly Tower, the ancient Seat of the Cairncrosses, where their Arms are to be seen on the Head of the Door, a Stag's Head cras'd, the rest of their Bearing being defaced: These Arms have been set up by Walter Cairncross. This Family had a great Interest in this Parish and in other Places: They lay claim to Robert Cairncross, Bishop of Ross, Treasurer and Abbot of Holyroodhouse in King James V.'s Time; though Mr Crawford says, in his Lives and Characters of the Officers of the Crown and of the State, that without Doubt he descended of the Family of Balmashanan. However, if the Character that Buchanan gives of him, both in his History and Epigrams, be just, and we have no Reason to doubt of it, it is no great matter what Family he belonged to. Hugh Cairncross of Hilslop, near to the Place, is the undoubted Representer of this ancient Family, since the Death of Mr Alexander Cairncross, Archbishop of Glasgow, and after the Revolution, Bishop of Rapho in Ireland. These Lands of Colmsly came afterwards to the Pringles, Hunters, Scotts, Lawsons, and Lithgows successively. At Hilslop there is a Road called the Abbeygate, Pilgrims being continually travelling to and from Melrose, because it was one of the four Head Pilgrimages in Scotland. On the East-side of this Rivulet, opposite to Colmsly Tower, stands Langshaw, a well repaired old House, with Gardens and Planting. This Barony of Langshaw has changed many Masters, such as the Hope Pringles of Smailholm, the Kers, Murrays, Scotts, Nicolsons. Mr Baillie of Jerviswood purchased it some Years ago, and it is now in the Possession of my Lady Murray and my Lady Binning, his Daughters. The many Changes of Possessors of Lands in this Parish may put us in Mind of what is said in Horace:

" Nunc ager Umbreni, sub nomine nuper Ofelli.
Dictus, erit nulli proprius, sed cedet in usum
Nunc mihi, nunc alii."

About half a Mile to the East of this, on the Road that leads to Edinburgh, is Mosshouses, where there have been several good Houses, but now ruinous, belonging to some ancient Feuars there of the Name of Notman: and about half a Mile from this to the North, on the same Road, is a famous Cairn, called the Blue Cairn, from the Colour of the Stones, where there is a large Space of Ground enclosed and fortified by Nature, which will contain a vast Number of People. About a Mile to the North-east of this are three Villages called Blainslies, remarkable for their fine Oats, which are carried to the most Parts of the Kingdom, and some of them to the South of London: They are regarded not so much for their Whiteness as for their Earliness and Increase; they are commonly sold three or four Shillings per Boll above the ordinary Rate of the Market. There are several of the Feuars here of a long Standing, particularly the Thymes, who perhaps have descended from the Botevilles in England, one of whom was called Tom at the Inne, and his Posterity had the Surname contracted into Thynne. By the bounding Charter of the Nether Town of Blainslie, it appears they have had a fine Chapel, called Cheildhelles Chapel; it has been built of hewn Stone, near a Mile from the Towns, on the March betwixt Lauder and them, where there is a large Dyke, called Monksdyke; as also that there have

been two Crosses on the Road to Edinburgh near
Leeder, the one called Lillies-cross, and the other the
High-cross.

Near Leeder, opposite to Bridgehaugh, there has
been a considerable Camp, but a great Part of it is
defaced by Tillage.

Near to Blainslies, on the West of the Water of
Leeder, is a Place pleasantly situated with a fine Bank
of Wood, from whence it has the Name of Broadwoodshiel, the ancient Possession of the Hunters, and since
of the Kers and Fairbairns.

The Parish of Melrose is here intercepted by that
of Lauder, till we come to Clackmae and Sorrowlessfield, the one opposite to Carolside, and the other to
Coldenknowes. These Lands belonged anciently to
the Humes of Coldenknowes, and were feued out by
John Earl of Haddington, about an hundred Years
ago, to Alexander Fisher, a Cadet of the Fishers of
Darnick Tower.

About a Mile to the North-west of Clackmae, there
has been a large Camp, with three deep Trenches; the
Space between the Trenches is so large, that it is
turned to Arable Ground: It is about half a Mile in
Compass, the Name they give it now is Ridgewalls,
there having been some Houses built within the in-
most Rampier, which are now ruinous. To the West
of this Camp there are three large Springs, very near

other. About a Quarter of a Mile to the East of this, there is another called the Chesterlee, about half a Mile in Compass, with one single deep Ditch; from this there appears a plain military Way to the South, but especially to the North, running through Chapel-muir and the Blainslie Ground till Cheildhelles Chapel. About a Mile to the South of Ridgewalls there is another small Camp on an Eminence, near Earlston, called Brownhill; this Camp lies in a direct Line with that of Chesterlee and that of Drygrange.

This Part of the Parish on the North side of Tweed is fruitful in Corn and Pasturage, particularly Pasturage, and well stored with numerous Flocks, and the Country is generally well provided with Peats and Turffs, which they have abundantly in the Muirs and Mosses, such as Threepwood and Blainslie Mosses, Places much frequented by the Moss Troopers under Cromwell's Usurpation.

The Patroness of this Church is the Right Honourable Lady Isabella Scott.

The Stipend 1400 Merks, and 100 Merks for Communion Elements. As to the Glebe it may justly be reckoned among the worst in Britain, being at an unusual Distance from the Manse, and scarce worth the labouring. The old Pasquinade with respect to the Corinthian Brass taken by Urban of the Family of the Barberini, from the Doors of the Pantheon, may

be applied to a great many things, " Quod non fecerunt
Barbari, fecerunt Barbareni."

The Number of Catechisable Persons will be about
one thousand and eight hundred, though by the Decreet
of Locality above an hundred Years ago, I find there
has been in this Parish two thousand Communicants
or thereby.

There have been baptized for the Space of seven
Years, two hundred and six Males, and two hundred
and ten Females.

Finis.

_N.B._—In the following pages relating to the present
town of Melrose, its ancient Abbey and classic environs,
we shall nowhere unnecessarily tread on the ground
so carefully trenched by the Rev. Adam Milne in his
History. There are a few inaccuracies which stand
corrected and explained in the following chapters, and
are of no great importance.

Chapter Second.

HISTORY OF MELROSE ABBEY.—OLD MELROSE.

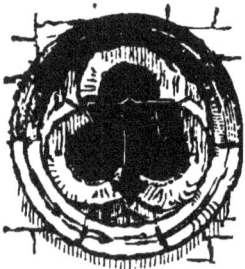

HE most ancient Monastery of Old Melrose stood beautifully situated on a peninsula formed by the waters of the Tweed, about two and a half miles from the present town of Melrose. It is still fringed round with high, abrupt, and rocky hills, adorned with bold overhanging woods, while a profusion of wild and variegated shrubs are seen to clothe the higher summits of the surrounding country. Its name was derived from two Celtic words—Mull, signifying bare, and Rhoss, a promontory, or Mulrhoss; in old chronicles spelt Mulros, Mulrais, and more recently Melrais, Melros, and Melrose. Coeval with the building of the first stone church in the city of Lincoln by Paulinus, this monastery was founded early in the seventh century, if not before it, but certainly during the reign of Oswald, Anglo-Saxon king of Northumberland. This monarch ruled from the river Humber to the Frith of Forth, and having embraced Christianity while enjoying an asylum

with the Picts, Oswald urged some of the Culdee brethren of the Monastery of St. Colombo, in the island of
Hy, commonly called Icolmkill, to come over and assist
him in the conversion of his subjects.

The Culdees were so named from the dress or black
habit they wore.

Oswald built a monastery, and established them at
Lindisfarne, since called Holy Island. He invested
Aidan, one of the missionaries from St. Colombo, with
the double office of Bishop and Abbot. It is most probable that King Oswald founded the Monastery of Old
Melrose, and that Aidan became first Bishop or President of it. So zealous was the king for the spread of
divine truth, that he ably assisted Aidan in his charitable office. At first, ignorant of the Saxon tongue,
Aidan preached in his own language, which the king,
standing by, interpreted to the people. Aidan is said
to have baptized 15,000 converts in seven days.

Aidan next took upon himself the instruction of
twelve* Saxon youths in the mysteries of the Christian
faith. They became proficients in learning, and fellow-
labourers with Aidan in the field of Christian teaching.

Many churches were now built, religious houses
erected, and various orders of monks founded, Dryburgh being already a settlement of Christian missionaries. One religious fellowship was established at
Old Melrose on the Tweed, and another at Coldingham

* BEDE, *Hist. Ecclesiast.*

in the Merse. This was about the year 640, or nearly two centuries before a similar society settled at Jedburgh. Eata, one of the twelve Saxon youths chosen by Aidan, was made first Abbot of Old Melrose. And Boisil, or St. Boswell, a monk famous for his piety and spiritual gifts, held the office of Prior.

Aidan, Bishop of Lindisfarne, died in 651, and was succeeded by one of the monks who accompanied him from Icolmkill. And about this time the brethren of Melrose were joined by Cuthbert, a name celebrated in the annals of monachism. Cuthbert was a youthful shepherd on the banks of the Leader, a stream that flows into Tweed a little above Old Melrose. He is said to have seen the soul of the holy Bishop of Lindisfarne borne up in triumph to heaven by a company of angels. Impressed by this vision, Cuthbert laid aside the cares of the world, and resolving to lead a religious life, joined the society at Old Melrose, embracing their rules of life and discipline. During his novitiate, he was carefully instructed by the good Prior Boisil, with whom he became a peculiar favourite, on account of his amiable disposition. A copy of the Scriptures, in which both had jointly read and meditated, was long preserved, uninjured by time, among other venerated relics in the Cathedral at Durham.*

In Butler's *Lives of the Roman Catholic Saints*, we read of a " copy of St. John's gospel, which Cuth-

* *Sim. Dunelm*, i. 3.

bert, after the example of his teacher Boisil, often read, and which was put into his coffin when he was buried, and was found in his tomb long afterwards." It is now, says Butler, in the possession of Mr. Thomas Philips, canon of Tongres, on whom the present Earl of Litchfield bestowed it.

In the British Museum (Nero, D. 4) is another MS. of the Gospels, beautifully written about the year 686 by Eadfrid, afterwards Bishop of Lindisfarne. Ethelwald, his successor, illuminated it with several elegant drawings. By the anchoret Bilfrith it was covered with gems, silver gilt, and gold, in honour of St. Cuthbert, to which Aldred the Priest afterwards added an interlineary version.

During the removal of St. Cuthbert's body in 885, this copy was lost in the sea, but recovered again three days afterwards. Simeon of Durham says it was not injured by the water, but Mr. Wanley thought he could perceive some stains upon it.

This book is still in the best preservation.*

Eata, first Abbot of Old Melrose, was sent to assist Alchfrid, son of Oswy,† King of Northumberland, in founding a monastery at Ripon, Yorkshire. A company of monks went with him from Melrose, and among them Cuthbert, who was made Prior of Ripon.

---

* Lingard's *Antiquities of the Anglo-Saxon Church.*

† Oswy, brother and successor to King Oswald.

Some misunderstanding shortly arose between this new colony at Ripon and the Church of Rome. Eata, being Abbot, declining, however, to submit to the Bishop of Rome with regard to the time of keeping the festival of Easter and other matters, they all returned to Melrose in the year 661. Eata resumed his former office again, and Boisil, who had been Abbot in his absence, became once more Prior. Boisil did not long survive, but died in 664 of "yellow plague or fever," a pestilence then raging in Britain. According to his dying request, Cuthbert succeeded him in the Priorate of Old Melrose, but resigned the office in 676. Cuthbert retired to lead a solitary life in the barren isle of Farne, about four miles off the Northumberland coast; and though called to the See of Hexham, declined to leave his retirement.

The See of York was for a long time included in that of Lindisfarne. In the year 685, Cuthbert was prevailed upon to accept the bishoprick of the latter. He was consecrated on Easter day at York, in the same year, by Theodore, attended by seven bishops. In 687 Cuthbert returned again to his hermitage, where he died about two months afterwards.

St. Cuthbert was the sixth Bishop in the Calendar; he founded the Bishopric of Durham, and many churches were built and dedicated to his name in various parts of the kingdom, and in distant countries.

Eata was translated to Hexham, and died there.[*]

It was about this time the visionary Drythelme retired to the Monastery of Melrose, where he spent the remainder of his life in the exercise of the most rigorous voluntary penance.   Of this man it is related, that in a severe fit of illness, towards evening, he became to all appearance lifeless, and upon his recovery in the morning, believed that he had actually passed a whole night in the state of the dead.   Recovering his health, he left off his former pursuits and pleasures. Disregarding the common concerns of life, he divided his substance, giving a third part to the poor, and the rest to his family.   Embracing a monastic life at Melrose, he obtained a cell from the Abbot apart from the other monks of the convent; and in order to mitigate the pains of purgatory by anticipating them, he immersed himself daily in the Tweed, summer and winter, without undressing, or afterwards changing his garments.

He had frequent visions of the unseen world, both of tormented and glorified spirits, some conceived in the wildest flights of mental hallucination and delusion. Like the patriarch Joseph, Drythelme was a mighty dreamer of dreams, the rehearsal of which terrified the ignorant, and mantled the superstitious with awe.

Odunald, a Saint, commemorated on the 26th of June, was also an Abbot of Old Melrose.   It is recorded of

* MORTON's *Monastic Annals of Teviotdale*, p. 187.

him, that when at the point of death, an angel appeared,
and encouraged him with the assurance of eternal glory.

Ethelwald, also canonized, and, according to Bede, a
disciple of St. Cuthbert, became Abbot in 696, and presided till 724, when he was made Bishop of Lindisfarne. He continued in this situation till 740, when
he died. He is said to have written a life of St. Cuthbert, and a treatise on the succession of the Abbots of
Mailros.*

About this time lived Winfrid, better known as St.
Boniface, the Apostle of the Germans. He is stated to
have been a Scotsman, and educated at Melrose. St.
Boniface was appointed Archbishop of Mentz, and
made Primate of Germany and Belgium, by Pope
Zachary, in 746. He disputed with Virgilius, an Irish
missionary, on the subject of the Antipodes, the existence of which Boniface denied. In his defence of the
celibacy of the Clergy and other papal dogmas, he was
skilfully opposed by three eminent Scotsmen, named
Claudius Clement, Samson, and John of Mailros.†

Thevuan, commemorated as a Saint on the 26th of
September, long presided as Abbot of Melrose. He is
named as having been Counsellor to Engenius VI., King
of Scots, who reigned from 688 to 697.

---

* Sim Dunelm Dempsteri Hist. Ecclesiast.

† MOSHEIM'S History of the Church. JAMIESON'S Account of the
Culdees.

Icolmkill was the burial-place of the kings at this period.

St. Grilbald or Gowibald, the first Bishop of Ratisbon, and very distinguished for his great eloquence and knowledge of the Scriptures, is said to have been a Missionary from the Monastery of Melrose. By the eighth century, however, Culdeeism was on the wane. Its simplicity of character and sincerity of purpose had become tainted and corrupt. Romanism began to infect primitive Christianity. John of Mailros accused an emissary of the Pope to Scotland as the "fabricator of falsehoods, the troubler of peace and of the Christian religion, and the corrupter of it both by word and writing." Such was the bold language of an intrepid and zealous ecclesiastic in those days.

In 839 the Monastery of Old Melrose was burned by Kenneth, King of the Scots, on his invasion of the Saxon territory, when he gained a lasting ascendancy over that power. Kenneth II., surnamed the Great, was a valiant prince, he utterly overthrew the Picts in several battles, and joined their kingdom to his own. The Commentator of Nennius, the British historian, speaks of the Monastery at Melros as having been formerly great and renowned. It seems probable it was rebuilt again in part, and inhabited toward the close of the ninth century. In the year 875 it became the resting-place of St. Cuthbert, whose body

G

was removed from Lindisfarne, on account of the invasion of the Danes. It was said to be uncorrupted, and was transferred from place to place for safety, by seven monks, for a space of seven years. It was at last suffered to rest at Chester-le-Street, but shortly removed to Durham Cathedral, where miracles were supposed to be wrought at its shrine. At the Reformation it was buried in that part of the Cathedral known as the Chapel of the Nine Altars. The following curious account of its accidental discovery appeared in the *Durham Advertiser,* May 1827:—"In carrying into effect several alterations at the east end of the Cathedral here, and in that part known as the chapel of the nine altars, an old oaken coffin was found, containing the remains of some distinguished personage, believed to be no other than the patron saint, St. Cuthbert. The skeleton was found to be remarkably perfect, and enclosed in the remains of robes richly worked with gold. A large and bright gold ring, having a crucifix, apparently of silver, appended, was found lying on the breast, and below it the remains of a book. A large comb was also found in the coffin. The wood of which the coffin was composed was about three inches in thickness, and strongly clamped with bars of iron."

The manner of removal from Melrose is of the marvellous, for tradition says, the body of the saint floated in a stone coffin down the Tweed to Tillmouth, where it stopped of itself. The ruins of a chapel may still be traced on the banks of the river where it was landed, and the alleged stone coffin was to be seen there till a recent period.*

Surtee, in his *History of Durham*, speaks of a stone boat, held popularly to be the coffin of St. Cuthbert, that floated with the body of the saint in it down the Tweed from Old Melrose, and came ashore at Tillmouth. It is described as still existing near the ruined chapel, though broken into two pieces, that it is finely shaped, ten feet long, three feet six inches broad, and four inches thick, and has been proved by experiment to be capable of floating with a weight equal to that of the human body.

Early in the eleventh century, William Douglas was Abbot of Melrose. He was a favourite of St. Fothad, Bishop of St. Andrews, who died in 962, and of Grime, King of Scots, who died in 1003. He was afterwards Confessor to Malcolm II., and an author of some repute in ecclesiastical matters.

While Eadmond was Bishop of Durham in 1021, a priest of the Cathedral named Ælfrid, alike remarkable for his moral virtues, religious zeal, and superstitious belief in the efficacy of relics, directed by a vision, began to collect the bones of holy men, from the ancient but ruined churches of Northumberland and other places.

* HUTCHINSON's *History of Durham*, vol. i. p. 55.

He is said to have paid a visit to Melrose, and removed the remains of St. Boisil, which he carried away, and had placed in a shrine near to that of St. Cuthbert at Durham.*

It appears, that about the year 1050, Old Melrose was a ruin and a desolation. That soon after it became the temporary abode of a few monks from Girwy (Jarrow†), among whom was Turgot, the historian. Turgot became Confessor of Margaret,‡ Queen of Malcolm the Third, and Bishop of St. Andrews.

Aldwine, Prior of Wincelcombe, Gloucestershire, was also one of them at this time. They shortly got into displeasure with Malcolm the Third; having conscientious scruples concerning the nature of an oath, they refused to swear allegiance to him, and were consequently compelled to quit Melrose in 1075. Meanwhile, Walcher, Bishop of Durham, had commanded them to return on several occasions; they now obeyed, and went to Monkwearmouth, where they settled. With the Bishop's assistance, they restored the ancient Monastery there, left in a ruinous state by the Danish invasion.

From about this period Old Melrose is only spoken

---

* *Sim. Dun.* iii. 7.

† Jarrow, county of Durham.

‡ Queen Margaret founded the *ancient* Church of Carlisle, and her husband those of Durham and Dunfermline.

of as a Chapel, dedicated to St. Cuthbert, and dependent on the See of Durham, until the founding of St. Mary's Monastery, Melrose, by King David in 1136. At this period, it is probable, that not only the relics, but all the other valuables of this ancient convent, were removed—that the cloisters were tenantless and without furniture—and that human tyranny and time had done their worst.

Old Melrose was long the resort of devout pilgrims, and there was anciently a sacred way to it, called the Girthgate; having the privilege of a sanctuary. Many traces of this Girthgate are still visible.

Many other roads and thoroughfares, from populous places in the kingdom, leading northwards, ran into it. Their junctions were distinguished by large, and frequently ornamental stone crosses, that directed the religious to the home of their pilgrimage.

Some of these crosses were in later times erected by the Monastery and monks of St. Mary, Melrose, who also availed themselves of the old Girthgate, and turned two of their approaches from the north-east and north-west into it.

It is highly probable that this Girthgate was originally a connecting military way of the Romans, by which victuals, pottery, fuel, water, and camp equipage, were conveyed from place to place for the service of the troops; as not less than seven hill-crowned fortifications of that people, rest or abut on this road at different points.

Some time previous to 1136, St. Cuthbert's Chapel was a dependency of the Priory of Coldingham. In that year King David recovered it, by giving in exchange for it the Church at Berwick; and so annexed it to the New Monastery founded by him two miles higher up the Tweed.

About the close of the reign of Alexander the Second, or beginning of Alexander the Third, Peter Haig, Laird of Bemersyde, engaged to pay to the Chapel of St. Cuthbert, Old Melrose, on St. Cuthbert's day annually, half a stone of wax, or thirty pence instead thereof, to light the said Chapel, for compensation for trespasses, committed by himself and others against the said convent. The aforesaid payment was in commutation of five fresh and five dried salmon, which Haig had previously been obliged to pay annually to the convent for the same trespasses.

The witnesses are, Oliver, Abbot of Dryburgh—Thomas Learmonth, of Ercildoun, (better known as Thomas the Rhymer), and Hugh de Perisby, Sheriff of Roxburgh.* The witness Learmonth was a poet in those days, and happening to foretell the death of Alexander the Third, which occurred according to his words, the country people were ready to ascribe to

* Catularium de Mailros.

him the tongue of inspiration and the gift of pro-
phecy. Many of his rhymes and predictions have
been handed down traditionally and otherwise to the
present age. For example, he said of the family of
Haig—

> "Tide, tide, whate'er betide—
> There'll aye be Haigs in Bemersyde."*

The Chapel of Old Melrose was finally destroyed by
the English in the reign of Robert the First. In
1321, Simon, Bishop of Galloway, granted remission
of penance, and promised indulgences to all who
would make a devout pilgrimage to the Chapel of St.
Cuthbert, at Old Melros, and contribute of their substance to rebuild the same. The Bishop stated that it
had lately been burned by the English. And Pope
Martin V., who held the Vicariate of Rome from 1417
to 1431, also promised remission of penance on all
the Festivals of St. Cuthbert, and some other holidays,
for seven years to come, and as many Lents, to such
as would assist in the restoration of this ancient monastery.†

---

* The Rhymer has not, however, proved a true prophet, the male
line of the Haigs having become extinct in 1854. The Misses Haig
still retain the estate of Bemerside.

· † The effect of this perdoun is, VII Zeir and VII Lentrynis, that is
to say, XXI Zeir of perdoun at the forenemit festis, as beforwrytyn,
procurit bedene Jhone of Cavertoun, mounk of Melros, at our haly
fader paip, Mertine the V. the Zeir of our Lord MCCCCXXXVII Zeirs.

We know little of the early architecture or construction of Old Melros. The Culdee erection was of oaken piles and boards, with a roof thatched with rushes. A stone edifice ,succeeded this. In early times the monastery was defended by a stone wall, stretching from that point of the Tweed on the south side to that on the north side of the Peninsula, where the land is narrowest.

It was difficult to remove the veneration shown by devout pilgrims to Old Melrose, long after the erection of the great monastery at Fordell. In its declining splendour and renown, persons flocked to its shrine from a great distance, and the way now only traceable at particular spots, known as the Girthgate, or Kirk-road, opened the communication to it from the northern districts by the great hospital of Soutra on the Hill, through Lauderdale, and the winding valley of the Alwent, now Allen, to the fair valley of the Tweed, for the accommodation of pilgrims to and from the Abbey.

The entrance to the Chapel was near the middle of this wall, where was a building called the Red-house or Porter's dwelling. Several spots about it still bear ancient names. The place where St. Cuthbert's Chapel stood, is called Chapel-knowe. And the "Haly Wheel," and "Monks Ford," are among the memorials of its antiquity, the site of which is now occupied by a modern villa.

The only antiquated remains of Old Melrose not already referred to, of which we have any knowledge, is the rudely carved head and cowl of a monk in stone, a mutilated head, of very coarse workmanship, symbolic of the Pascal Lamb, and the letter B cut in most antique character, upon what appears to have been the head stone or tablet of a tomb. On the left side of this letter are two cross-bars with four masonic points, surrounded with a single fleur-de-lis at their terminations. This very ancient stone may represent Boisil, Bosil, or Bosuel, a renowned monk and abbot of this convent, and to whose name the town of St. Boswell owes its derivation. Lessuden is a similar example, derived from Aidan the Culdee, Bishop of Lindisfarne, and next to the royal founder, the first patron of Old Melrose, and anciently called Lis-Aidan.

In its early development and the character of its occupants, Old Melrose resembled the parent institutions of Iona and Lindisfarne, but eventually eclipsed them in learning, zeal, and activity. Its missionaries were intelligent, painstaking, and persevering; learning and religion were disseminated by them far and wide. Economy in dress and living, simplicity of character, and impressive earnestness, were their genuine charac-

teristics. Long after the celebrity of Lindisfarne began to wane, the Monastery of Old Melrose enjoyed a
flourishing position, and was justly celebrated throughout Christendom. Milne describes it most correctly
where he observes, that it was "a famous nursery for
learning and religious men, who were filled with zeal
for propagating the Christian religion."

Some part of the foundation of Old Melrose was
opened up early in the last century, and only a few
years ago, some small pieces of stone were dug up,
which had the quaint dog's-tooth carving upon them.
As a monastery, it was not finally extinguished till the
reign of Robert the Bruce, when the English mercilessly
ransacked it, and afterwards burnt it to the ground.
We are convinced that a stone erection of some magnitude succeeded the early wooden fabric of Culdee construction. After the final overthrow of the former, the
materials composing the ruins were carried away and
used for domestic purposes by those who thought
proper to fetch them.

Lindisfarne must ever be regarded as the parent
source of the See of Durham. For, as Iona shed the
bright and cheering light of Christianity over Ancient
Caledonia, and savage clans and roving barbarians derived the benefits of knowledge and the blessings of
religion, so Lindisfarne, in its apparent solitude and
isolation, shone on the Saxon land, diffusing learning

and piety amongst a race cradled in ignorance, super-stition, and poverty.

Next to Melrose, among the far-famed Abbeys of Teviotdale, must be mentioned Kelso, Jedburgh, and Dryburgh. That of Kelso was founded in 1128, and first occupied by monks who had previously enjoyed a temporary residence at Selkirk, this latter settlement being henceforth discontinued. Kelso particularly suffered from the disastrous incursions by the Earl of Surrey in 1523, and the Earl of Hertford in 1545. The Monastery of Jedburgh was founded about the middle of the twelfth century for monks of the Benedictine Order. It is probable some religious houses had pre-viously occupied the same site. At Dryburgh the Druids long performed their pagan rites. A colony of Culdees settled there about 522, under a presbyter, whose name was Modan, and in 1150 Sir Hugh de Morville, under the auspices of David I., founded a Premonstratentian Abbey, and which was first colonised with monks from Alnwick. Dryburgh was burnt by the army of Edward II., but restored by Robert Bruce. The town of Dryburgh was also burnt, and never resumed its former position and opulence.

Thus we learn that the four ancient monasteries, whose glorious remains ravish the eye of the antiquary and historian, had their original consummation at about one and the same period.

The three monasteries of Melros, Melrose, and Dryburgh were built of red-sandstone obtained in the district, known in ancient times as the quarry of Dryburgh. Its chief peculiarity was, that it cut soft in the bosom of the strata, but afterwards, on exposure to the atmosphere, became so hard (not brittle), as to preserve indelibly the severe and artistic lines of the sculptor's chisel, and even now exhibits but few traces of decomposition, after the lapse of centuries.

The ancient quarry is no longer worked. In the tenth century the wages for lifting this stone was only one penny per man per diem. The Pinnacle and Eildon quarries now supply the neighbourhood.

The estate of Old Melrose was long possessed by a family of the name of Ormistoun. It is now the property of George K. Fairholme, Esquire, and the delightful residence of Lady Charlotte Forbes. Adjacent is Ravenswood, a handsome modern castellated building, rising from a lovely belt of forest trees and sylvan glades, also the property of George K. Fairholme, Esquire, and at present occupied by Gideon Pott, Esq., younger of Dodd. On the north bank of the winding Tweed, stands Gladswood, rising gracefully from the very skirts of that noble river, into a proud and lofty eminence. Studded with majestic trees, and dotted with greenwood shaws, from which are seen bold rugged summits and sylvan vistas, Glads-

wood is rendered doubly ornamental by its natural
loveliness of position.   Deeply sequestered, yet bold
and elevated, it affords the finest views from its green
slopes of the almost magic peninsula of Old Melrose.
Gladswood is the property and residence of John
Meiklam, Esq.   The picture is that of a vast amphi-
theatre,—   "Where greenwoods grow, and rivers row,
                  Wi' mony a hill between."

Charmed by the harmonious numbers of the rippling
Tweed, the song of birds, the shepherd's voice, and the
minstrelsy of bees—far as the eye can see is beautiful,
—a glorious diorama.   From its lofty eminence may
be seen the Northumberland Hills and "bonny Cowdenknowes," the seat of Robert Cotesworth, Esq.—

            "Oh, the broom, the bonnie broom,
              The broom o' the Cowdenknowes!"

Many are the vicissitudes the Monastery and Chapel of
St. Cuthbert's, Old Melrose, passed through, during the
eight centuries of its eventful history.   Saints, sages,
and princes of this world, sought its sequestered
courts, and trod its antiquated aisles and cloisters dim.
Once the abode of spiritual histories—a place of visions
—a receptacle of relics, mightier and more prophetic
in the estimation of pilgrim and devotee, than the
stalwart lines of the mountain chiefs, or the feudal
blast of trumpets.   Held long sacred by the sign of
the cross, (Pagan, Barbarian, and Saxon only ex-

cepted).   Burnt, scattered, demolished, obliterated, lost.   Indulgences, graces, ordinances, of no avail— in vain the worshippers desire to restore it—it lay a wreck, a chasmed city, which the destroying lava of years and dire vicissitudes has left at length enveloped in a coat of grass, forming now a gentle undulating field.   No gospels read, no matins sung—the idols de-throned, and the worshippers long gone to their account—a dream, a phantom, a subterranean mono-gram—doomed, fated, irrevocably lost, extinguished.

The contemplative mind can hardly refrain from lamenting over the last expiring grandeur of ruined temples, and the almost annihilated conservatories of primitive Christianity; once the oracles of God, and the sanctuaries of our forefathers.   What sublime lessons rise up from their departing shadows, pointing us to the instability of human greatness; and prophetically reminding us, that dust and ashes crown the end of all.

> " The ticking wood-worm mocks thee, man;
>   Thy temples, creeds themselves, grow wan;
>   But there's a dome of nobler span—
>   A temple given;
>   Thy faith—that bigots dare not scan—
>   Its space is Heaven ! "

As we pass on, at the opening of the vale of Leader, amid tall ancestral trees, stands Drygrange, the seat of Thomas Tod, Esq., one of the most beautiful residences in the vicinity of Melrose.

DRYGRANGE AND NEWSTEAD.

Drygrange was the chief granary of Melrose Abbey in ancient times. Its pastoral beauties are celebrated in the old song of "Leader Haughs and Yarrow:"—

> "Sing Ercildoune and Cowdenknowes,
>   Where Homes had ance commanding;
> And Drygrange wi' the milk-white ewes,
>   'Twixt Tweed and Leader standing."

Pursuing the course of the river westward, we cross the Tweed by Drygrange Bridge, or, as it is called, the Fly-bridge, from a fly-boat plying here formerly. Near the bridge is a pleasant mansion, the residence of Mrs Tod of Kirklands, not far from which the classic Leader pours itself into the Tweed. The scenery from the mansion is most imposing; and the family are deservedly honoured by all who reside in the neighbourhood. A mile still further westward stands the village of Newstead, near which may be traced the remains of another sacred edifice,* called Red Abbey Stead, probably from the colour of the stone. The great extent of its foundations shows that the building must have been of magnificent proportions. We are led to believe, that this, which is doubtful, if a religious establishment, flourished between the overthrow of the Culdee establishment of Old Melrose, and the rise of the

* MILNE'S *History of Melrose.*

New Monastery at Fordell.   Close to Newstead has
been a Roman Pottery and Tile-yard.   Numerous coins
have been found here; one dug up in 1821 bears the
inscription, "Augustus Nero."   That Newstead was
peopled during the Roman occupation, seems evident,
from the remains of decorated and other kinds of pottery found there, such as altar-pieces, figures, and frag-
mentary parts of the wild boar and other animals.   The
figure of a wild boar was emblazoned on the escutcheon
or standard of the twentieth Roman legion.   Newstead
is justly famed for its Roman relics and antiquities.

Round Newstead immense foundations of Roman
buildings have been ploughed up—hewn stone, from
the Dryburgh quarry, sufficient to build a good house,
has been collected in a single field.   There is a place
called still the Well-meadow, where numerous pits have
been discovered at various times.*   In all parts of the
village, and on every occasion, the land is trenched and
drained, fresh discoveries of buildings are made.   Several arched vaults, substructions, and arches for the support of upper works, have been laid bare, also, of Roman
origin.   For only to the Romans, at that early period,
could be known the key and mystery of the arch.

---

* It has been surmised by Dr John Alexander Smith that these
pits were the burial-places of the Roman town, the depositories of
the ashes of the dead, and of those other animals sacrificed in the
performance of their pagan rites.

In the primeval splendour of the present Melrose Abbey, a great wood of oaks called the Prior-wood extended from Newstead to the precincts of the former. Anciently, about midway, stood a notable cross, known as the Priorwood Cross. At Drygrange was the principal store-house and granary of St. Mary's, Melrose.

In the possession of the family of Drygrange, is the tablet of a Roman altar, which is by far the most interesting relic of antiquity yet discovered among the Roman remains of Newstead. It bears the following inscription,—

"Deo Silvano pro salute sua et suorum Carrius
Domiti Annus.   Leg. XX. V. V. V. S. L. L. M.*

During the construction of the Edinburgh and Hawick Railway in 1846, extensive Roman remains were brought to light, a little to the east of Newstead. A group of circular shafts or pits was laid open, two of which were twenty feet deep, and thirty inches in diameter. The others were of various dimensions. In one of the shafts the skeleton of a man was found standing erect, with a spear beside him, accompanied with remains of Roman pottery. Alexander Mitchell, Esq., and Captain Smith have each delightful villa residences in Newstead. The gardens and farms here are in the highest state of cultivation.

* Or thus: "Deo Silvanus, pro salute sua et suorum Carrius Domitianus, Centuris Legionis Vicesimæ Valentis Vistrius votum solvit libentissime merito."

H

Newstead was early noted for a society of masons that settled there. Their craft was in high repute, and what they bequeathed to us, although in ruins, fully sustains their ancient reputation. The early masons were chiefly of French extraction, and were probably sent from rising continental countries, to build the Monastery of St. Mary, Melrose, and the other ancient monasteries of Teviotdale. The institution of St. John's Lodge of Freemasons, Melrose, is said to be as far back as the building of Melrose Abbey in 1136,—one John Mordo, who by the Chronicle of Melros, had in keeping all mason work, at the building of St. Mary's Monastery, having been the first Grand Master.

Several years ago, Dr John Alexander Smith brought before the Scottish Society of Antiquaries some interesting accounts of an incised sepulchral stone, which had been found previously in the same field in which the Roman altar dedicated to Silvanus was discovered.* This stone was given by Thomas Tod, Esq. of Drygrange, to Sir David Erskine, who placed it in the north wall of the choir of Dryburgh Abbey, where it still remains. "It had been considerably broken, is now irregular in shape, measuring about thirteen inches in length by eleven and a-half inches in breadth. It has

* Another votive altar, also dedicated to the forest deities, has been found in the same locality.

.cut on it a portion of a large-sized double-edged sword of ancient form, the guard being bent at its extremity towards the blade. At the sides of the handle we have, in old English characters, the letters A. P., apparently the initials of the person's name to whom the monument had been placed. On the right of the sword-blade is sculptured a mason's square, and on the left a pair of compasses. Below these emblems runs on each side the upper part of an ornamental wreath, formed apparently of ivy, or perhaps the more sacred emblem of the vine." From the appearance of the letters, and the shape of the sword hilt, Dr Smith estimates this stone to belong to the latter part of the fourteenth or beginning of the fifteenth century, which we coincide with. As he observes, the initial letters may be read Alexander or Andrew Pringle, which was a common name in the vicinity. That the individual, whatever his name, was a freemason, admits of no doubt, and the two-edged sword and wreath may indicate that he was a knight-templar or crusader.

The ancient Watling Street of the Romans, which connected Yorkshire with the Frith of Forth, after traversing the basin of the Teviot by way of Jedfoot, crosses Newstead and the Tweed, leading on to Lauderdale and Soutra Hill. Across the Tweed at Newstead there stood anciently a very fine stone bridge of massive construction and great dimensions, the building of

which was excellent in masonic skill and workmanship.
The piers were standing in the seventeenth century,
and have been carted away to repair mills and sluices
with.   The stone required for the building of Melrose
Abbey was carried over this bridge, and the site of its
abutments is traceable on both sides the river.*   A
mile to the westward stood another bridge upon Tweed,
of a much lighter construction, which was called Melrose Bridge.   The Red Abbey seems to have had no
connection with any of the neighbouring institutions
that we can discover.   If it was an hospital of the
Templars, their distinguishing badge was a red cross,
and the Red Cross Knights were all of the masonic
fraternity, which was their mysterious link of brotherhood.   The masons of Newstead might have given
vitality to such an institution.   The early orders of
chivalry augmented masonic emblems, rites, and associations; they instituted the rules of hospitality, and
blended an agreeable courtesy with their knightly
bearing.   Many curious and interesting stones have
been found here,—the dog-tooth pattern in carved
stone, amongst the rest.   In the now rural village of
Newstead, on the outer walls of gardens and houses,

---

* Although we have no correct data to guide us, it is probable
there existed a bridge of Roman construction at this place at an
earlier period, leading from their town "Tremontium," east to
Leader Vale, and west to Soutra Hill.

may still be traced many ancient and rudely-sculptured stones found in the neighbourhood. Hand-mill stones for triturating corn and preparing flour have frequently been found at Newstead.

We copy the following highly interesting extract on the remains of an ancient stone building, discovered near the village of Newstead, Roxburghshire, by permission of John Alexander Smith, M.D., Sec., S.A. Scot. :—

"This building was discovered by a man when cutting a drain in the spring of 1845, in a field near the village of Newstead, a short distance to the south of the Roman road and other remains afterwards exposed by the railway cutting; which I have already brought before the notice of the Society. On visiting, at a later period, the field, which was then under turnip crop, I found the only trace of the building still remaining, was the hollow from which the stones had been all dug out, and in which the stronger growth and darker green colour of the turnips distinctly pointed out both its peculiar size and shape.

"The building was rather more than two feet under the surface of the ground, and consisted of two low, apparently sunk or face walls about three feet deep, built of hewn stone (reddish sandstone) laid in courses, and enclosing an elongated space, increasing gradually in breadth from the opening to the other extremity, which was shut in by a semicircular wall; the whole forming, from being bent considerably, a figure somewhat resembling a chemist's retort. The walls were formed of only one stone in the thickness, and each stone is described as varying from about six to ten or twelve inches in depth; they seem to have been built *dry*, as no appearance of lime or mortar was observed. The entrance or doorway was turned towards the north-west, and was four feet two inches in width; seventeen feet from this the building was five feet four inches wide; eighteen feet further up the interior, it was six feet nine inches; and eighteen feet still further, it was seven feet in width; the whole length of the interior, measured along the centre, being fifty-four feet; and a line drawn from the outside of the entrance across to the beginning of the curved extremity was thirty-six feet in length. Nothing was found within the space enclosed by the walls of the building, except dressed stones of various sizes and shapes; some of them simply flat pavement-like slabs, which were most numerous near the entrance; others, flat stones bevelled on one side, along which a notch was cut longitudinally. These last were about seven and a half inches thick, the bevelled projection being seven inches in length; they were indiscriminately mixed with the pavement-like stones, which were about the same thickness; but the bevelled ones were found in greatest number in the wider portions of the interior, or from about the middle to the closed extremity. Two larger stones were also found, having a rich moulding cut on one side; they measured about four feet in length, two feet three inches in width, and eight inches in thickness. One of these moulded stones was given, I believe, to Lord Polwarth, and the other was cut and altered for some economical use; I was fortunate enough to get a small portion of the latter (which was presented to the Society's Museum): it distinctly shows the central member of the moulding, the well known rope or cable pattern,—one that frequently occurs on various Roman ornamental stones or tablets, and also forming part of a moulding in almost the same or at least a corresponding position to this, in some of the Roman altars that have been discovered in Scotland. The moulding was considered by some of my friends, architects, to be undoubtedly Roman in its character. The stones found in the interior of the building may have been merely a coping to the walls, or, what is more probable, the remains of the roof which had covered the vault; this latter opinion is strengthened by the fact of several of the stones being found apparently *in situ* on the top of the wall, so as to favour the idea of its being covered by a somewhat arch-like or flattened roof,—one row of stones being placed with the bevelled part projecting inwards, and

others in a similar way above it; thus corbelling in,
or encroaching on the central space, and shortening
the bearing of the roof, so that a flat stone or two on
the top would complete the enclosure, and thus do
away with the necessity of long stones, which are by
no means plentiful in this neighbourhood;—and reminding one of the ancient so-called Cyclopean edifices,
which were arched in a somewhat similar way. In
favour of this view, I may refer to the position which
the stones occupied in the interior of the building; the
bevelled ones being found in most abundance towards
the widest parts; and the flat stones being possibly the
covers of the whole, were many of them rather in short
lengths, having apparently been broken by the falling
in of the roof. The two moulded stones were found
near the inner or closed extremity of the building, and
as they can scarcely be supposed from their totally
different character to have formed part of the roof, they
had probably been portions of some enclosure which
may have existed at that part of the interior.

"Another ruin, said to have been of a somewhat
similar kind, was found in the adjoining field in the
spring of 1849, about a hundred yards to the east of
the building mentioned. It was described as having
resembled the other considerably, except that it was
built of whinstone as well as sandstone, and the stones
were not so neatly dressed, being altogether of a ruder

character. The materials of which it was composed were dug out for economical purposes; and after following it for some ten or twelve feet, further progress was arrested by its passing apparently under an adjoining road, which formed the boundary of the man's field, and consequently put a final conclusion to his operations.

"Various shallow flat-roofed buildings, formed of hewn stone, have been found at different Roman stations in Scotland, as at Duntocher (vide *Caledonia Romana*), which consisted of circular vaults, and were believed to have been granaries; the Newstead buildings had, however, a much closer resemblance to those described by Pennant as existing at Borthwick in this county, and others found near Coupar-Angus. These, though of much the same general shape, and having their entrance apparently also turned towards the north-west, were much ruder in their character, being built of stones in their natural state, and not cut or dressed. They enclosed within their walls a black mould containing the remains of animals (bones and teeth), considered to belong to cattle and sheep, and none of them to be human; with charcoal and burnt earth interspersed throughout; and also, it is said, ' some stones which must have fallen from the surrounding walls,' but which may possibly have formed part of a flattened roof; and were supposed by Pennant

'to be the Repositories of the ashes of the sacrifices
which our Ancestors were wont to offer in honour of
their deities.' It is an interesting fact that these
buildings appear to have been in the neighbourhood
of Roman remains ; and although others of a somewhat
similar character have also been found in distant parts
of the country, I am of opinion, that the one just
described might be of Roman workmanship ; and, when
we remember that it was at no great distance from the
pits and beds of burnt materials formerly described, I
imagine it might have been connected with the religious rites of the people. Because, even if we suppose
buildings of this peculiar shape, which are much ruder
in their details, to have been the work of the natives
of our country ; still, from their mysterious character,
their length, and apparently, at least in some instances,
their total absence of the light of day, it seems to me
not impossible they were either used as places for the
safe keeping of their most valued property, or had more
probably been connected with the secret rites of a native
priesthood. The same style of building might have been
adopted by the Roman invaders, who, with the facility
so remarkable in that people, may have continued in its
gloomy recesses the superstitious ceremonies of its first
architects, or engrafted on them their own dark Mith-
raic worship ; and, for want at least of a better explanation, I can only say, it reminds me of the dark under-

ground Sacella or smaller temples which the Romans dedicated to the god Mithras or the Sun. There is one described by Hodgson, in his *History of Northumberland*, as having been found at Housesteads or 'Borovicus,' the general character of which somewhat resembled this building : he says, 'the cave itself seems to have been a contemptible hovel dug out of the hillside, lined with dry walls and covered with turf or straw ; for the ruins of the walls and roof had not been sufficient to hide the altars from the action of the weather.' It is also worthy of notice, that in it the altars, with the exception of a small one, were ranged along the western wall ; corresponding, as it seemed, to the position in which the moulded stones were found in the Newstead building. In conclusion, Dr Smith alludes to the fact of several coins of Constantine the Great, formerly exhibited to the Society, which were stated to have been found in the immediate neighbourhood ; having on the reverse a male figure of the Sun, standing, with radiated crown, his right hand raised, and left holding a globe ; with the inscription, '*Soli invicto comiti*,' the sun the invincible companion ; '*Imperit comes*,' I suppose, of the emperor. These coins might serve to show that the worship of the sun was by no means unknown here. And Hodgson has referred to the same fact, when he says that 'Mithraism had become common among the Romans during the reign of

Commodus, and in the time of Severus had extended over all the western part of the empire.'"

From the foundations of numerous buildings, and the quantity and variety of Roman coins, discovered around Newstead, of which several are before us, relating to the period of Roman occupation, and referring to Nero, Vespasian, Trajan, Hadrian, Antoninus Pius, Marcus Aurelius, Severus, Constantine the Great, and others, we may conclude, that the place now called " Red Abbey Stead" is none other than the ancient site of the " town of the three-peaked hill," the "Mons Tremontium," or rather, Colonia Tremontium, of the Romans.   Add to the former, the remains of fine glazed Samian ware, embossed and pictured with field sports; coarse red, grey and yellow kiln pottery and tile found there in abundance ; paved roads, substructions, and the stronger testimony afforded by Roman altars with lettered tablets, we are encompassed by a cloud of witnesses, which, with the elevated and noble position of the ground in proximity to the Eildon, draws us to the same conclusion.

At one period, both cavalry and infantry composed the Roman army of occupation, whose head quarters were at Eildon, and it was not till the close of the fifth century they finally quitted Scotland.

In the pits previously referred to, the bones of various orders of animals were discovered, such as

the horse, dwarf-ox, red-deer, and also of man.   And
when we consider the vestiges of camps, diverging at
all points from Newstead as a centre, the good supplies
of fuel and of water in the district, we are irresistibly
led to the conclusion, that this was once a Roman
settlement, and of considerable importance.

GATTONSIDE.

The pretty suburb of Gattonside, with its extensive
and productive gardens, its fruitful orchards, in the
spring-time white with living bloom—its immediate
proximity to Melrose by an elegant chain bridge—rising
on the north banks of the Tweed, greatly embellishes
our view from Newstead. R. B. Maconochie, Esq., is
the owner, and Colonel Duncan and family the occu-
piers of Gattonside House, and its demesne, which
skirts for a considerable distance the silver edges of
the Tweed.

In olden times a chapel stood here; but, excepting
vaults, hewn stones, and leaden pipes, little else remains
to point out its former proportions, which are said to
have been beautiful and extensive.

On the south of Gattonside was the Grange, which
Fordoun mentions, still called the Grangegate.   Around
Gattonside are such places as the Tytheyard, the
Cellary Meadow, the Smyddie Croft, the Abbot's Mea-

dow, the Vineyard, the Abbey Orchard, and Friar's-close, which had been originally so named. A few modern villas have sprung up about this village, to which the owners still continue the ancient monastic names.

Gattonside was long the residence of several families of good standing, feuars of the place, under the regality of Melrose. There was a period when its inhabitants were much more numerous than at present; and, with the exception of the Boston family, still living there, almost all the early feued and chartered families are either extinct or have passed to other localities.

In very early times, Gattonside was famed for the weaving, spinning, and bleaching of fine linen, and in the sixteenth century had a high reputation for the domestic manufacture of woollen cloth. Amongst its other residents were upwards of fifty weavers, living there as recently as the seventeenth century. Horticulture flourished here in very remote times, under the skill and management of the monks of Melrose, to whom even the cultivation of the turnip seems to have been known. Early as the thirteenth century, the vale of Melrose was unequalled in the south of Scotland for its skilful agriculture and great productiveness, and it is doubtful whether its present fertility surpasses that of the period we refer to.

The antiquities of the Borders are most interesting. The district around Melrose abounds in tumuli, cairns,

military stations, remains of Roman villages, ruined
castles, fortalices, and other strongholds, and the ruins of
several religious houses.   The Monastery of Lindisfarne,
for four centuries the seat of the present See of Durham, was undoubtedly the first institution of the kind
in the North of England.   From it, all the churches of
Bernicia, from the Tyne to the Tweed, had their begin-
ing; and also many of those in Diera, or from the
Tyne to the Humber.   The Nunnery of Coldingham is
the oldest in Scotland.   Thus, Coldingham and Lindisfarne, only by priority of erection, take precedence of
all other religious houses on the Borders.   But Melrose
Abbey, of classic fame, by universal consent occupies
the first place, and the link which binds her to Old
Melrose, and makes the chain of history complete,
must ever impart a thrilling and unwearied charm to
both.

Chapter Third.

HE Monastery of Melrose was ten years in building. It was finished in 1146, and with great pomp and solemnity dedicated to the Virgin Mary, on Sunday, the 28th July. The Cistertian Order were now acquiring great celebrity throughout Europe. They were introduced into England in 1128, and had their first settlement at Waverley in Surrey. Melrose became the residence of a community of monks from Rievalle, in the North Riding of Yorkshire. This colony was the first of the order introduced into Scotland. They had for some time been instituted in France on the Benedictine principles, and were spreading rapidly throughout every country in Europe. Possessing considerable knowledge of agriculture, the Cistertians settled in pleasant secluded places. They were given to pastoral pursuits. They admired sequestered val-

leys, and broad, deep, winding streams. Their primitive
lives and manners were adorned with great simplicity.
The King, by a charter, which was confirmed by his son,
Prince Henry, gave them lands, forests, and rights of
fishing. The latter were of great value in those days.
Many convents sold fish, and laid out the proceeds in
stock. Some sold as much annually as bought from
ten to twelve head of store cattle, besides having ample
supply for the convent. After David I. had established Melrose and the southern abbacies, he transferred large portions of the crown lands to their use.
They became nurseries of religion, training, and labour.
The seclusions of the cloister were allied to the work of
the field. The cultivation of letters and the practice
of horticulture formed pleasing recreations, after severer
labour in the open fields, and during the intervals of
devotional routine. Patrons of art and skilled in
design, the monks, with the assistance of lay brethren,
embellished and extended the churches erected by that
remarkable order of chivalry, Freemasonry. A love of
the bold and beautiful was deemed not incompatible
with the love of truth. Faith expressed itself with
grandeur, and the arts of the age were made subser-
vient to the one great exulting thought—the exaltation
of ecclesiastical architecture. The nobles of David's
court, following his example, vied with each other in
their gifts to Melrose, so that in a short time this

I

monastery became very wealthy, and enjoyed a princely revenue.

The Cistertians promoted learning by every means in their power. The transcribing of books was one of their chief occupations. A number of the brethren were always employed in the scriptorium or writing-room. They furnished the common library with copies of the most esteemed works then to be had. They could not write a new book, however, without permission from the general Chapter. The most remarkable events of each monastery were recorded in the Latin language by the monks. This was styled the Chronicle of the place where it was kept. Matters of general and local interest were often registered in it, as well as the affairs of the convent. Only part of the Chronicle of Melrose Abbey was preserved; it is written with brevity, but the style is somewhat barbarous. It commences with the year 735, and breaks off abruptly in 1270. The first part of it is said to have been compiled by an Abbot of Dundrennan.* Should this be true, he was probably a monk of Melrose previously; as we read that Dundrennan in Galloway was founded in 1142, and colonized with monks from Melrose.

The Cistertians were at this period a reformed class under monachism. They were so named from their first and chief monastery at Cisteaux, in France, founded

* NICOLSON'S *Eng. Hist. Library.*

about the close of the eleventh century. They embraced the rules for monastic life instituted by St. Benedict at Monte Cassino, in Italy, five centuries before. And they revived in all their primitive simplicity and integrity, at this time, the rules laid down by their patron and exemplar. Those rules had fallen into disuse. In short, abuses had crept in, and neglect followed. They were now to be proclaimed anew, and a great revivalism of faith and duty was expected to be achieved thereby. Seven times in every twenty-four hours devotions must be performed. The first service was at two o'clock in the morning; second, Matins, or Prime, at six o'clock; third, Tierce, at nine o'clock; fourth, the Sexte, at twelve o'clock; fifth, the None, at three o'clock; sixth, Vespers, at six in the evening; seventh, the Compline, which was said after seven o'clock. The monks went to bed at eight, so they had six hours rest before the nocturnal service began.

They were to fast daily in Lent till six in the evening. They all slept in the same dormitory, which was a long open room, undivided by cells. Each monk had a bed to himself, and was furnished with a mat, blanket, coverlet, and pillow. The latter was to be only eighteen inches long. They never went abroad alone, but always two together, to guard and witness each other's conduct, and prompt each other to good thoughts. In the year

1134, two years prior to the foundation of Melrose Abbey, a general Chapter of the Cistertian Order was held in France. It was then resolved, that the rules of St. Benedict, with regard to food, dress, morals, and religious observances, should be enforced. Luxury, if not wholly suppressed, was to be prevented as much as possible. Their monasteries were to be in the most solitary and retired situations. The monks were to live by labour. They were to cultivate the earth and keep cattle; and they were permitted, for this end, to possess lands, woods, vineyards, meadows, and fishings; sheep, oxen, horses, goats, and other domesticated animals. But prohibited from having deer, hawks, bears, or such animals as are kept for amusement only.*

They were forbidden to possess tithes, revenues, or advowsons of churches, dues of milns or ovens, bond-servants, or even the rents of land. Regulations were thus made, that they should not live by the labour of others. To enable the monks so disposed for greater retirement, study, and abstraction from the world, it was deemed convenient to admit into their community a certain number of persons, such as lay brethren, or converts, as they were sometimes called. Their office was to manage the secular business of the convent, including the cultivation of its lands, and all other pastoral duties. These lay brethren were not called

* *Annales Cistertionses.*

upon to take the monastic vow, but in every other respect they were treated exactly like the monks.

The dress of the Cistertians was a white cassock, with a narrow scapulary, over which they wore a black gown when they went abroad, but a white one when going to church. They also wore hoods of plain cloth, fustian, or linen. Great simplicity and frugality was to be observed also in their church ornaments, and the dress of their ministers. The altar cloth was to be of plain linen. The stole and maniple, which at first was of cloth, were afterwards allowed to be of plain silk. Palls, capes, dalmatics, and tunics were forbidden. The crosses were to be of wood and painted, not carved, nor of silver or gold. The chalice might be of silver gilt. The candlesticks must be iron, and the censers of iron or copper. Pictures and painted glass were not allowed in their churches, and all churches under this order were dedicated to God, under the invocation of the Virgin Mary.

With respect to their food, variety of dishes was forbidden. Flesh was allowed only to the sick. They observed a rigid abstinence. Fish, eggs, milk, butter, and cheese were not common things, but only used as pittances or dainties. None but the sick, or guests, were allowed any other than brown bread. They used the common herbs of the country, but foreign spices and pepper were forbidden. No convent would send to colonize a new monastery unless the community consisted of at least sixty monks. License also was required of the general Chapter, and the Archbishop or Bishop. The convent was to consist, at least, of twelve monks and their superior. Before they could be brought to their new abode, the following buildings must be provided: an oratory, a refectory, a dormitory, a stranger's cell, and a porter's lodge. The books required for divine service must be ready also. The superior of the new establishment was bound to pay a visit to the parent monastery once a-year. All abbots of this order were obliged to attend the general Chapter, held annually at Cisteaux, except those who were excused on account of sickness or distance. Abbots in Scotland and Ireland need only be present every fourth year, and delegates were allowed in some cases.

No candidate desiring to become a monk could enter upon his noviciate under fifteen years of age. He must first petition to be admitted. This done, after the space of four days, he was brought before the abbot and a select number of monks, in the Chapter-house. Being asked of the abbot what he wanted, he replied, " The mercy of God and yours." The abbot then explained to him the great strictness of their rules, and the large amount of self-denial required in keeping them; after which he asked him if he was willing to submit to the restraints they imposed. Upon his replying in the affirmative, the abbot again admonished him, concluding with these words, "May God finish the good work that he hath begun in thee;" all present saying, "Amen." The candidate hereupon bowed, retiring to the guest-chamber. He now had permission to read the rules of the order, and went through a similar ceremony on being introduced into the Chapterhouse, on the following day. On the third day he was admitted into the cell of the novices, and began the year of his probation. He now received daily instruction from the master of the novices, who was usually one of the oldest and·most learned of the monks. Twelve months were considered a sufficient trial of their discipline and manner of life, and if to further interrogatories now put, he persisted in his request, he was allowed to make his profession, and become a regular member of the order. Such was the simple ceremony from first to last, about which such monstrous rites of admission have been given to the world by various authors.

When King David founded the monastery of St. Mary's, Melrose, the ground on which the present town and 'ruins stand, was a village called Little Fordell. Such was its ancient name, probably at a remote period a Roman village also, like Newstead.

Old Melrose had attained great celebrity in the annals of monachism, not less by the learning and eloquence of some of its brethren, than by the miraculous fame and canonization of others. Whatever the king might think with respect to rebuilding Old Melrose, the situation of Fordell was far better for the purpose. It was secluded, still more *apropos* of display, and better calculated to defend itself and be defended. In honour of St. Cuthbert, and veneration for the old monastery, Melrose was the name the king chose to confer on the new locality.

Many changes in church government were effected by David I. Under his reforming hand many minor churches, such as Lindean, and others, lost their importance. The king was bent on establishing great monastic institutions. He wished to see an extended episcopacy, branching to all parts of the country. He saw the advantages likely to result from the formation of churches on the Borders. An enemy might have reverence for an edifice of an ecclesiastical character, who would otherwise sack and destroy it. He foresaw the benefit of annexing extensive possessions to monastic churches. Endowments to communities which fostered intelligence and order, would be productive of more good than increase of wealth and power in the person of nobles and courtiers, not more ignorant than selfish, deceitful, and quarrelsome. With such views were founded the monastic institutions of Teviotdale, including that of Melrose. Great favours were bestowed upon them by David, and his successors on the throne, till the reign of James V. They gradually increased in importance and political status, while their churches became the chief ornaments of the kingdom. For ages both commerce and agriculture flourished under monachism. The people grew wiser. They were both wiser and better in worldly circumstances than they had been hitherto. While war and faction disturbed the state, the wealth, wisdom, and learning of the ecclesiastics kept the throne steady, and gave to society a balance which the dissensions of warlike chiefs only tended to unsettle and overturn. In their primitive simplicity and mission, these establishments were not such nurseries of evil as some writers wish us to believe. Like some of the states of old, wealth and luxury paved the way to degeneracy, and -degeneracy to their destruction. The guileless manners of their lives became corrupted with the too frequent gifts of loaves and fishes, and the worm that lies hidden in all human institutions, pride, ultimately fed upon the vitals of their morals, and darkened their declining power and waning influence likewise. Such was the munificence which kings, princes, and nobles, had favoured this monastery with, that in the latter part of the thirteenth century, the convent possessed more than one hundred saddle horses, and as many more for agricultural and other purposes, and threefold the number of both in outlying mares and foals.

The monks had two thousand acres of arable land, and one thousand acres of meadow in cultivation, under their own surveillance. They had also fifteen thousand acres of forest, common, and pasturage lands. They had herdsmen, hinds, and labourers, at hired rates from a penny to twopence per day, besides a numerous staff of lay brethren. They had two hundred cows, three thousand head of oxen, eighty bulls, nearly as many calves under one year old, and upwards of twenty thousand sheep. They had also deer, swine, capons, and other poultry. At this time they bought, sold, and exchanged lands. They advanced money by way of mortgage on the security of lands or buildings. They bestowed lands on their brotherhood or those of the same order. They had access, free of tollage and dues, to markets all over the kingdom. They bred, bought, and sold horses, cows, oxen, sheep, and pigs. They sold fish, fruit, and grain of all kinds. They exported from Berwick twenty thousand fleeces of wool, or three thousand sacks, in a single year, the produce of their own flocks. They made butter and cheese, and sold both. They had fishings in the principal rivers, and even on the sea-coast. They had potteries and tile-works, public mills

and ovens or bake-houses; church livings and benefices, in all directions. They had forty granges and
herd-houses situated in various localities; private property in distant counties. Gifts of all kinds came in
annually, such as wax for tapers, white flour for holy-
day and pittance bread, as well as benefactions in
money. They were empowered to travel through
foreign countries and states free of taxes and dues
therein. Their sacred vessels became of silver and
gold, their sanctuary clothed in purple and fine linen.
Grand was the pageant, and sublime the warning. All
went on, thoughtless and merry as a marriage bell.
The scene shifted. Another oligarchy envied their
lands, another class of people their revenues, another
their pageants and the costly splendour of their churches;
and lastly, another and far greater class in number than
all the others, excited by declamatory agitation out of
doors, threw their weight into the great reforming
movement of the times. Some there were who sighed
deeply for more religious toleration, a less corrupt
church, and a more catholic spirit. Ultimately, as with
giant grasp, the great cordon of public opinion surrounded not Melrose only, but every similar institution
in the kingdom. Pillage, forfeiture, spoliation, ruin,
followed. One extreme ushered in another. Popery
was to be crushed at all hazards and consequences,

however dreadful to the pursuer or pursued. The strong
and the mighty estranged the abbey lands and possessions, and called them after their own names. The
monasteries were broken into forcibly, their wealth
stolen and distributed, the sacred vessels of their chapels
carried away, their ornaments defaced, their statues
mutilated and thrown down, and the inmates and houses
generally maltreated and dispersed. The monks were
incapable of offering any resistance. Priestcraft was
ignominy—monachism at an end. The handwriting
had been seen on the wall, but disregarded till too late.
Within was discord, and without were foes. In a
moment, powerful as the elements that urged them on,
and fierce as the retribution that fell on every hand,
Romanism was to be eradicated, root and branch, and
its expiry marked with terror and desolation. So it
was, the strong and the powerful cheering each other
on by

> "The good old rule, the simple plan,
> That he should take who has the power,
> And he should keep who can."

Such was plainly the motto of the times. At the
period of the Reformation all kinds of reproaches were
cast upon Romanists. They became a jibe and a bye-
word. The songs of the streets were about them.
We extract the following verse as a sign of the times,

and leave it to others to determine its truth or fiction
for themselves:—

> "The monks of Melros made fat kail
> On Fridays, when they fasted:
> But wanted neither beef nor ale,
> So long's their neighbours' lasted."
>
> *Old Ballad.*

The early monastic institutions of Britain have, by
a recent writer, been denominated "moral fortresses."
They were indeed the nurseries in which religion and
learning found refuge, at a time when the cottage
afforded no protection, and when the baronial residence
echoed no sound save that of brutal merriment and
ferocious warfare. By the religious awe they inspired,
they tended in some measure to render the incursions
of hostile armies less destructive. In perilous times
the peasantry of the neighbourhood found an hospitable
shelter within their walls, for themselves, their wives,
and their little ones; while the food and alms which
the monks regularly distributed, must have preserved
the existence of many who would have otherwise
perished. They were skilled in pharmacy, they had
an extensive knowledge of botanical science and medicinal plants, and observed, in a distinguished manner
at Melrose, the most courteous rule of hospitality to
rich and poor.

Chapter Fourth.

MELROSE TOWN.

Hail to thy ruins gray—all hail! Melrose!
Thy thriving town, and ancient market-cross,
Thy tap'ring spires, that crown the wat'ry glade,
And modest villas to the Tweed displayed.

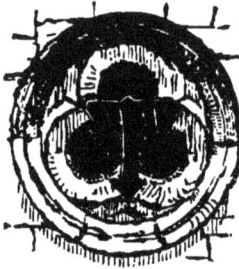

HE small, but pretty and retired town of Melrose, stands in an imposing and charming situation; surrounded by high hills on every side, and warmly sheltered from the cold north winds by the Gattonside range. It expands on a gentle acclivity from the south banks of the Tweed, towards the base of the northern slopes of the Eildon hills, once the Trimontium of the Romans, and in the upper ward of the county of Roxburgh. The air is remarkably dry and salubrious, and the prospect from all quarters of the town rich and inviting.

The town is a burgh of barony, has a capital weekly

market on Mondays for the sale of grain and stock, and is abundantly supplied with all kinds of agricultural and garden produce. Of late years, the town has made great progress, and is rapidly improving in extent, accommodation, and enterprise. The market-place is very capacious. In the centre stands the Cross, a structure bearing the marks of great antiquity, and on which is the date 1642. The shaft is twenty feet high, having the rampant figure of a unicorn on its apex, sustaining the arms of Scotland. For the support of this relic there is a piece of land in the vicinity, termed the Corse Rig. The upper part of this cross was changed at the Reformation; else, prior to this, it was supposed to be coeval with the Abbey. The old-fashioned flight of steps was removed, and an octagonal base substituted, which was anything but tasteful or appropriate, and vandalises this otherwise curious monument of antiquity, which is to be regretted. There is a prosperous farmer's club here, established in 1832. Its meetings are held the first Monday of each month; the attendance is numerous, and the business ably conducted. There are also a curling club of considerable local repute, and a spirited cricket club; several excellent educational institutions; horticultural, benevolent, and benefit societies.

The town of Melrose rests principally on the grey-wacke formation, the superincumbent strata consisting of good friable loam, interspersed occasionally with rich beds of clay, evidences of a warm and healthy locality, perfectly free from miasma and local atmospheric derangement. The inhabitants are both healthy, and look so, and strangers frequently observe, that in the oldest the lines of age come late in life, or seem deferred.

The rich, champaign, beautiful, and highly-cultivated vale of Melrose, occupies the site of what was once an ancient lake. From east to west, whenever the ground is turned up, this is manifest by the deposits met with, which consist of pebbles, water stones, and fresh water sand-beds, lying in many places quite contiguous to the surface. The general formation is Graywacke, especially northwards; to the south we find whinstone, conglomerate, and other varieties of sandstone.

This once magnificent sheet of water extended at one period from the bight of land by Melrose bridge to beyond Newstead, a distance of two miles, and from the grassy slopes of the Eildon to the fertile ranges of Gattonside. It was, in fact, a great basin or reservoir of the Tweed, and so existed for a long period until some phenomena burst the eastern barrier and liberated the pent-up waters. The Tweed has not always pursued an undeviating course in this locality. At one period it sallied on, in joyous mood, much nearer the town and abbey of Melrose than at present. In some places it has retired nearly a hundred yards from the south, and gained correspondingly on the north side, so that of the ancient Galtonside as it was called, now Gattonside, some inconsiderable portion has been detached, and lies south of the river, known as Gattonside haugh, and is thus separated from its ancient borders by the deviations made in the track of the river.

In dry seasons the volume of water in the Tweed is not nearly so great as formerly. In very rainy seasons, too, the subsidence of the water is far more rapid than it used to be. Agricultural improvements, more especially draining, passes the surplus water from the land with an amazing rapidity. A few days of dry weather entirely drains the land, and the best pools, which the fisherman knows, are thereby seriously affected. Supposing these changes and improvements continue, and ultimately embrace the mountain slopes and high uncultivated districts of the Tweed and some of its tributaries, the time may come when the heads of the weirs or caulds must be lowered at the overshot, or many must go wholly to rest, and the mills and machinery dependent on them. It becomes more apparent, year by year, that the salmon high up Tweed cannot pass the caulds and be gone to sea, to return again in a jolly, well-fed condition, let them try their best. Thus they are compelled sometimes to remain long in the same locality, and too often become a prey to the lawless and mischievous reiver

K

Within a few years, to the west of the town of Melrose, there has sprung up a long line of very handsome and superior suburban villas, enjoying on the south a romantic view of the Eildon, and on the north the bosom of the softly gliding Tweed, and a lovely range of rich upland cultivated fields and orchards stretching far beyond it.

Most conveniently situated, and near the business end of Melrose, stands the railway station, which is both a handsome and capacious structure, in excellent keeping with the picturesque locality that surrounds it. An omnibus runs twice a-day from the railway station to Earlston, and other omnibuses are in constant attendance on every train that arrives and departs.

Of late years, Melrose has become a favourite haunt of the tourist, and an inexpensive resort of the middle and upper classes. To families or individuals seeking retirement, the town and neighbourhood offer all that can be desired, and the distinguished advantages also of good and well-bred society.

Melrose is of easy access north or south; by rail, it is distant from Edinburgh 37 miles, from Kelso 15, Hawick 16, and Berwick $38\frac{1}{2}$ miles. It is within thirty minutes' drive of the far-famed Abbotsford, the romantic seat of the late Sir Walter Scott, Bart., and of Dryburgh Abbey, the scene of his boyhood and his grave; to either of which favourite places, as well as to

the ancient houses of Bemerside and bonny Cowden-
knowes, good posting accommodation at moderate rates
can be easily obtained in Melrose.

The population of Melrose town proper has risen
from 964 in 1851 to 1141 in 1861. The continued
growth of the town in size and proportion is attributable to the many natural advantages of the district of
which it is the centre. The parish is now divided into
two districts, viz., Ladhope district, with 4154, and
Melrose district, with 3557 inhabitants, the latter consisting of 1643 males, and 1914 females. The united
population of the parish of Melrose is now, therefore,
7711. At the census of 1851 it was only 7365. Many
new residents have contributed to this increase.*

---

* The growth of population has, however, been retarded by incidental
circumstances. The town has been improved in general appearance,
and has witnessed an influx of the middle and higher classes, with a
diminution of the poorer and industrious ones. In our estimation of
the philanthropic principles so nobly advocated by the friends of
social science, this is matter of regret. Within the memory of the
present generation, a row of cottages existed where the present wall
of St. Cuthbert's garden is placed. A similar line of houses extended
down the east side of Abbey Street, where the wall of Priorbank
nursery stands. And a considerable street, known as Dingleton
Wynd, occupied the situation now covered by the railway station
and its approaches. These clearings have compelled many of the
inhabitants to resort to the neighbouring villages to procure suitable
house accommodation. Some steps have already been taken in the
right direction, and we shall be glad to see this anomalous state of
things altered, and good two-storey tenements erected for the industrious poor.

The parish church is a large and most substantial building, crowned with a spire, and ornamented with a clock, standing upon a conspicuous eminence called the Weirhill, a little west of the town.*

Nearly opposite, looking from the Established Church northwards, stands the Free Church, a very neat edifice;† and a little beyond it, close to the highway leading to the sequestered village of Darnick, is a small but elegant Episcopalian Church, of which the Rev. John Gabriel Ryde, M.A., is incumbent, and was ordained in 1847. The High Cross, as it was called, and which was much noted in ancient times, and directed the pilgrim from the Abbey to Bridgend and the Girthgate, stood near the present site of the Episcopalian edifice. This cross pointed out the great Edinburgh road by the Girthgate. There is also an Evangelical Union Chapel, of which the Rev. William Crombie is minister, ordained in 1850; and a United Presbyterian Church in the centre of the town.‡

Near the Free Church, on the higher ground, is a new and well-enclosed cemetery, with good carriage way, purchased and laid out by the parochial board of Melrose.

---

* Rev. William Murray, ordained in 1836. Patron, the Duke of Buccleuch.

† Free Church. Rev. William Cousin, ordained in 1840.

‡ U. P. Church. Rev. Hugh Stevenson, ordained 1860.

In the immediate vicinity of Melrose are the splendid estates and residences of the most distinguished families, a goodly number of remarkably pleasant villas, villages, and hamlets, scattered amongst smiling fields and gardens, presenting an appearance of great fertility and loveliness. Within easy distance is the ancient manufacturing town of Galashiels, noted for its tweeds, shawls, and tartans; the town of Earlston (Ercildoun), not more famed for the ruins of Thomas the Rhymer's tower than for its ginghams and hosiery; and the ancient towns of Selkirk and Jedburgh, with the beautiful monastic ruins of the latter. About the close of the seventeenth century, there were a great many public breweries and malt-houses in Melrose and the vicinity. Melrose also stood in high repute for its domestic manufacture of shirting and fine linen cloths. These were bought by the first houses in London and Edinburgh; some were so costly that the rich and luxurious could only afford to wear them. This useful occupation has entirely ceased, and agriculture is the chief source of local industry.

Around Melrose, the most eligible sites of land for building purposes can be readily obtained. Land is feued at an easy price, and materials for the erection of dwellings are both cheap and plentiful. As a speculation, building has become profitable; as an investment, it affords capital interest and security; houses are taken up as soon as finished, and frequently before. Of late years, many good families have erected houses here for their summer occupation only. The roads are everywhere in good order and preservation, soon dry again after rain, and whether for season visitors or permanent residents, few places possess so much attraction with so much quiet and seclusion.

The joyous river with its silver falls, Melrose bridge, its sylvan scenery and wooded slopes, the busy corn mill on the Weir, the chain suspension bridge, and here and there some angler with his cunning fly and dexterous hand,—one varying prospect,

" Ever charming, ever new ;"—

the church, the grassy knoll, and amorous music of the waters wimpling on beneath our feet. Sequestered oft in shady nook and greenwood shaw, some village farm gives to the landscape round a matchless and unbroken charm.

The lover of piscatorial pleasures may revel here. They who delight from lofty eminences to catch enchanting scenes, and lift the veil of nature to behold her when "unadorned, adorned the most," will discover many worthy of admiration and the pencil likewise. The retiring and contemplative may here enjoy heavenly tranquillity, and woo the balmy breeze of blithe invigorating health at morning, noon, or night, while perambulating the lovely walks that everywhere crown the margin of the river.

The town of Melrose contains four good libraries, many first-class shops, and numerous private houses for the accommodation of temporary residents, two excellent family hotels and posting houses, besides comfortable inns; and is well supplied with both water and gas of superior quality. Lammas fair, which is annually held on the northern slopes of the Eildon, attracts buyers of sheep and horned cattle to Melrose from a considerable distance. The fair is a notable one.

The Duke of Buccleuch is superior of Melrose. Many places in Melrose and its vicinity still bear monkish names, as the Cloister Close, the Abbot's Meadow, and Cuddie's (St. Cuthbert's) Green; and the principal wells and water-springs still retain the names of Romish saints, as St. Mary's, St. Helen's, St. William's, St. Dunstan's, and others. The wooded bank south of the Abbey is still called Prior's Walk, and a small rivulet that runs thereby, the Malthouse Burn. The ancient name of Dingleton was Daniel's Town.

In the High Street, Melrose, stands a very ancient two-storied tenement, with thatched roof, directly opposite the King's Arms Hotel. It has one gable jutting out upon the pavement. This was formerly styled the " Westport," and about fifty years ago formed the western extremity of Melrose, whereas it now stands in the centre of the town. Above the door is the date 1635. In this house slept General Leslie, the night before the battle of Philiphaugh in September, 1645: After the battle of Naseby, Sir David Leslie was sent to seek out the Marquis of Montrose and crush him. The commander of the Covenanters left Melrose early on the following morning, and, favoured by a dense fog, marched unobserved on Philiphaugh, where he fell in with the infantry of Montrose, and hostilities commenced briskly on both sides. The cavalry of Montrose, which lay in Selkirk the previous night, shortly came up, but too late, the infantry being already in disorder, which the cavalry increased, until at length all the adherents of Montrose gave way together, those who could escape taking full flight up the Yarrow, and across Minchmoor to Peebles.

Two very ancient holidays are held annually in the town of Melrose, viz., Fastren's E'en and the Eve of St. John.

Fastren's E'en is celebrated annually after the Border fashion, in the month of February, the day being fixed by the following antiquated couplet—

> " First comes Candlemas, syne the New Moon;
> The next Tuesday after is Fastren's E'en."

On these occasions the town presents a most

singular appearance, from the windows of the shops
and dwellings in the main streets being barricaded.
This precaution is necessary to prevent breakage, as
football playing on a most indiscriminate and unlimited
scale is the order of the day. The ball is thrown up
at the cross at one o'clock, when the young men of
the town and neighbourhood, with a sprinkling of the
married *athletes*, assemble in considerable numbers.
The footballs used are previously provided by a general
public subscription, and from one o'clock the sport is
kept up with great spirit, until darkness sets in and
puts a stop to the game. Business throughout the
town, as a matter of course, is almost entirely suspended
during the day.

The eve of St. John witnesses a masonic comme-
moration of great interest. The institution of the Melrose St. John's Lodge of Freemasons, is said to be of
equal antiquity with the Abbey—"John Mordo, who had
in keeping all mason work" at the building of it, being
the first Grand Master of the lodge. The anniver-
sary is celebrated on St. John's festival of each year.
Immediately after the election of office-bearers for
the year ensuing, the brethren walk in procession
three times round the Cross, and afterwards dine together, under the presidency of the newly elected
Grand Master. About six in the evening the members
again turn out, and form into line two abreast, each

bearing a lighted flambeau, and decorated with their peculiar emblems and insignia. Headed by the heraldic banners of the lodge, the procession follows the same route, three times round the Cross, and then proceeds to the Abbey. On these occasions the crowded streets present a scene of the most animated description. The joyous strains of a well-conducted band, the waving torches, and incessant showers of fireworks, make the scene a carnival. But at this time, the venerable Abbey is the chief point of attraction and resort, and as the mystic torch-bearers thread their way through its mouldering aisles, and round its massive pillars, the outlines of its gorgeous ruins become singularly illuminated, and brought into bold and striking relief;

"That deeper seem their shadows still."

The whole extent of the Abbey is, with " measured step and slow," gone three times round. But when, near the " finale," the whole masonic body gather to the chancel, and forming one grand semicircle around it, where the heart of King Robert the Bruce lies deposited near the High Altar, and the band strikes up the patriotic air,

"Scots wha hae wi' Wallace bled,
Scots wham Bruce has often led,"

the effect produced by the associations of the music

and the scene is sublime and overpowering. Midst showers of rockets and the glare of blue lights, the scene closes, the whole reminding one of some popular saturnalia held in a monkish town during the middle ages.

Melrose has long been the great central artery of Border antiquity, history, literature, and romance, ramifying in all directions to a distance of twenty and thirty miles. It was rendered immortally classic by the songs of Burns and the *Seasons* of Thomson, to the lore of which has been added the *Adventures and Travels* of Parke, and the undying wreaths woven by the industrial genius of Scott, Wilson, Hogg, and Dr Leyden.*

No single district of equal extent in Christendom is so rich in the spoils of time—so full of interest to the antiquarian and historian, and so redundant and over-flowing in legendary lore and tradition. It is replete and teeming with the essence of romance, and pre-eminently artistic and beautiful in its outward diversity of form and general character.

Once a mystic cycle of the Druids, dyed with their bloody immolations and forest sacrifices ; early held of

---

* Sir Walter Scott; Professor John Wilson, Author of *Noctes Ambrosianæ ;* James Hogg, the Ettrick Shepherd ; and Dr John Leyden, the poet and linguist, who was a native of Denholm, but died in India.

the Romans, their Tremontium, on the barren Eildon,
a General's quarters, with connecting roads and inter-
cepting ramparts; next sought of the Religieuse and
Monachism; how often the very theatre of Border
strife and sanguinary foray; trodden under foot of
that merciless horde of barbarians, the pagan Danes—
it has witnessed the strife of battle and the greater
triumphs of peace. In the dark ages of our history,
and while the genial rays of religion were bursting but
slowly upon the mental surface of the national character, it became too frequently the cradle of heroic
valour, and the mausoleum of vanquished greatness.

More exquisitely beautiful, however, than fairy ever
dreamed, the wonder of the beholder, the joy of the
eye, immortalized by immortality itself in song and
fable—skilfully enigmatical to the grandest conception
—a superhuman relic of the past—sublimely harmonious in all its parts—a charm—a glory, are the sumptuous ruins of the ancient and renowned Monastery of
St. Mary's, Melrose. Fire, sword, and rapine have
done their worst, while time seems only to have
wrinkled its beauty, in order to give the grand outline
of its past pomp and magnificence more striking effect
to the beholders of the present age. Roofless in part
—annihilated in portion—stript—denuded. The inimitable chastity of its decorated doors, windows, and
columns, with its flowery carvings and symbolic deco-

rations, are gorgeous and fascinating in the extreme—
they are, in truth, a life's study—and when treading
its now silent and deserted aisles, the mind instinctively
reverts back to its appearance when graced with vir-
ginal bloom and primeval splendour.

MONACHISM, ITS ORDERS, DUTIES, HABITS, AND EMPLOYMENTS.

As order and economy were the mottoes observed
in all monastic institutions from an early period, it
will be interesting to enumerate the office-bearers and
their duties, also the habits and employments of the
monks, thus rendering more intelligible the following
history.

1. The Lord Abbot ruled over the whole convent
with absolute sway, living in great state in private
apartments, but more generally in a separate hall or
palace. He had servants, horses, hawks, hounds, boats,
gardens, lawns, orchards, and could entertain knightly
guests with sumptuous dinners and any individual of
the convent at his private table. He had a chaplain,
who, besides his spiritual duties, managed his household.
Both he and the monks were held accountable, however,
to the parent monastery. Melrose being a mother
church, and the chief of the four pilgrimages of Scot-

land, was subject to a Chapter of the general order only, whose decisions required the confirmation or rejection of the Pope.

2. The Prior was chosen by the Abbot, and acted for him; he also kept up considerable state in his private apartments. He presided in the choir, chapter-house, and refectory, when the Abbot did not choose to do so himself: he knew the revenues of the convents, both fixed and fluctuating, the produce of the harvests, the grants and benefactions bequeathed from time to time, and was in fact a monastic chancellor, with ample power and recognised authority.

3. The Superior was the Prior's assistant and occasional deputy. He had the general supervision of the convent in matters of discipline, noting those who were guilty of any neglect of duty, or were absent without leave; took care the doors of the convent were kept locked from five in the evening to five in the morning, and when he visited the dormitories at night, read over the names of the monks, who were bound to answer to them.

4. The Cellarer had charge of the cellar, storehouse, kitchen, and refectory; in this respect he superintended them, and saw that nothing necessary was wanting.

5. The Refectioner had care of the furniture of the table in the refectory eating-room.

6. The Chamberlain had charge of the wardrobe and bedding.

7. The Secretarius, or Sacrist, had charge of the sacred vessels and ornaments of the church, provided the candles, also bread and wine for the Communion.

8. The Almoner distributed food and clothing to the poor, especially the fragments left at meals.

9. The Infirmarier watched over the interest of the sick in the convent ward, administered to their wants, and on urgent occasions was their confessor.

10. The Hospitaller received pilgrims, strangers, and wayfaring poor, and provided for their entertainment and wants in a suitable and appropriate room, called the hospice or guest-chamber. Strangers of rank were entertained by the Abbot only.

11. The Chantor, or Precentor, conducted the service of the choir, instructed the singing boys, had the custody of the archives or records, and sometimes of the library.

12. The Librarian kept the books in a room built for the purpose, adjoining which was the scriptorium or writing-room, where some of the monks were constantly employed making copies of books.

13. The Commendator, Steward, Seneschal, or Baillie, was the Abbot's depute, in the exercise of his seignorial rights, as temporal lord of the abbey lands, &c.

This office was usually held by a layman of distinction in the neighbourhood, and, in later times, became almost hereditary in their families.

14. The Treasurer received the rents and paid accounts and wages.

15. The Porter had a lodging at the gate, with power to admit pilgrims, strangers, and all proper persons, and to exclude others.

16. The Kitchener, or chief cook, was sometimes a layman.

17. The Master of the Noviciate superintended the education of the young persons who were on trial for admission into the order. He was sometimes styled master of the converts; persons who, having lived long in the world, afterwards took the monastic habit, being called converts.

18. The Lay Brethren were also sometimes called Converts; they were the servants of the community, performed the menial offices, and were employed in the labours of husbandry. They were attired like the monks, this being ordained as a token of the humility of the latter.

19. Hebdomadaries, or weekly officers, was a name given to any of the monks while employed in waiting at table or in other services, performed by weekly turns. Such were the readers who stood at a desk

in the refectory, and read, while the rest were at their meals.

20. A master Mason* or builder was either kept in the monastery or adjacent to it, and many other persons who exercised useful employments, such as potters gardeners, tool-makers, smiths, and habit-makers.†

LIFE AND CONDITION OF A MONK OR FRIAR IN ANCIENT TIMES.

Their lodgings cost them nothing in the Abbey, and the dress of each individual was scarcely worth more than fifteen shillings; the chief part consisting of coarse woollen stuff, being manufactured by themselves. The colour of the hood and tunic (white or black), indicating at sight the brotherhood of the wearer. In general they had neither linen nor stockings, they wore sandals with boot legs, and wooden soles for shoes. Although never distressed for eating or drinking, clothes or lodgings, their lives were hard and uncomfortable.

They rose early every day, very early, to sing matins in the choir, say masses, and attend confessionals.

---

* A society of masons always settled, and instituted their lodge or club in the neighbourhood of a monastery, from the very commencement of its erection.

† For further information, see Fosbroke's learned work on *British Monachism.*

L

The business of the latter is often tiresome, because
the largest number of the penitents are wholly unknown to them; many repeat the same story over and
over again; the priest can seldom see their faces; and
many who commit grievous and singular sins seldom
go to confess them.*

When the fatiguing task of the morning was over, the
monks went to dinner at twelve o'clock exactly, which
was always frugal and scanty. While they dined they
kept silence, and listened to one of their brethren, who
read aloud some book all the time of dinner.

After dinner, a full hour was given for recreation,
which usually consisted in walking about their garden
in summer, or sitting round the refectory fire, which is
in the middle of the great hall, in winter, chattering,
telling stories, or disputing with each other. They had
now to go sing again for another hour, and when this
was over, those who wished to go out beyond the precincts of the Monastery, had to kneel before one of
their Superiors, kiss the hem of his garment, and ask
permission, which was seldom denied. Those who
chose to stay at home, retired to their cells, to read,
write, or practise some manual work.

At sunset, they must always be within doors to
sing prayers before supper. After supper they all
withdrew, and went immediately to bed if they chose,

* Baretti.

or looked over their books, or mended their garments, for an hour or two. Their beds consisted of a simply contrived mattress, usually stuffed with straw, chaff, or leaves, with a coarse coverlet of cloth, but no sheets. At midnight, they were called up from all parts of the Convent by lay. brethren appointed for the purpose. They went to prayers for about an hour, after which they retired to rest till daybreak. This interruption of sleep was felt a great hardship, unnatural, and detrimental to health. Their unaltered temperance and regular manner of living, alone compensating for it. And in a general way, they all looked florid, robust, and contented, the outward world attributing their appearance to plentiful diet and gross indulgences.

We will now say a word or two about nuns. Soon as morning appeared, and in winter, long before, they got up and went to sing their prayers in the choir. Then to breakfast, which consisted of a bit of bread and a glass of water. Their dinners were most frugal, and their suppers still scantier. During Lent and Advent they fared still worse, for they had but one meagre dish in the morning, with undressed salad, and bread and fruit in the evening.

They sat down to a bountiful board only on the most particular occasions, such as when they received a new nun at Easter, or at Christmas, and on their Patron Saint's day, once a-year.

They fasted on Fridays and Saturdays all the year round.

Some received small pensions from their families, others were very ingenious and industrious. Fancy articles, such as ribbons, garters, flowers, buttons, lace, knitted stockings, and many other things, occupied their leisure time, by the sale of which they were enabled to procure themselves some little delicacy, to regale their visitors with.

The daily life in the cloister would have been strangely monotonous but for the constant series of devotional services, acts of charity and munificence, the inmates were continually called upon to exercise and contribute to.

The occupants of the Convent enjoyed uninterrupted communication with their friends; they were permitted to receive visits from relatives, and to entertain them on those occasions.

Exterior View of South Transept.

Chapter Fifth.

CARTA REGIS DAVID DE ABBATIA DE MELROS.

AVID, Dei gratia, Rex Scottorum, episcopis, abbatibus, comitibus, · baronibus, et probis hominibus suis, et omnibus fidelibus suis totius regni sui, Francis, et Anglicis, et Scotis, et Galwensibus, salutem : Sciatis me pro anima mea, et animabus patris et matris meæ, et fratris mei Ædgari, et aliorum fratrum et sororum mearum, et uxorus meæ Matildæ, et etiam pro anima Henrici filii mei et hæredis, et antecessorum et successorum meorum, concessisse et dedisse Deo et Sanctæ Mariæ de Melros, et monachis ibidem · Deo servientibus, Cystertiensis ordinis de Rievallis, et suis successoribus, annuente et concedente Henrico, filio meo · et hærede, et per cartam suam confirmante, in perpetuam elemosinam, totam scilicet, terram de Melros, et totam terram de Eldune, et totam terram de Dernewie, per terminos et rectas divisas suas, in bosco et plano, in pratis et aquis, in pasturis et moris, in viis et semitis, et in omnibus aliis rebus, liberas et quietas, et solutas ab omni terreno servitio et exactione seculari, perpetuo tenore possidere.

Insuper, autem, sciatis me dedisse prædictis monachis, et hac mea carta confirmasse, in terra mea et in forestis meis, scilicet de Seleschirche, et de Tranequair, omnia aisiamenta sua; pasturam, scilicet ad averia sua, et ligna, et materiam, et pasnagium ubique ad suos, proprios usus, sicut ego ipse melius habeo ad opus meum, et nominatum, intra Galche et Leder.   Præterea, in aquis de Tweda, infra terminos eorum, piscaturam, tam ex mea parte fluminis quam ex eorum parte ubique.   Præter vero, omnia supradicta, dedi et confirmavi eis, ad incrementum, Galtuneshalech, et totam terram et boscum de Galtunesside, sicut ego ipse, et Henricus filius meus, et abbas Ricardus ejusdem ecclesiæ, perivimus et circumivimus, die veneris crastino ascensionis, Domini; anno, scilicet, secundo quo Stephanus Rex Angliæ captus est.   Testibus ad hoc præsens donum, Johanne, episcopo; Willielmo, nepote regis, Hugone de Morevilla; Willielmo de Sumervilla; Henrico, filio Swani; Gervasio Ridel.   Volo itaque ut ipsi omnes has predictas terras et res suas ita libere et quiete teneant et possideant, sicut aliqua elemosina liberius et quietius, perpetuo tenore, teneri potest et possideri.   Teste, Henrico, filio meo; Johanne, episcopo; Willielmo; nepote meo; Willielmo, cancellario; Madd. comite; Roberto, de Humframvilla; Hugone de Morevilla; Waltero filio Alani; Hugone Britone; Osberto de Ardene; Gervasio Ridel, Willielmo, de Sumervilla; Ricardo, Gernim; Ricardo Anglico; Willielmo, de Lindes. Accelino, archidiacono; Jordane, clerico; Estmundo, elemosinario; Præterea, hominibus de eadem terra; Gospatricio, comite, Ulfchillo, filio Ethestan; Osolfo, filio Huctred; Macco, filio Unwain; Huctredo, filio Sioth; Huctredo, filio Gospatricii; Orm, filio Eilaf; Eilaf, filio Gospatricii; Eduso, filio Norman; Osolfo, filio Edine; Osolfo, filio Elfstan; Roberto Brus, Meschin; Radulfo, filio Turstaini; Rogero, nepote episcopi. Apud Ercheldon. In Junio.

[TRANSLATION.]

CHARTER OF KING DAVID TO THE ABBEY OF MELROSE.

"David I., by the grace of God, king of the Scots, to all bishops, abbots, counts, barons, and to all good men and faithful allies of his kingdom, in France, England, and Scotland, greeting. Be it known to you, that I, for my soul, and for the souls of my father and mother, and for the souls of Edgar and my other brother, and for the souls of my sister and wife Matilda, and likewise for the soul of Henry, my son and heir, and for the souls of my ancestors and successors, Have granted and given to God, and to St. Mary of Melrose, and to the monks of Rievalle, serving God, of the Cistertian order of that place, and their successors, my son and heir, Henry, confirming it by his charter for a perpetual possession, that is to say, the whole land of Melrose, the land of Eildon, and the whole land of Darnick, divided by their proper bounds, into level parts by meadows and watery pastures, and ploughed land, by highways and footpaths, and other things of that sort, free and delivered from all landed servitude and exaction, to be possessed by them in a perpetual secular tenure.

"Be it known to you, moreover, that I have given to the aforesaid monks, and confirmed by this my charter, all the fruits and pasture and timber in my land, and in the forest of Selkirk and of Traquair, and between Gala and Leader Water, besides both, the fishery of the Tweed, everywhere on their side of the river as on mine. Besides all that has been already mentioned, I have given and confirmed to them in addition, the whole land and pasture of Gattonside, which I myself, along with my son Henry, and Richard, abbot of the said church, surveyed on Friday morning, the ascension of our Lord, and the second year of the captivity of Stephen, king of England." Present as witnesses of this gift, John, Bishop, William, nephew of the king, Hugo de Morville,* William de Somerville. Henry, the King's son, Gervasius Riddel, and others.

" I wish, therefore, that they may hold and possess the aforesaid lands and their appurtenances, that is to say, with greater freedom and stability than any other tenure could be held - and possessed. Witnesses, Henry, my son, John, Bishop, William, my nephew, William, Chancellor," &c.

David I., commonly called St. David, on account of his piety, was the youngest son of Malcolm III., king of Scotland, surnamed Cammoir, son of Duncan I. David began to reign anno 1124 ; he was a valiant, honourable, and religious prince. The abbeys of Holyrood, Kelso, Jedburgh, Melrose, Kinloss, Dunfermline, Newbattle, and Dryburgh, were either founded by him or under his auspices. He also built two religious houses at Newcastle, and one at Holm-Cultrum in Cumberland, and he created the Bishopricks of Ross, Brechin, Dumblane, and Dunkeld. His queen was Maud, daughter of Waldeosus, Earl of Northumberland and Huntingdon, whose mother was grand-daughter of William the Conqueror. David I. died in peace at Carlisle, in the twenty-ninth year of his reign, and was buried at Dunfermline.

* Nephew of De Morville, one of the murderers of Thomas à Beckett.

Chapter Sixth.

CHURCH SYMBOLISM, WITH REFERENCE TO THE
SYMBOLISM OF ST. MARY'S CHAPEL, MELROSE.

FROM the earliest ages, the structural design of monastic churches was
peculiarly symbolic, both in outward form and internal appearance.
Within, the ornaments bespoke
grace, beauty, solemnity, and holi-
ness. Without, pleasure, worldiness, deformity, and
sin. The churches were cruciform above the ground
and below it—they were an allegory. This occurred
in the first erections of oaken walls and thatched roofs.
This was apparent in the great simplicity of the early
Anglo-Saxon style, and existed where Christianity was
winning its way, long before the combined treasures of
Greece and Rome had fallen to the lot of the ancient
occupants of Britain.

How much more exquisite and elaborately wrought
out, in some of these more recent majestic temples; in
what remains of our beautiful Abbey, where all that

wealth could bequeath was poured forth a willing offering
to prosecute and accomplish—all that art could devise
and genius impose, to array a solemn structure in
unequalled grandeur and immeasurable charm.

But the sign of the Cross was that which gave the
greatest scope to symbolism. Churches were multiplied
on this sign. So the symbols have continued the same
throughout all ages of the Christian church. The dis-
ruption of empires, the rise and fall of some, the dis-
memberment of others, have not affected them in any
way. They have grown old with civilization itself, and
are commensurate with it.

The Chapel of St. Mary's, Melrose, represents a cross
of St. John. The arrangement of a material church
resembles that of a human body. The chancel, or
place of the altar, represents the head ; the transepts,
the hands and arms; and the nave and aisles towards
the west, the rest of the body; the sacrifices of the
altar, the vows of the heart. By the length of the
church is meant fortitude; the breadth, charity; and
the height, the hope of future retribution; the door is
obedience; the pavement, humility. The open court or
porch signifieth Christ. The door is Christ: "I am
the door;" "Knock, and it shall be opened." The
triple breadth of nave and aisles, the triple height of
pier-arch—triforium and clerestory; the triple length
of choir, transepts, and nave, again set forth the Holy

Trinity; and what besides is there that does not tell of our blessed Saviour!—that does not point out to "Him First," in the twofold western door—"Him Last," in the distant altar—"Him midst," in the great rood—"Him without end," in the monogram carved on boss and corbel, in the Holy Lamb, in the Lion of the tribe of Judah, and in the mystic fish;—the ascension of Christ is expressed by the flying bird, as martyrs are signified by birds let loose.

The extended hand signifies providence. Spire, pinnacle, and finial, the upward curb of the sculptured foliage, the upward spring of the flying buttress, the sharp rise of the window arch, the high-thrown pitch of the roof—all these overpowering the horizontal tendency of string course and parapet, teach us that, vanquishing earthly desires, we also should ascend in heart and mind.

Again, the transepts stretching out crossways, tell of the atonement. The communion of saints is set forth by the chapels clustering round choir and nave. Lessons of holy wisdom are written in the delicate tracery of the windows. The union of many members is shadowed forth by the multiplex arcade; the duty of letting our light shine before men, by the pierced and flowered parapet that crowns the whole. As we enter the church, close by us is the font, for it is by regeneration we enter. It is deep and capacious, for we are buried in baptism with Christ. It is of stone, for He is

the rock. The massy piers are the apostles and prophets; they are each of many members; for many are the
graces in every saint. There is delicate foliage round
the heads of all, for all were plentiful in good works.

The saints are usually the attributes of great moral
power, as St. Martha, the patron of industry.

Within we are compassed about, as it were, with a
mighty cloud of witnesses. The rich, deep glass of the
window teems with saintly forms, each in its own
fair niche. There is the glorious company of the
apostles, the goodly fellowship of the prophets, the
noble army of martyrs, the shining band of the con-
fessors, and the jubilant chorus of the virgins.

But on none of these things do we rest. Piers, arch
behind arch; window, light behind light; arcades, shaft
behind shaft; the roof, bay behind bay; the saints
around us, the heavenly hierarchy above, with dignity
of pre-eminence still increasing eastwards, we are led,
eye and soul and thought, to the image of the crucified
Saviour, as displayed in the great east window. Gazing
steadfastly on that, we pass up the nave, that is the
church militant, till we reach the rood screen, the barrier between it and the church triumphant. The screen
itself glows with gold and crimson;—with gold, for the
redeemed have golden crowns: with crimson, for they
washed their robes in the blood of the Lamb to obtain
them.

The resurrection is set forth by the Phœnix rising immortal from its own ashes; the meritorious passion of Christ, by the pelican feeding its young with its own blood; the sacrament of the holy eucharist, by grapes and wheat ears; the Christian's renewal of strength, by the eagle; and the Christian's purity and innocence, by the dove.

The piscina or lavacrum, denoted the pity of Christ.

The chapter-house, the secret of the heart.

The refectory, the love of holy meditation.

The cellar, Holy Scripture.

The dormitory, a clear conscience, and the oratory a spotless life.

The garden of trees and herbs, the cultivation of virtues.

The well, heavenly gifts, the " water of life." " Ho, every one that thirsteth, come and drink."

The cloisters, signified the celestial paradise, or separation from the world.

The choir, the harmony of the church triumphant.

The altar signified the heart.

The bells, the preachers.

Harpers there are also, harping with their harps, for one is the song of the church in earth and in heaven.

Outwardly the hideous forms that seem hanging from the eaves, speak the misery of the hardened and impenitent, and of those who are cast out of the church.*

The figures of the blind carrying the lame, richly attired nuns, musicians of all kinds, monks with strings of beads in their hands, saints, martyrs, and apostles, the ornamental rosettes that decorate the whole structure, the family of Ham represented in the sculptured head of the negress, have each their proper and peculiar meaning. None of these things are by chance, but design, and being such, admit of unequivocal interpretation, and have been conveyed, from age to age, with unimpeachable fidelity. With the ancient religieuse, the rose was emblematic of the "flower of life," its withered leaves the ashes of good men, and their perfume, immortality itself. Stars and crosses signify saints and martyrdom. The fox signifies cunning—the Evil one; and the geese, the unwary, credulous, easily tempted and ensnared. The owl and the mouse admit of a similar interpretation.

* For further information see "*Church Symbolism,*" by DURANDUS, sometime Bishop of Mende.

Chapter Seventh.

AN ARCHITECTURAL DESCRIPTION OF THE RUINS OF MELROSE ABBEY.

RE we unfold the pages of history, emblazoned with the devices of monachism and invested with pathetic incident, let us patiently examine what the hand of time and the destroyer has left us.

The structural form and character of all monastic edifices had its root in ancient symbolism, which we have described in the previous chapter.

In the year 1136[*] this monastery was founded by King David, and enriched beyond all similar institutions in Britain. The most valuable possessions and privileges were bestowed upon it. Of the first erection perhaps nothing remains, as it is said to have been wholly destroyed by Edward II. in 1322. For this

---

[*] The Monastery of Dryburgh was founded in 1150, and occupied by the monks in December 1152.

Interior View of Chancel and Oriel Window.

and other barbarous acts, Robert the Bruce severely punished Edward at Bannockburn, and expelled all the English out of Scotland. He rebuilt the abbey in 1326, in the most magnificent architectural style of the period, the mature, graceful, decorated Gothic. The old Gothic style, after the massive Roman, was coarse and heavy. The later Gothic, as exhibited in these ruins, is wonderfully grand and of the most elaborate and accurate execution. But it is only since the twelfth century that this style, by some called the flambuoyant, developed itself. The Egyptian style had its origin in the cavern or mound—the Chinese in the tent. The Grecian was derived from the wooden cabin, hence the exquisite chastity of their leaf ornament, but the Gothic from the bower of trees. It would seem to have originated in the imitation of groves and bowers, under which the Druids performed their religious ceremonies.

Its most striking characteristics are its pointed arches, its pinnacles and spires, its large buttresses, clustered pillars, flying shafts and vaulted roofs, a profusion of ornament, and general predominance of the perpendicular over the horizontal; in other words, its bold, lofty spirit and expressive harmony of parts. The pleasing landmark of our cities and villages, the spire, is exclusively Gothic.

We may here observe, that antecedent to the twelfth

M

century, neither tabernacle work, nor niches with canopies, statues in whole relief, pinnacles, pediments or
spires, nor tracing in vaultings, were used. Towards
the close of the thirteenth century a new epoch commenced. Pillars, supporting sharply-pointed arches,
of slender and graceful proportions, were introduced.
Ceilings sustained by groined ribs, resting on the
capitols of pillars, and windows lighted by several
openings, instead of one.

Such was the era of Gothic architecture when what
we still behold of St. Mary's Chapel was constructed.
Massive columns and semi-circular arches were dis-
pensed with, also the archivolts and imposts of Roman
architecture.

The Norman Conquest brought lofty vaultings and
pillars with capitols more elaborately finished; towers
of large dimensions and great height, placed either in
the centre of the cross, or at the west end of ecclesiastical erections. In both north and south transepts
we see an admirable illustration of these several par-
ticulars.

The first transition of the arch seems to have taken
place towards the close of the reign of David, King of
Scots, the circular figure becoming slightly pointed,
and the heavy single pillar transformed into a cluster;
the archivolts still retaining many of the Saxon ornaments.

The fifteenth century was greatly distinguished by the study and revival of ancient architecture in Europe; and in the fourteenth century, indeed, great improvement was manifest in Italian construction.

The first erection of Melrose abbey, destroyed by Edward II., would be vastly inferior to the second in splendour and detail. The substantial part of the latter was probably executed with rapidity, but to complete the decorative portions must have occupied a period extending over one or two centuries. The style of decoration then prevailing differed from everything previous, and formed the last era of Gothic architecture. After the rebuilding of Melrose abbey, under the auspices of King Robert Bruce and his successors, we have an account of the burning of Melrose by Richard II., after he and his generals had slept one night in the abbey, anno 1385, when he gave it to the flames on the following morning. We think the damage was partial on this occasion, and that the western portion only was severely injured. The German or romantic style had succeeded the early or coarse Gothic, and was consonant with the spirit of the middle ages. The great Italian churches, even St. Peter's and others, were henceforth to be raised in a sublimity of style hitherto unapproachable.

This latter style, better known by some as the perpendicular, presents us with a splendid example in the great eastern or 'prentice window of the abbey. The mullions, instead of waving at the top, as in the decorated style, run up in perpendicular lines. And although the day-light of this window is thirty-six feet. by sixteen, it is simply divided by four slender mullions, eight inches in thickness—the arch lines being straight, and not curved as usual. This window presents us with a magnificent study, in the richness of its tracery, the sharpness of its outline, and the extreme beauty of the work. Beyond all, the sublime harmony of its parts demands our warmest admiration. Indeed, the splendid composition displayed throughout the whole of the east end of Melrose abbey is not exceeded in the kingdom. It exemplifies to us at the present day the most finished, graceful, matured, and elaborate culmination of Gothic architecture the fourteenth century produced.

The stone is similar in tone and texture to that of which Strasburg Cathedral is built, and there is some similarity of style between the two; more particularly do we notice this in the light open ornamentation and tabernacle work.

The chapel of this monastery, which is all that now remains to us, was built in the form of St. John's Cross. The ancient town of Melrose was in this respect similarly built. The west end of the nave is gone, so that we cannot state with certainty the length of that portion

of it. It is reasonable to infer, however, that the west
door or entrance would front and abut upon the
ancient line of street running north and south by it.
This would necessarily be the common and ordinary
gateway to and from the chapel. It would be also
the most vulnerable and easy of attack in perilous
times. To this western gate, however, must both
pilgrims and alms-askers have come, as being the stated
entrance of approach and egress for all such as lived
without the walls of the monastery. The almoner,
hospitaller, and porter would have suitable offices at the
western termination—the former to distribute alms and
broken victuals, the other to entertain strangers and
devotees, and the latter to exercise general supervision
over all who entered the convent, or returned from it
by this way.

The western portion of the nave, and the public
offices and gateway, seem to have shared most bitterly
the last convulsion (prior to the Reformation) which
befel it. The three first chapels, numbered 1, 2, and 3
on the Ground Plan, are of more recent erection than any
other portion now remaining, and rather point to the
sixteenth century. The connecting or continuing line
to the westward seems abruptly broken, as if the pro-
secution of the work had been stayed by some unfore-
seen irruption. Probably it was so, and that prior to
the general dispersion, neither time nor opportunity

happened to complete its restoration. A careful examination of the stone shows it of more recent facing than is found in other parts of the ruins; at the extreme west end the tusks are most conspicuous; in fact, the stone is fresh, the carvings of the capitols coarse, as if executed hastily, and the whole indicating a much more modern period of erection than the eastern end of the abbey by two or three centuries.

The nave, as now seen, would lead us to believe that it had never extended full and completely on both sides, up to the point where the eighth chapel now terminates. The effort to carry it out was evidently frustrated, it being manifestly the last undertaking begun, and abruptly terminated, without accomplishing the object intended. We must therefore admit that the extreme west end is comparatively of recent origin.

There are in all sixteen chapels still traceable in this church, eight of which breast the south aisle of the nave, and four stand right and left of the chancel, on each side. There are piscinas in each chapel or baptistry, and altars; the latter are all broken, but show remains of exquisite workmanship. The roofs of these chapels are supported with groined ribs, and embellished with carvings, each differing from the rest. The roof of the high altar is uncommonly beautiful, the soffit being covered with delicately groined tracery. On the key-stones are a number of quaintly carved figures.

In the centre is a sitting figure supporting our Saviour on the cross; the others hold swords, staves, and crosses. This roof covers the tombs of several illustrious men.*

Within the walls of the chancel are fonts for holy rites, sedilia, and recesses for containing the vessels of the sacristy. The groined ribs of the chancel roof spring from corbels, carved with figures, and as they diverge across the ceiling, the intersections are beautifully carved with large twisted knots of flowers.

The grand east window, with its slender shafts, in this part of the building, is exquisitely put together, and of matchless beauty, and has been appropriately described by Sir Walter Scott.

The floor of the chancel was lower than any other part of the sacred edifice. This was not unusual in monastic churches, its symbolic signification teaching with what humility the priest should enter the "Holy of Holies."

In the north transept is a circular window at an elevation of sixty feet, representing a "crown of thorns." We give a drawing of it, which is exceedingly beautiful and novel in design, notwithstanding its apparent simplicity of architectural character. (See p. 176.)

The plan of the nave is uncommon, having a very narrow but lofty north aisle, and a double south aisle;

* See Ground Plan.

Crown of Thorns.

the outer one being much lower than the other two, and
divided into eight square chapels, before alluded to,
running the whole length of the nave. Each chapel
has a decorated four-light Gothic window, except the
east one, which is a three-light. These windows differ
from each other in their tracery. There is a buttress
between each window, and those which are still complete, run up in several diminished stages towards the
top, and terminate with pinnacles, from which spring
flying buttresses over the roof of the side aisle, supporting the main wall of the nave, and balancing the interior
arches. This arrangement involves a scientific principle

admirably understood by Gothic architects and builders in those days. In the year 1618 the nave, from the

Corbel in North Aisle.

rood-wall or screen, was fitted up as the parish church, and in this part marked innovation is seen.

The decorated capitols of the columns yet standing in the north transept, are deeply and artistically carved with representations of the leaves of curled brocoli or Scotch kail. They deserve especial notice.

The narrow north aisle is conspicuous for the neatness of its pointed roof, and the row of massive pillars from which it springs. Their capitols, representing leaves of plants and flowers, are all classically chiselled, and have opposite them branches of foliage, equally well carved, from which spring the groins of the north side of the roof. We give an illustration of a beautiful corbel in the north aisle. (See p. 177.)

Of the chapter-house, dormitory, and refectory, which were all on the north side of the chapel, not a vestige remains; although occasionally, in digging, their foundations are discovered.

The cloister formed a quadrangle on the north-west side of the chapel, and stretched alongside the whole of the nave. Beyond this was an arcade or piazza, 150 feet long each way. And further northwards were numerous massive buildings, occupied by the officers and wealthy lay brethren of the convent, surrounded with gardens, and bridges crossing the dam, that extended to the very confines of the river. We annex an illustration of the east wall of the cloister.

The Cloister—East Wall and Angle.

Seven of the seats in the cloister remain. They are covered with false Gothic arches, composed of various members, along the extremity of which a wreath of flowers, springing from the pilasters at the sides of the arches, runs upwards to an ornamental frieze. The frieze appertaining to each sedile, contains six square compartments, representing with truthful delineation, clusters of plants, flowers, and other objects, such as oak-leaves and apples, lilies, houseleeks, ferns, scallop shells, and quatrefoils.

The choir of the chapel is short, and the transepts have only side aisles, along the east side.

A finely arched door-way leads from the angle formed by the north transept to the cloister. The grand or principal entrance is on the south side, and contains a noble window we shall describe hereafter.

The great square tower which rose from the centre of the cross, and crowned the gorgeous fabric, was a splendid specimen of ancient architecture. The west side only is standing. It is raised to an height of eighty-four feet, upon a lofty pointed arch. Two of the pillars are yet standing that support the western side, the two which supported the east are gone.* A stone balustrade, ornamented with beautiful rose work, surmounted the whole.

The magnificent pillars which support the remain-

* See Ground Plan.

ing portion of the tower are a study. The light and elastic grace of their springing shafts are peculiarly architectural, and harmonize well with the elegant

One of the Columns which support the Tower.

chasteness of the whole interior. We give a drawing of one of the remaining columns that support the tower, which is the finest specimen of sculpture in the abbey.

The noble south window and doorway are of great size and magnificent proportions. The window is twenty-four feet in height within the arch, and sixteen feet in breadth, divided by four principal mullions, each only eight inches in thickness. The exquisite tracery of this window is perfect, and rises in graceful interlacing curves to a glorious wheel of seven compartments. This window and doorway we have described at considerable length in our description of the ruins.

We have gazed from the roof upon the ruins with delight and admiration—there is not a corner without its decorations, invisible though it may be to all who look upon the exterior from below. The frieze that runs underneath the eaves of the south side of the nave is very beautiful, we have counted upwards of a hundred ornaments in it, consisting of roses, stars, crosses, shells, flowers, plants, &c., each different from the rest, and forming a distinct and chaste design of itself, studied and chiselled with care and exactness — so much so, that each might be a pattern, executed for some future study.

Ascend the stair, which winds like a snail-cap, and look in every direction across the ruins from the roof, there notice the profusion of embellishment that everywhere prevails, invisible to those who look on the church from beneath. Even the private galleries have their ornaments and grotesque figures winning the eye at every step.   The annexed engravings represent two grotesque heads of monks from the staircase.

Two Grotesque Heads in the Staircase.

Exterior View of the East Window.

To the architect and builder, the very stones of the ruin present features of more than ordinary interest. The trade marks of the masons are distinguishable in many places upon them—the same working signs being in common use at the present day. The mark of the chisel on the best-carved stones is sharp, light, and wonderfully accurate in touch and tone. The stones lie disposed in the building as they chiefly lay in the bed of the quarry—they rest on the horizontal line, and are consequently only compressed thereon—and we notice no signs of decay through the agency of time, only where this principal rule has been deviated from. The grooves are all exquisite, and the jointure of parts clean and faultless. The poetry and sculpture of ancient Greece were related to each other—so in like manner was her painting and architecture. So painting, sculpture, and architecture were twin children in more modern times, and nearly reached perfection under the fostering care of Rome, whose ecclesiastical system became the living sentiment or poetry of the three. The chapel of Henry VIII. is a striking example of this. Its beauty of combination, simplicity of conception, and richness of emblazoning, has never been equalled in the kingdom. Flaxman estimated, that at one period it possessed three thousand pieces of statuary. And the Abbey Church of St. Mary's Monastery, Melrose, in its original bloom and purity, has

N

contained several hundred pieces; for the interior would not be much less profuse in statuary and ornament, than was the exterior of its once lofty and beautiful walls. The exterior of the ruins contains seventy niches for statues.

We are not certain the tower of St. Mary's, Melrose, ever supported a spire or lantern; if it did, it is gone, and we know little of its form or composition. If it had a spire of any kind, it was a wooden one, for the lightness of the tower walls precludes the idea of them ever having supported a massive stone spire. In all ancient Gothic ecclesiastical buildings the spire was of wood. The vane was almost invariably a cock, which denoted watchfulness, or signified ' the preacher.'

Alas! for these turrets, which in days of yore gladdened the eyes of weary pilgrims, from many an alpine summit of the Border land! Alas! for that tower, three parts of which are no more, and the other fast hastening to destruction! And the bells, where are they? For ever hushed. No more their cadence floats on the fragrant zephyrs of the evening gale— they summon not again for ever to holy ordinances and flaming sacraments—they ring no festival in, nor chime some sainted vigil out—they hymn no requiem for the departed—they pour forth no theme to the solitude and triumph of monastic life, heard as in the days of old, far beyond Gala Water and bonnie Leader foot.

Where now are the ecstatic dreams of absolution that soothed the stricken conscience of the wayfaring soul? They have fled. The hard penance of the weak and disobedient is past. The horrid tortures of the offending moss-trooper, cooped up in the gloomy dungeon, are balmed with the waters of oblivion. Here the brave and the base lie down in perfect equality. The dreams of insatiate ambition are dispersed. Even the foundling has found parental solicitude at last in earth and stones; and the weary of hope, rest, in a narrow cell of tranquillity. The terror of all, and to whom all were foes, has obtained a free pardon; while kings and nobles are but a carnival for dust and worms. Time bears their effigies mantled in cobwebs. Oblivion is the pall bearer—these stones are the weepers, and the secrets of their bosoms as well as the lineaments of their mortality, have found shade and seclusion in the dust we tread on.

Whoever will take the pains to examine the elaborate monument erected to the memory of the late Sir Walter Scott, in Edinburgh, will not fail to discover, in its beautiful details, an application and embodiment of many of the ornamental details of Melrose Abbey. The late Mr Kemp made Melrose Abbey his study, and we give him infinite credit for choosing so sublime a prototype.

As we read the chronicles of this aged pile, and

gaze on the sepulchral earth in its consecrated chancel, we are ready to exclaim in the words of prophetic poesy,

> " How sweet to sleep, where all is peace,
>   Where sorrow cannot touch the breast—
> Where all life's idle throbbings cease,
>   And pain is lull'd to rest:
> Escap'd o'er fortune's troubled wave,
> To anchor in the silent grave."

In concluding this chapter, we may briefly observe, that the masonic display and decorative work of this abbey has been admirably executed beyond all praise. The mouldings are sharp, the pillars elastic, light, and graceful, the perpendiculars slender and harmonious, the carvings elaborately correct and classically severe; fresh to-day, as if new from the artist's chisel. The minute veins of leaves, and the diminishing and almost imaginable edging of fruit and flowers being exquisitely worked out and delineated. As though line upon line had been traced by some magic pencil (such as Buonarotti and Barozzio could only grasp), and the spell worked out by enchantment, in inexpressible delicacy of loveliness and truth. The quality of the stone is excellent, well assorted from the liver of the rock, but few soft and foliaceous stones are to be seen, which discover themselves by their pale yellow appearance and chalky outline.

The light touch of the Greek artist is pre-eminently

conspicuous in the east end—the massive Roman and coarse Gothic are everywhere subdued; and the architect seems to have varied his style with each succeeding subject, similar or not, and has throughout displayed consummate talent in composite design, and produced the most chaste and captivating effect.

The architect and antiquary may read invaluable lessons, by studying the anatomy of this ancient structure, unrivalled for its beauty and interest, its historical associations and medieval splendour: and which is indeed capable of affording a highly intellectual treat to the enlightened and appreciative mind.

Mr Hutchinson's opinion of the ornamental decorations is thus expressed: "Nature is studied through the whole, and the flowers and plants are represented as accurately as under the pencil. In this fabric there are the finest lessons, and the greatest variety of Gothic ornaments that the island affords, take all the religious structures together." And Mr Smith has expressed a similar opinion.

The ornamentation met with in these ruins is worthy of our warmest admiration and deep attention. Even at the early period of its execution, the draftsmen and the sculptors must have been inspired with the highest achievements of Greek and Roman art. Look at the foliage and plant work—curvilinear gems! Mark the starting points! The basis of Egyptian art was founded on cups and stalks. The cup was the flower of the lotus or water-lily. The beauty of Grecian ornament lay in its equality of foliage, stalks, starting points, and groundwork. And the glory of the graceful, mature, elaborate Gothic before us, lies in the expressive delicacy, inimitable chastity, and elaborate carving of its tracings, ornament, and tabernacle work.

Its ruins are glorious at the present time, they are a gem, conveying a sublime and touching allegory— an affecting monument of the instability of all human institutions.

Chapter Eighth.

HISTORICAL SUMMARY, AND BIOGRAPHY OF THE ABBOTS OF MELROSE.

ITHIN a short period after the settlement of the monks from Rievalle, Yorkshire, at St. Mary's, Melrose, they began to colonize other newly erected abbeys. In the middle of the twelfth century the abbey of Dundrennan, Galloway, was colonized by monks from Melrose. The Chronicle of Melrose Abbey comprises a period of little over five hundred years. It was spared from the destruction that befel most monastic records at the Reformation, and is written with brevity, but not in a style equal to the learning of the place.

1. Richard, first abbot of Melrose, appears to have been a man of strict piety and integrity, and a rigid disciplinarian. He was installed in 1136, being the same year in which it was founded by King David.

He was greatly esteemed at court on account of his learning and eloquence. He ruled in monastic matters with authority. The same spirit which might have endeared him to churchmen of an earlier period, rendered him obnoxious to those over whom he now presided. After repeated complaints respecting his harshness to the abbot of the parent convent of Rievalle, he was removed from his office in 1148, after he had ruled the abbey twelve years.* Richard died the following year at the abbey of Clairvaux, in France, whither he had retired. He opposed, without effect, the appointment of William Cumin, Chancellor of Scotland, to the see of Durham, having discovered, through one of Cumin's agents, that the letters he produced as from the Pope, confirming his election, were artfully forged.†

2. Waltheof, or Waldeve, was second abbot. After his death he was canonized and honoured as a saint. He was as much beloved by the monks as Richard had been disliked. Mildness of manner and acts of beneficence succeeded, where rigour and coercion failed. He was the younger son of Simon de St. Liz, Earl of Northampton, by his wife Matilda, daughter of Waltheof, Earl of Northumberland, who inherited the earldom of Huntingdon from her mother, Judith, niece to William the Conqueror, who had it for her

---

* *Annales Cistertienses.*   † *Chron. Mailros.*

dower. Earl Simon falling under the displeasure of Henry I., by whom his lands were forfeited, assumed the cross, went to Palestine, and soon after died, leaving two sons, Simon and Waltheof. Simon became Earl of Northampton, and Waltheof abbot of Melrose. The Countess Matilda, Earl Simon's widow, and mother of Waltheof, afterwards married David, Prince of Cumberland, brother and successor to Alexander, King of Scotland, who resided at this time chiefly at the English court, his sister Matilda, being Henry the First's queen.* Waltheof became of great note in the calendar. Josceline, a monk of Furness Abbey, Lancashire, wrote a life of Waltheof, which contained many marvellous stories. Numerous miracles are recorded of him. His personal encounters with Satan, and his visitations from heaven, were doubtless the ridiculous imaginings of legendary compilers. Angelo Manriquez tells us, that from a child, Waltheof was remarkable for his meekness, humility, and gentleness, and showed early a predilection for the diversion of building baby churches. Waltheof's step-father, David I., took him to Scotland in 1124, when he ascended the throne of that kingdom. He there completed his education along with Baldred, afterwards abbot of Rievalle. David offered his step-son the amusements of the chase, but Waltheof had no taste for them, He rather

* *Scotichron,* vi. 3–6.

chose to stray away unseen into the bosom of the woods, to sit down on some shady bank and read or meditate. The king knew his love of study, and habitual piety, and formed the design of promoting him to some high office in the church. Waltheof had other views than becoming a secular priest. He resolved to embrace monastic life. Circumstances tended to confirm this resolution. He fell in love with a beautiful young lady at court, who felt an equally tender passion for him. Some expressions used by her, however, on presenting him with a ring, and the remarks of others on seeing him wear it, awakened him to a sense of what he considered to be his danger. Warned by this, as he thought, he withdrew from the world, retiring to St. Oswald's Priory at Nosthill, near Pontefract, Yorkshire, where he was admitted into the order of canons regular of St. Augustine. While holding the office of Sacristan in this monastery, he was called to the priorate of Kirkham.* Here he won the hearts of all the brethren, although he greatly increased the strictness and severity of their discipline. Kirkham was founded in 1122, by Sir Walter Espec, a powerful baron, who endowed it with great possessions in Northumberland; among which were the churches of Carham, Ilderton, and Newton, in Glendale. He

---

* Kirkham is a pleasant village, standing on the river Derwent, near Malton, Yorkshire. The ruins of the priory may still be seen.

also founded the monastery of Rievalle, Yorkshire, in 1131, and that of Wardon, Bedfordshire, in 1136. About two years before his death, Sir Walter took the monastic habit in Rievalle.   His death happened in 1153.

It was about this period of Waltheof's history that stories of visions, miracles, and many fabulous things, were reported of him.   We give one or two, as illustrating the state of religious belief at the period when they were written.

" On Christmas day, as Waltheof was celebrating mass alone in the church at Kirkham, while in the act of elevating the host, he beheld the consecrated bread changed into the likeness of an infant, more beautiful than the sons of men, crowned with a diadem of gold and jewels, who, with a look of ineffable sweetness, embraced him, kissed his lips, gently touched his face and head with his hands, and then making the sign of the cross over him, suddenly disappeared."

Thinking the life of a canon-regular not sufficiently austere, Waltheof resigned his priorate, and entered the Cistertian convent at Wardon, Bedfordshire, where he commenced his noviciate.   This step greatly displeased his brother, Simon, Earl of Northampton, and in order the monks of Wardon might not suffer on his account, he removed to Rievalle, where his brother's influence did not reach.   At this latter monastery his resolution became fixed. He was soon reconciled to the insipid food, coarse garments, manual drudgery, and long fasts of the first Cistertians. The year of his probation expired, he took the vows, and became, by his cheerfulness and self-denial, a bright example of monastic virtue. He continued at Rievalle till the year 1148, when he was elected abbot of Melrose. In this advanced position he was more than ever venerated and beloved. His kindness to the poor was gratefully spoken of, and when he had occasion to find fault with any of the inferior officials, his paternal mildness gave him sovereign sway. At this period the religious were accustomed to confess with their backs bare, in token of their willingness to submit to whatever stripes their spiritual director might think fit to inflict, before giving them absolution. Waltheof's constant friend was St. Everhard, his confessor, who, being a canon-regular at Kirkham, embraced the Cistertian order along with him at Wardon, and removed with him to Rievalle and Melrose. He afterwards became first abbot of Holm-Cultram in Cumberland, founded by David I. in 1150.*

Waltheof's miracles obtained great celebrity, after his removal to Melrose Abbey. Upon one occasion we

---

* St. Everhard is reported to have written the life of Waltheof, also, the life of Adamnan, abbot of Icolmkil, and other works.— DEMPSTERI *Hist. Eccles.*

are told, during a severe famine, four thousand starving
people, inhabitants of Teviotdale, came to the monastery
imploring food.   Many, destitute and houseless, built
huts for themselves in the fields and woods adjacent.
The charity of the benevolent monks was severely tried.
It was a time of great scarcity.   Their stock of corn
was barely sufficient for their own wants till harvest.
They had a resource in their cattle, to be sure, but to
kill them, as was proposed by Tyna, the kind-hearted
cellarer, would be ruinous to their tillage and future
hopes of increase.*   While the convent was delibera-
ting upon this alternative, Waltheof rose up, and desiring
Tyna to accompany him, they proceeded to the store-
house at Eildon, where the abbot struck his staff into
a heap of wheat which lay in the granary, and prayed
for a blessing upon it.   This done, they passed over
the Tweed to the storehouse at Gattonside, which also
belonged to the abbey.   Here, in like manner, Waltheof
blessed a heap of rye, designed as bread for their servants, and commanded that daily rations of grain
should be dealt out to the starving multitude.   They
were thus fed continually for three months, from the
stores of grain the abbot had blessed, which lasted till
the corn in the fields was ready for the sickle.   Tyna,
the cellarer, stated that the convent at this time pos-

* Tyna was the author of a life of Waltheof, a treatise on alms-
giving, and a series of sermons for Lent.

sessed great store of oxen at pasture, as well as sheep and well-fed pigs, with plenty of cheese, butter, and vegetables.   In a time of general scarcity, this conveys a most favourable idea of the good husbandry and management of the whole fraternity, and of the benefit which the country must have derived from their skill, influence, and example, in the cultivation of the land.

Upon a similar occasion, when the monks, by Waltheof's suggestion, agreed to share their daily allowance of bread with the hungry, the loaves were no sooner cut in two, than each half was converted into a whole loaf.*

The monastic rule, which enjoined the exercise of hospitality, was nowhere better observed than at Melrose. Strangers, pilgrims, wayfaring men of every description and of every condition, from the king to a peasant, found a welcome and shelter there, and at all times such cheer as the monastery afforded.   For charity the hospice was renowned.

In 1152 the monastery of Melrose had to regret the death of a great patron of the religious orders—Henry, eldest son of David I.   The king himself did not long survive the loss.   He was found dead, in a posture of devotion, and his virtues and liberality to the church procured his admission into the catalogue of holy men. Perhaps David did more by the beautiful and religious

* *Annales Cistertienses.*

tone of his character to merit eulogium, than if he had achieved many warlike exploits.   The youthful successor to the throne, Malcolm IV., proved a warm friend to the monastery of Melrose also, seeking through the churchmen to improve the condition of his people.   He was surnamed the "Maiden," because he would never marry.   He built the abbey of Cupar, died at Jedburgh, and was buried at Dunfermline.

It is related, that one day when some guests had arrived, and Walter, the hospitaller, had set food before them, it happened that some other strangers came, who were also invited to partake at the same table.   And although the viands were not more than might have sufficed for the first number of guests, yet when all had partaken, they appeared undiminished, and only began to decrease when one of the company, in the middle of the repast, called the attention of the rest to the miraculous circumstance.*

One evening, three strangers knocked at the abbey gate, and were admitted to lodge there for the night. They were immediately conducted into church, according to the rules of St. Benedict.   When their devotions were concluded, they were led back to the guest-chamber, and taken care of by brother Walter, the hospitaller. By the time they had washed their feet, they were summoned to supper in the refectory, but had scarcely sat

* *Annales Cistertienses.*

down when it was discovered that one was missing, and his place vacant. Walter asked the remaining two what had become of their companion, the third person, when, with surprise, they affirmed that no third person had been in their company. The friar now insisted that he had placed three of them at table. The porter and another monk who had received them at the gate, declared that they had let in three persons. Nobody had gone out, yet the third stranger could nowhere be found. The following night, however, a person of angelic appearance showed himself to the hospitaller, in a dream, and said: "Dost thou know me, brother Walter? I am the stranger whose sudden disappearing from amongst you yesterday nobody could account for. The Lord has appointed me to watch over this monastery, and I am come to certify to you that the alms and prayers of this community, and especially of your abbot, are accepted, and ascend unto heaven like the odours of sweet incense."*

On the eve of the Epiphany, when the convent was singing the praises of God in the choir, the abbot had a vision of the Virgin Mary, with the infant Jesus on her knee, and the three wise men of the East coming, preceded by a star, to offer him gifts and worship; and it is recorded that, on Easter day, at early matins, Waltheof had a vision of the sufferings, death, and resurrection of Christ.

* *Annales Cisterticnses.*

It is also said of him that, by his blessing and touch, he healed three of the brethren on one occasion, who lay dangerously sick in the infirmary.

In 1159, on the death of Robert, bishop of St. Andrews, the clergy of that cathedral, with many of the principal noblemen of Scotland, came to Melrose, to announce the election of Waltheof, and conduct him with honour to the episcopal city. But he who, in the days of youth and strength, was deaf to the charms of worldly distinction, shrank from it now in the season of age and feebleness. In vain did the abbot of Rievalle endeavour te persuade him to accept the call, to which Waltheof but pointed with his fingers to the ground, at the entrance of the chapter-house, where he had fixed upon a spot for his grave. In allusion to his having laid aside all earthly cares to prepare for death, he said: "I have put off my coat, how shall I put it on? I have washed my feet, how shall I defile them?"

Thus Waltheof kept his resolution, and continued to exercise his functions at Melrose till the day of his death, an event which he joyfully anticipated, and often prayed for.

The peace of the convent had often been disturbed by the rude behaviour of one of the brethren, named Simon, a man of great muscular strength, and a good artificer. This person having fallen asleep, during the hour of rest at noon, dreamed that a gigantic being with terrible aspect,

o

and armed with a scythe. stood before him, and, in a voice that made him tremble, reproached him for his wicked life; after which, hewing him to pieces, he put the several limbs into a basket which he carried, and was preparing to depart, when a being of glorious appearance came suddenly and drove him away, after he had compelled him to fit again all the dissevered pieces to each other. Then the angelic being, having restored Simon to life, and exhorted him to amendment, put into his hands a written scroll, charging him to deliver it faithfully to his abbot, to whom it was sent from God and the holy Mary.

Simon, awaking, found the scroll on his breast, and did with it as he was directed, at the same time giving an account of his vision. Waltheof with reverence unfolded the epistle, and kneeling down, read it with tears of thankfulness. The words were these—" Jesus Christ, and Mary his Mother, greet their beloved Waltheof. Know that thy prayer is heard, and, between the two feasts of John the Baptist,* thou shalt come to us to live forever: prepare thyself. Farewell."†

On the feast of the nativity of John the Baptist, the biographer informs us that Waltheof was seized with mortal sickness; that, on the 1st of

---

* The nativity of John the Baptist is commemorated on the 24th of June, his martyrdom on the 29th of August.

† *Annales Cistertienses.*

August, feeling himself worse, he received the last sacraments of the Church, and bade his assembled friends farewell. On the 3rd of the month, at the hour of tierce, the convent was summoned to witness his departure. As the custom then prevailed, the dying saint was laid upon a hair-cloth, while those around sung the psalms and litanies proper for the occasion. He lived, however, till the hour of sext, when, the monks being re-assembled, and singing as before, he expired. According to custom, his body was washed, clothed in a monk's habit and hood, and then wrapped in a wax-cloth, prior to burial. The use of the wax-cloth, however, was contrary to the Benedictine formula, on such occasions. His funeral obsequies were performed by the bishop of Glasgow, attended by four abbots, and a great number of religious men of different orders, and he was buried on the spot he had himself pointed out in the Chapter-house.

Several literary works are attributed to Waltheof.

III. William, one of the monks, was the next abbot of Melrose. He was elected on November 27th, 1159, in a chapter held by Baldred or Ailred, Waltheof's friend, and abbot of the parent monastery of Rievalle. William soon became unpopular with the monks. He appears to have been somewhat incredulous of the miracles said to have been wrought at Waltheof's tomb. He also endeavoured to put a stop to the superstitious

practices founded on them. Waltheof was no sooner
dead than the most supernatural visions were seen by
different people. Walter, a lay brother, and sick inmate of the infirmary, was wonderfully restored to
health by the abbot, who appeared to him in a vision,
and informed him that he was now a partaker of the
joys of paradise. Henry, another lay brother, beheld
Waltheof, with St. Benedict and St. Bernard, borne
through the air, each in a splendid litter, and was mira-
culously told that they were on their way to the abbey
of Kinloss, to rescue from Satan the soul of Robert, one
of the monks, who was to die on the morrow.*

Pilgrimages from all parts were now made to the
tomb of St. Waltheof. His beatification was fully believed in. Those who hoped for favour by prayer and
fasting gave donations to the convent—such as money,
wax-tapers, lamps, wine, and other gifts which they
had vowed. Bernoul, a wealthy citizen of Rothbury,
was restored from sickness to health and strength, by
watching one night beside the tomb of Waltheof.
Josceline, the recorder of this legend, conversed with
Bernoul's son, who became a monk of Melrose.†

Whatever support these stories received out of doors,
the abbot William does not seem to have credited all of
them; for he shut up the chapter-house, and refused
admission to the crowds who came daily to perform

* *Annales Cistertienses.*   † *Ibid.*

their devotions at Waltheof's grave.   The monks now
accused him of harshness.   He was warned by Sylvanus
abbot of Rievalle, to be less severe, and he ultimately
resigned his office on the 23rd of April, 1170, and retired to the abbey of Rievalle, where he died fifteen
years afterwards.*   He was an author of repute.   The
brethren of the convent most distinguished in his
time were: Ralph, who, in 1171, was made abbot of
Cupar; Simon de Tonei, or Thondei, who became abbot
of Coggleshall, Essex, and continued some years, but,
returning to Melrose, resumed his station as a private
monk, till elected bishop of Moray, in 1171, in which
situation he died in 1184.

IV. Josceline, the prior, was made abbot the same
day that William retired.   He had defended Waltheof's
beatification with such zeal, that he must now endeavour to justify the part he had acted.   The common
belief of the times was that, when the soul had entered
into immediate felicity, the body would not see corruption.   Josceline resolved to test this, in respect of his
deceased patron and friend.   A new slab of polished
marble was prepared to replace the stone-covering of
the tomb.   On May the 2nd, 1171, Ingelram, bishop of
Glasgow, four abbots, monks of different orders, all the
brethren of Melrose, besides a goodly company of sober
and religious men, being assembled in the chapter-

* *Chron. de Mailros.*

house, the grave was opened in their presence. The
body, and the garments in which it had been buried
twelve years before, appeared to have suffered no
decay.* The bishop, stooping down, touched the garments and different parts of the body, at first gently,
and then with greater pressure, to assure himself that
every joint and limb was flexible and sound. Peter,
the chanter, who doubted the propriety of so accurate
a scrutiny, could not help saying, " In sooth, my lord
bishop, saving your reverence, methinks you handle the
body of the holy man somewhat roughly." When some
present approved of Peter's remark, the bishop thus
addressed them : " Be not offended, my dear children,
that I have scrupulously examined into this matter,
but rather praise God, since I have thereby clearly
ascertained and made manifest that this is indeed a
miracle, which proves that you have now another saint
belonging to you, and that your venerated father,
Waltheof, is become a companion to the holy Cuthbert,
who also was once a monk of Melros." At these words,
we are told, many of the brethren shed tears of joy, all
present gave vent to some expression of thankfulness,
and at the suggestion of the abbot of Kelso, a Te Deum
was solemnly chanted.

Josceline was made bishop of Glasgow in 1174.
While abbot of Melros, he established a house of hos-

* *Chron. de Mailros.*

pitality on the banks of the Teviot, at Hassendean, for the entertainment of strangers and pilgrims coming to Melrose. With the consent of King William, he gave for its support the patronage of the church of Hassendean, with all its lands, tithes and possessions.* Josceline is praised for the kindness and urbanity of his manners. His elevation to the episcopal dignity gave universal satisfaction. He began to rebuild and enlarge the cathedral church of Glasgow in 1180, which was finished in a magnificent style in 1196, three years before his death. Josceline, who had been distinguished for his learning and piety, was buried at Melrose. One of the friends of Josceline at Melrose, was St. Nervus, or Nerva, the patron usually invoked by travellers, in consequence of a miracle believed to have been done by him. Two pilgrims, it is said, having been found murdered on their way to visit the holy places in Scotland, this devout monk restored them to life for a short space, that they might confess their sins, and receive the sacrament of the Eucharist. In 1174, Nervus became abbot of Kinloss, where he rebuilt the cloister, and secured it with a high wall.

V. Laurence, or Laurentius, one of the monks and a person of great meekness, was elected abbot on the 14th May, 1175. He had previously been abbot of a monastery in the Orkneys, and is said to

* *Cart. de Mailros.*

have been a skilful and learned theologian   He died
in 1178.

VI. Ernald, the next abbot, received the benediction
from Bishop Josceline, on the day of the Epiphany,
1179. During the reign of William the Lion, a keen
struggle was maintained by the Scottish clergy with
their more southern ecclesiastical brethren. The King
of England succeeded in obtaining a recognition of
temporal authority from William and his barons. The
ecclesiastical supremacy of the question was disputed
with much success; and the Church of Scotland was
declared to be the daughter of Rome by special grace,
and immediately subject to the apostolic jurisdiction.
William was spirited enough to dispute the Pope's right
of interference in the appointing a bishop to the diocese of St. Andrew's. This opposition finally brought
down the vengeance of his holiness, and the kingdom
of Scotland was subjected to excommunication. A
reconciliation was set on foot, and Bishop Josceline, with
Ernald, abbot of Melrose, were the principal persons
sent to Rome to effect it. A compromise was made,
and the country freed from the pontifical curse.

While these disputes were in existence, dissensions
of another nature were not uncommon in reference to
the territorial rights of different churches. The extensive forests of the shires of Selkirk and Roxburgh were
the theatres of frequent quarrels. The increasing im-

portance of the religious communities was opposed to the warlike power of the barons. The district of Wedale, situated between the rivers Leader and Gala, was the scene of frequent disputes. Cattle-drivers and swine-herds · indulged in quarrels. The respective claims of the bishop of St. Andrew's, the family of the Morvilles, and the monks of Melrose, required adjustment, and royal intervention was called for. Richard de Morville, constable of the kingdom, and twelve other jurors, were ordered by the king to perambulate the boundaries. They did so, and being sworn upon the holy relics preserved at Melrose, attested that the royal forest extended to the highway leading to the westward of the church of Wedale, and that the right of pasture belonged to Melrose as far as the marches of Wedale, and the rivulet called Fasseburn. Thus King William established what was emphatically called " The Peace of Wedale."*

Ernald was chosen abbot of Rievalle on the second of March, 1189, upon the resignation of his predecessor, Sylvanus.†

VII. Reiner, abbot of Kinloss, once a monk of Melrose, succeeded Ernald. In 1194 he resigned his charge of

---

* William, surnamed the Lion, was a valiant king. He built the monastery of Aberbrothock ; and his queen, Emergarda, daughter of Earl Beaumont, built that of Balmerinoch. William died at Stirling, and was buried at Aberbrothock.

† *Chron. de Mailros.*

Melrose abbey, and again became abbot of Kinloss, where he died in the year 1219. A monk of Melrose, named Reginald, who lived about this time, is mentioned as a distinguished person. Reginald became bishop of Ross, and was made cardinal. Another monk of Melrose, named Gilbert, became abbot of Holy Island, and died in 1200. He was the author of eight elegant sermons upon the Song of Solomon.

VIII. Ralph, or Radulph, also an abbot of Kinloss, succeeded Reiner, two days after his resignation. Another dispute had arisen between the monks of Melrose and those of Kelso abbey, whose lands of Bowden lay close to theirs in Eildon and Darnwick. Certain boundaries required adjustment. The Pope's legate, John de Salerno, being in Scotland, visited Melrose in 1201. He had been attending a general council at Perth for the reformation of the clergy. In the settlement of the boundary question, however, he acted with duplicity. He made himself merry and comfortable for a couple of months at the expense of both parties in dispute. He received from them valuable presents of money and horses, deluding both with the hopes of a favourable decision ; he settled nothing, but went off to Ireland, took with him Ralph, abbot of Melrose, and made him bishop of Down. Cardinal Gualo must have noticed this consummate piece of Italian trickery, for shortly afterwards he made a bold attempt to enrich himself, and succeeded, at the expense of the nation. Ralph was at Melrose in 1211, and there gave the episcopal blessing to three abbots on St. Lucia's day, viz., of Fountain's abbey, Yorkshire, Furness, and Caldeia. He died in 1233, and bequeathed to posterity several works on ecclesiastical polity.

IX. William, formerly master of the novices of Melrose, and now abbot of Cupar, was brought back, and succeeded Ralph as abbot of Melrose in 1202. He died in 1206, and such was the opinion of his sanctity, that it was agreed to bury him near his sainted predecessor, Waltheof. There is a story about brother Robert, a mason, whose curiosity led him to raise the cover of the tomb, in order to look into it, when a most fragrant odour of drugs and spices issued from the opening. It being dusk a lighted taper was brought, and a dozen or more monks and lay brethren looked in, and saw the body of the holy man laid uncorrupted, and the grave-clothes fresh and beautiful.

X. Patrick, the sub-prior, was chosen abbot on the 8th of June, 1206, but died the following year.

XI. Adam, prior of Melrose, was elected abbot in 1207. Next year the differences between the monks of Melrose and those of Kelso, referred already by Pope Celestine to the arbitration of King William, were finally adjusted. The future boundaries between the grounds of Eildon and Bowden were minutely described, drawn up in writing, and attested by the abbots of Jedburgh, Dryburgh, Newbattle, and Cupar.

Adam was elected bishop of Caithness, August 5th, 1213. He did not vacate his office at Melrose till the 11th May, 1214, the day of his consecration. In the ninth year of his episcopate, his days were cut short by the people of his own diocese. A dispute arose with the bishop and his flock respecting a more equitable adjustment of tithes. The people refused payment, and it is said, that in the heat of the moment, Adam excommunicated them. This harsh and cruel measure inflamed them, and, on September 11th, 1222, a mob of three hundred men surrounded his house at Hawkirk at an untimely hour in the morning, broke open the doors, and slew a monk of Melrose, named Serlo, a companion to the bishop, also a servant of the house, dragged the bishop from his chamber, bound him hand and foot, beat him with sticks and stones, shut him up in the kitchen, and set fire to the house, where he was burned to death.* When the flames were extinguished the body of the bishop was found under a heap of stones unconsumed. It was buried in the parish church, and in 1239 disinterred and removed to a more honourable tomb in the cathedral church of the diocese.

---

* *Scotichronium*, ix. 37. *Wyntoun*, viii. 7. The monk Serlo was a reputed saint, and the author of several books, among which was one on "Tithes."

Intelligence of this outrage was brought to King Alexander, who was then at Jedburgh, preparing for a journey into England. The king was exceedingly vexed, and postponing every other concern, proceeded to the spot, and punished the murderers with death. The conduct of John, Earl of Orkney and Caithness, who lived near, was not void of suspicion, and his lands were confiscated in consequence by the king. Strange to say, in 1231 the Earl was murdered by his own servant, who, to conceal his guilt, burnt the house in which lay his mangled body. Bishop Adam was the reputed author of many literary productions.

XII. Hugh de Clippeston, one of the monks, was elected abbot of Melrose in 1214, but resigned his office in the following year, at a general chapter of the order.*

XIII. William de Curry, abbot of Holm-Cultram, Cumberland, succeeded Hugh on the 16th of November, 1215; and on August 30th, 1216, William was translated to Rievalle, the monks of that abbey having chosen him for their superior.

XIV. Ralph, the cellarer of Melrose, was made abbot on the 14th September, 1216, which he held till the 1st of June, 1219, when he died.† He was of a kind and gentle disposition, and greatly beloved of the monks.

The King of Scotland had not been an uninterested

* *Chron. Mail.*   † *Ibid.*

observer of the contests between King John and his
barons, the issue of which secured, on an indestructible
basis, the foundations of the liberty of Englishmen.
On the 11th of January, 1216, King Alexander met the
Yorkshire barons, with those of the northern counties,
in the chapter-house of Melrose abbey. They swore
fealty to the king, and engaged to put him in possession
of Northumberland and the city of Carlisle, upon his
agreeing to assist them in the assertion of their rights.
John had, in the meantime, advanced northwards,
destroyed their lands and castles, invaded Scotland, and
was now laying waste the country between Roxburgh,
Dunbar, and Berwick. The King of Scotland retaliated
with equal devastation. John died, leaving his kingdom
to the Pope's protection. Gualo, on the plea that the
King of England was a vassal of the Pope, now excommunicated the king and people of Scotland. The
churches were therefore shut up, and all the clergy
ceased exercising their functions, except the monks of
the Cistertian order, who held themselves exempt from
the apostolic curse on account and by virtue of their
privileges. Subsequently, almost all the abbots of the
Cistertian order attended a general chapter at Cisteaux,
whence several churchmen were sent as delegates to
Rome, where they succeeded in obtaining the recall of
Cardinal Gualo, and getting the order confirmed in the
possession of all its former rights. The historian

Buchanan says, that the plunder amassed by the crafty cardinal, in sums paid by the opulent churchmen for absolution from the curse, was ordered to be divided among the complainers, who were sent home laden with fine words, but saw none of the gold.

XV. Adam de Harkaris, abbot of Newbattle, and a relation of Patrick, Earl of March, was translated to Melrose abbey on the 6th of August, 1219. He presided twenty-six years, and during this period the convent greatly increased in wealth and importance. Many of the members were promoted to episcopal offices, or chosen to preside over other monasteries. The dignitaries of the order were becoming remarkable for their position and influence in the state. Pilgrims to their shrines were numerous. Persons of distinction, in their old age, were admitted as novices. Donations were showered upon the abbacy. Bequests were left in all directions. Dying persons left their property to it. The habit of the order alone seemed sufficient to ensure eternal salvation. Superstition appeared in its most pleasing forms. Political influence followed the acquisition of property. Temporal objects weakened spiritual exertion and self-examination.

We read that Patrick, Earl of Dunbar, when near dying, assembled his friends and neighbours together in his castle at Christmas, 1231, and having kept festival with them during four days, he then sent for the abbot of Melrose, who gave him extreme unction, and invested him with the Cistertian habit on the 30th of December, when he affectionately bade his friends farewell, and died the next day.

It was said that the Virgin Mary changed the black habit originally worn by the Cistertians into white, upon the person of Alberic, the second abbot of Cisteaux.* ·

The reign of Alexander II. witnessed the steady progress of Melrose abbey.† Its possessions were augmented in 1235 by a grant of the lands of Ettrick Forest. In 1240, the remains of all the abbots buried at the entrance of the chapter-house at Melrose, except those of St. Waltheof, were disinterred, and removed to a place prepared for them in the east side of the same building.

Waltheof's tomb was opened, and when it was found that his body was now reduced to bones and dust, it was covered up again. Some of the persons present selected some of the small bones to keep as relics. William, son of the Earl of Dunbar, got a tooth, by which, as he affirmed afterwards, many sick persons were cured. The abbot, Adam de Harkaris, died in 1245, after a most peaceful, prosperous, long, and contented administration of the affairs of the abbey.

---

* *Annales Cistertienses.*

† Alexander II. was, at his death, interred in an elegant chapel on the right side of the chancel.

XVI. Matthew, the cellarer of Melrose, was chosen abbot on the 19th of April, 1246. In July 1261 he resigned, from infirmity. Matthew had behaved with great kindness to the monks, and they were warmly attached to him. He had increased their comfort in many ways, and by the erection of convenient buildings and offices. He also built a fine hall on the south banks of the river for himself and his successors. During the reign of Alexander III. the revenues of the church reached their zenith. After his death, a series of national calamities weighed heavily on the monasteries of Teviotdale, exposed as they were to the hostile attacks of the English nation.*

XVII. Adam de Maxton, abbot of Newbattle, and formerly cellarer of Melrose, was chosen abbot, August 1, 1261. He was deposed in 1267 by a general chapter of the order, on account of his pride and obstinacy. He had deposed Henry, abbot of Holm-Cultram, without consulting his brethren. Henry was at the same time restored again to his former position.

In 1265, the Western Isles, long held by the Norwegians, were granted to Scotland by treaty. Alexander III. was to pay the King of Norway four thousand marks within four years, and one hundred marks a-year

---

* Alexander III. built the Cross-kirk of Peebles. He met his death by a fall from his horse, in the thirty-seventh year of his reign, and was buried at Dunfermline.

P

ever after, for possession of them. Reginald of Roxburgh, a monk of Melrose, went as ambassador to the
court of Norway, and conducted the negociations on
the part of Scotland.*

XVIII. John de Ederham, master of the novices, was
the next abbot of Melrose. In 1268, John, with many
of the monks, was excommunicated. At a council of
Scottish clergy held at Perth, it was proved that they
had broken the peace of Wedale, by violently entering the houses belonging to the bishop of St.
Andrews, killing one ecclesiastic, and wounding
many others. The monks of Melrose had frequent
quarrels with the men of Wedale, or Stow, about their
marches.

XIX. Robert de Keldeleth, or Kildalach, was chosen
abbot of Melrose in 1268. He had passed through
strange turns of fortune,—originally a Benedictine
monk at Dunfermline, then abbot of that monastery,
afterwards chancellor of Scotland, and confessor to
James the First. At length, charged with conspiracy
to procure from the court of Rome the legitimacy of a
marriage that was invalid—his accusers being the
Earls of Mar and Monteith. He now resigned the
seals of office, and retired to the abbey of Melrose.
Disgraced at court, the monks respected him not, so
that he soon left Melrose, entered the Cistertian

* *Chron. Mailros.*

monastery of Newbattle, and became a private monk again. He died in 1273.

XX. Patrick de Selkirke, one of the monks, was now chosen abbot of Melrose. How long he held office we know not, as the *Chronicle of Melrose* extends no farther. This Chronicle relates to the affairs of Old Melrose, rather than the new monastery of that name. In the year 1291, Edward I., acting upon his usurped authority as feudal lord of Scotland, granted a letter of protection for one year to the abbot and convent of Melrose. He also renewed this assurance to them annually for several years. During this eventful period in Scottish history, the ecclesiastics of the abbeys of Teviotdale played a most important part in national affairs. The usurpation of Edward, and the rival claims of Bruce and Baliol, called forth all the talents of the churchmen. We find them in these perilous times asserting their privileges before those in authority, compromising royal disputes, and personally protecting their property from the ravages of invasion. In 1296 the monasteries of Jedworth, Kelso, Dryburgh, and Melrose, severally, swore fealty to Edward I.

In 1303, Hugh Audley, who attended the King of England in his expedition against Scotland, being lodged at Melrose abbey, with sixty men under his command, was attacked in the night by Comyn, Regent of Scotland, who forced the abbey gates, and killed several of the English within the building. Sir Thomas Grey fled over the bridge, and defended himself in a house, until it was in flames over his head, when he came out and surrendered.*

King Edward's letters of protection availed but little during this period of strife and foray. The monks continually made their losses known to him. They obtained confirmation of their charters ; also permission to cut down forty oaks in the forest of Selkirk, to repair such buildings as had been burnt and demolished in the war. They called the king's attention also to the fact, that they had never received payment for fifty-five sacks of wool, bought from them on his account, by Sir Hugh de Cressingham, when he was treasurer of Scotland. And for fourteen sacks of wool, and one last of leather, bought from them for his account by Sir Osbert de Spaldington, Sheriff of Berwick. For settlement of these debts, Edward, in his reply, coolly referred them to his chamberlain of Scotland.†

When the plan of government and police for Scotland, as a dependent state of England, was settled at Westminster in September, 1305, the abbot of Melrose was one of the ten commissioners chosen by the National Council of Scotland to confer with the twenty

---

* *Scala Chronica in Lel. Col.* i., 541.
† *Rolls of Parliament,* vol. i., 473.

English commissioners of parliament, appointed for that purpose.*

William de Foghou, or Foggo,† was abbot in 1310, and his name appears in connection with many charters until the year 1329. He had letters of protection granted him by Edward II. on various occasions. One to go to visit the king at York; another to pass to Holm-Cultram, to preside at the election of an abbot. That abbacy was founded by David I. in 1150, and colonized with monks from Melrose; therefore Melrose was its maternal house. In 1319 Foghou had another letter of safe-conduct from the king, who wished to see him in the north, where he was preparing with a hostile army to enter Scotland. The design of the king failed, and he was only able to lay siege to Berwick, without effect. His last invasion of Scotland, in 1322, met with even less success than his former attempts. After reaching Edinburgh, he was obliged to retreat, and we find him passing homeward through Roxburghshire, with a dispirited and discontented army, defeated more

* RIDPATH, 293.

† It was about this period, 1318, that the first association was made between King Robert Bruce and " good Sir James Douglas." Shortly after the return of the former from Ireland, they went and burnt the towns of Northallerton and Boroughbridge, spoiled Ripon, but spared the church, and levied five thousand marks upon the monks they found there. In this disastrous mission they also burnt Scarborough, and burnt and sacked the town of Shipton in Craven, Yorkshire.

by famine than by military prowess. Intending to
lodge at Melrose, he sent forward three hundred men to
prepare for his reception. Here Edward received a
check which greatly irritated him. Lord Douglas was
at the time, with a company of Scots, planted in a
neighbouring forest, and having intelligence of their
movements, got unobservedly to the abbey before them.
When they came up, he attacked them suddenly, killing
a great number of the three hundred, the remainder
having fled to rejoin the main army.

According to Barbour, a sturdy friar on horseback
was set to watch the enemy's approach, and that, armed
with a spear, he began the fray himself, as soon as they
reached the abbey wall.

Annoyed at the issue of the fray, and smarting under
the losses and privations already sustained, the soldiers
wreaked their vengeance on the inmates of the abbey,
slaying and wounding the monks; they ransacked the
monastery, carried off or destroyed the valuables, and
leaving behind them ruin and desolation, the English
army proceeded southward, destroying all the religious
houses in their route.

It is stated that when Edward's main army came up
to Melrose, they showed no mercy. William de Peblis,
the prior, was slain, many of the aged and infirm monks
were sabred, two of the lay brethren, who were blind,
were cruelly butchered, and several of the monks were

wounded. On their route, the abbey of Dryburgh was set on fire, and burnt to ashes, by command of the king.

The good government of Robert the Bruce ultimately triumphed, after Scotland had experienced great misery and oppression. The monks of Melrose began to think of restoring their ancient church and monastery again. Robert endeavoured by his liberality to make good what the English soldiery had destroyed. Peace was favourable to the design, and prosperity once more swelled the resources of the convent.

At Scone, March 26th, in the year 1326, King Robert granted the sum of L.2000 sterling to enable the monks of Melrose to rebuild their church. This sum, equal to fifty thousand pounds of the money of the present day, was to be chiefly raised in the county of Roxburgh from fines and forfeited lands ; from the baronies of Cessford and Eckford, forfeited by Sir Roger de Mowbray; and the lands of Nesbit, Longnewton, Maxton, and Caverton, forfeited by William, Lord Soulis, both for treason and conspiracy. Soulis was confined in Dumbarton Castle, where he died; Mowbray died about the time the plot was discovered, and his dead body was suspended on a gallows and afterwards beheaded. William de Soulis had aspired to the throne of Scotland.

In the Northampton treaty of peace, between England and Scotland, in 1328, it was stipulated that there should be a restitution of the lands and possessions of the religious houses in both countries. The claims of Melrose, and the other abbeys of Teviotdale, were particularly attended to.

King Robert augmented the revenues of the abbey with other considerable gifts. In 1329, a few weeks before his death, he wrote a most paternal letter to his son, recommending to his favour the monastery of Melrose, and directing that his heart should be buried there. This latter direction was superseded by a wish, expressed ere he died, that his heart should be deposited in the Holy Sepulchre at Jerusalem. James, Lord Douglas, faithful in his attachment to his sovereign and friend, undertook to execute his last request. The following year, Douglas, accompanied with a splendid retinue of knights and men of note, set out for Palestine, with the royal heart enclosed in a silver casket. Passing through Spain, the Douglas offered his services to the King Alphonso, then engaged in a war with the Saracens. To fight against the enemies of Christendom suited the chivalrous spirit of Douglas, who, after exhibiting prodigies of valour, fell in battle. It is recorded of him, that being surrounded by the enemy, he took the casket containing the heart of Bruce, and casting it before him, exclaimed, " Now, pass onward, as thou wert wont, and Douglas will follow thee, or die!" These were the last words of James, Lord Douglas. Sir William Keith brought back the heart of King Robert, which was deposited near the high altar of Melrose abbey. The body of Bruce was magnificently interred under the grand altar of the church of Dunfermline abbey. The body of Lord Douglas was also brought back from Spain, and buried in the graves of his ancestors.

> "The Earl Murray, that had the cure,
> That time of Scotland haillily,
> With great worship he gart bury
> The king his heart at the abbay
> Of Melros, where men prayeth ay
> That he and his have Paradise."

Melrose abbey sustained but little injury during the stormy period which comprehends the minority of King Robert's successor.

After Edward Baliol's ineffectual attempt to seat himself on the Scottish throne, the abbot and convent of Melrose swore fealty to Edward III., and had letters of protection granted, dated Berwick, July 26, 1333 *

Thomas de Soltre was abbot of Melrose about this time. In a grant made to the abbey of Dryburgh by Sir William de Feltoun, Sheriff of Roxburgh in 1338, his name appears thereto.

On December 24, 1338, Lord William Douglas, surnamed the "Flower of Chivalry," arrested the English

---

* *Rotuli Scotiæ.*

convoy, carrying Christmas fare from Melrose to the castle of Hermitage, and after losing many men, got possession of the victuals. He then went and laid siege to the castle of Hermitage, which he took, and provisioned with the victuals he had taken from the English convoy previously.

Of Lord William Douglas it was said, that " he was terrible and successful in armes, meek, mild, and gentle in peace, the scourge of England, and sure buckler and wall of Scotland, whom neither hard success could make slack, nor prosperity slothful."*

In the winter of 1340, after the siege of Tournay, Edward III., after making an excursion to Ettrick Forest in very stormy weather, returned to Melrose, celebrated Christmas at the abbey, and gave a tournament. Sir William Douglas and other Scottish knights attended. Douglas joisted, in the king's presence, with Henry of Lancaster, Earl of Derby, who, having heard of his valorous deeds, desired his acquaintance, and for that purpose had challenged him to this chivalrous sport. The tilting was at Roxburgh, where the king's lieutenant, Derby, lay with his forces.† In the first course Douglas's spear broke, and a splinter of it hurt his hand, whereupon the Earl of Derby, then one of the most courteous, brave, and generous men of England

---

* HUME of Godscroft.
† KNYGHTON, *Charter of Mel. Abbey. Cart. Kel.*, 199, r.

at the time, would not suffer him to joist any longer. Another tilting match took place at Berwick in the Easter following, between twenty English and twenty Scottish knights, which lasted three days, when two English knights and a knight and a squire of Scotland were slain.

William is the name of the next abbot of Melrose. He is mentioned in charters dated 1342 and 1343.* About this time lived Peter Fenton, a monk of Melrose, who wrote a poetical history of the life of King Robert the Bruce. In 1342, David II. returned from France, and assumed the reins of government. In 1346, he was taken prisoner by the English, at the battle of Neville's Cross, near Durham. The southern counties of Scotland were again overrun by the English. During this period the monastic institutions, in particular, felt the inconveniences and vexations incident to such an unhappy state. In 1365, the monks of Melrose were accused of selling wool and victuals to their countrymen, and of traitorously defrauding the King of England of his customs and dues. In 1375, Edward gave them liberty to buy in Norfolk or Suffolk two hundred quarters of barley or malt, for the use of the convent, for prompt payment, and to carry it by sea from the port of Lynn to Berwick, and thence by land to Melrose. They had

---

* SIMPSON's *MS. Collections, &c.*

similar permission to buy food in England, anno dom. 1377. These were periods of great scarcity.

In the year 1353, shortly after the disastrous battle of Durham, Sir William Douglas, the Dark Knight of Liddesdale, known also, from his exploits, as the "Flower of Chivalry," was beset and cruelly murdered in Ettrick Forest, where he was hunting, by William Earl of Douglas and his adherents. The Earl was a kinsman of Sir William's, and the murder, which was perpetrated at a place called Galeswood in the forest, had its origin in jealousy. Godscroft says, the Earl had become jealous of the Knight and the Countess. So says the old ballad,—

> "The Countess of Douglas, out of her bower she came,
>   And loudly there that she did call:
> 'It is for the Lord of Liddisdale,
>   That I let all these tears down fall.'"

The ballad goes on to say how the Countess wrote love-letters to the knight to persuade him from the hunting on this occasion; and how he was killed, and by whom and where. The body was carried the first night to Lindean Kirk, a chapel in the forest, not far from Selkirk, whence, on the day following, it was transferred to Melrose, and interred in the abbey. The ruins of Lindean church, now almost obliterated, are still to be seen near Abbotsford.

About this period, William, first Earl of Douglas,

had been chiefly instrumental in retaking all the castles
and strongholds of Teviotdale, which the English had
kept since the disastrous battle of Durham, the Castle
of Roxburgh only excepted.   Douglas also purged the
country of brigands and robbers.   Soon after these
exploits he died of fever, and was buried in Melrose
abbey, 1384.   His son James, the second Earl of
Douglas, succeeded him; he was also a most heroic
chief, but was slain at the battle of Otterbourne.   His
two natural sons, William and Archibald, became the
progenitors of the houses of Drumlanrig and Cavers.
William of Drumlanrig's second son, Archibald Douglas,
married a Pringle of the house of Galashiels, who bore
to him twelve sons, and, after his death, married again
to one Colonel Wallace, and bore twelve more to him
also.*

Annoyed by the predatory excursions of the Borderers,
and determined to check the turbulent spirit of the
Scotch, who, by the exertions of the Earl of Douglas,
had succeeded in wresting the frontiers from the enemy,
in 1385, Richard II., with a great army, invaded Scotland, and spread devastation on every side.   The inhabitants, according to custom, removed their corn and
cattle, and retreated to the hills and inaccessible places
of the country.   The nobility shut their families up in
castles for safety.   Distressed for want of provisions

* GODSCROFT.

Richard's army laid waste the villages and burned the monasteries. Melrose and Dryburgh shared in the destruction. After obtaining shelter for one night in Melrose abbey, Richard gave it to the flames on the following morning. Newbattle shared a similar fate. It is recorded he intended to spare Melrose and Newbattle, and that he caused his banners to be affixed to the gates of those abbeys, but that some soldiers, forming part of the rear-guard of the army, as it advanced, having been killed, in revenge he commanded that they should be burned and destroyed.*

Richard seems to have repented of these sacriligious acts; for, in October, 1389, after the battle of Otterbourne, and when a truce was concluded, he granted the monks of Melrose a reduction of two shillings of the duty on each sack of wool, to the number of two thousand sacks, which they should send for export to Berwick, the latter being at this time a seaport of the English. He also gave them protection from plunderers, and likewise license to buy and sell leather and farming stock in Northumberland and Cumberland.

Forays and combats did not cease on the withdrawal of Richard's army. Predatory warfare continued, and inroads were made into England with various success. Not the least remarkable of these was the battle of Otterbourne, in Redesdale, in 1388, of which Froissart

* KNYGHTON, 2675.

says: "Of all the battles, this was the bravest and best contested, for there was neither knight nor squire, but acquitted himself nobly, doing well his duty, and fighting hand to hand, without either stay or faint-heartedness." Tytler says, that Henry Percy, surnamed Hotspur, left Newcastle after dinner, and arrived before the Scots encampment by sunset. Much of the fighting was by moonlight. For many hours the battle raged with undiminished fury. Banners rose and fell. The voices of the knights shouting their war cries, were mingled with the shrieks and groans of the dying. The ground was literally covered with dead bodies and shreds of armour. Slippery with blood, it scarcely afforded room for the combatants, so closely were they engaged, and so obstinately was every foot of earth contested. It was at this time that the Earl of Douglas, the hero of the fray, wielding a battle-axe in both hands, and followed only by a few of his household, cut his way into the press of the English knights, and throwing himself too rashly upon their spears, was borne to the earth, and soon mortally wounded in the head and neck.

Douglas thus died heroically in the field, requesting his friends to bury him in Melrose abbey with his father, not to suffer his standard to be lost or cast down, and to avenge his death. Victory ultimately declared the battle of Otterbourne in favour of the

Picts, but the loss of Douglas was the more lamented as he had fallen in the prime of manhood.   The whole army mourned for him, and the march to Scotland was like a funeral procession.   In the midst of it moved the car that bare the body of this brave man, and conveyed it to the abbey of Melrose, where they buried him in the sepulchre of his fathers, with the military pomp of the whole army, and they hung his banner, torn and soiled with blood, over his premature grave.   Burns truly says,

> " One Douglas shines in Home's immortal page,
>   But Douglases were heroes every age."

One Patrick Hepburne, captain of a Lothian regiment, valiantly distinguished himself at Otterbourne, and was slain June 11th, 1401, in a sharp encounter at West Nisbet.

David Benyn,* or Binning, is the next abbot whose name is found on record.

He had leave from Henry IV., December 2, 1409, to go, with twelve servants in his company, to Canterbury, abide twelve months there, and so return to Scotland without hurt or molestation.   In 1422, he excommunicated John Haig of Bemerside, and his servants, for trespasses committed by them upon the

---

* The Binnings and Binnjies take their derivation from the above name.

servants and cattle of the convent, on their land at Redpath.

John Fogo was abbot in 1425, and was sent to Rome, with other prelates, on an embassy from King James I. Fogo was a monk of Melrose, confessor to the king, a doctor of divinity, and a man of great eloquence and learning. Symptoms of disorder were at this time manifest in the Church. The doctrines of Wickliffe and Huss were receiving attention in many places. Fogo was particularly active in confuting their opinions, and is said to have had the principal hand in obtaining the condemnation of the unfortunate Paul Crawar, the Bohemian, who was burned at St. Andrews in 1433.

The habits of the clergy were altogether changed, monastic discipline was relaxed, and industry and temperance gave way to sloth and luxury. All earthly institutions are liable to decay, and the abbeys of Teviotdale shared in the degeneracy of the Church, and their abuses needed a serious reformation.

Richard Lundy is named in the Chartulary as abbot in 1440. He was a monk of Melrose in 1428.

Andrew Hunter, abbot of Melrose, in 1844, and confessor to James II., was much employed in affairs of state. At one period he was Lord High Treasurer of Scotland.

His arms are carved on one of the buttresses of the church, near the west end; they are two crosiers, and two

Q

hunting horns, with a rose in chief and a mallet in base. The initials A. H. are on the right and left of the shield, which is supported by two singular figures.

In 1452, Alexander Geddes, one of the monks, was elected teacher of philosophy in the newly established University of Glasgow.*

STATE OF THE COUNTRY IN 1446.—History informs us, that shortly after this period, mischief reigned so common in all parts, that society was thoroughly disorganized. Lawlessness and ruffianism was in all the land. Numbers of good families, seeing there was no regard paid to the king, the law, nor the religion of the land—neither to the Earl of Douglas, nor the forces under him—retired, and shut themselves up in castles and strongholds, and left their flocks and goods they could not put away in places of security, to thieves and robbers, to take them as they thought good, thinking, if they saved themselves, they had sufficient till a better fortune. Lindsay of Pitscottie also says, " that about 1455, Donald (Lord of the Isles and Earl of Ross) gathered a company of mischievous and cursed limmers, and invaded the kingdom in every airth, wherever he came, with great cruelty, neither sparing old nor young, without regard to wives, aged, feeble, and decrepit women, or young infants in the cradle, which would have moved a heart

* M'CRIE's *Life of Melville.*

of stone to commiseration. Donald burnt villages, towns, and corns, so much thereof, as might not goodly be carried away, by the great prize of goods that he took."

William was the next abbot. He was a commissioner of truce in June, 1460.

Richard, abbot of Melrose, was a commissioner of truce in 1473, and his name occurs as witness to a charter of James III. to the church of Glasgow, in 1476.*

John Frazer, abbot of Melrose, was descended from a good family of the name in Tweeddale. He was much respected for his worth and hospitality. Made bishop of Ross in 1485, where he completed the building of the cathedral.

He was a privy counsellor and lord of session, and died in 1507, aged 78 years.†

Bernard was abbot of Melrose in 1487 and until 1499. ‡

So grievous had the errors of the Cistertian brethren become about this period, that Innocent VIII. convened by his injunction, a general chapter of the order, to be held at Cisteaux. The abbot of Cupar was commissioned to visit and reform the monasteries in Scotland, and did so. He deposed the abbot of Melrose

---

* *Rotuli Scotiæ.*   † KEITH's *Catalogue of Bishops.*
‡ *Original Charters of Melrose Abbey.*

among others, and found the complaints but too true that were brought against them. The offices of the church were now becoming matters of merchandise. Many of the dignitaries were characterised by idleness and indifference to all that concerned their high calling. The abbots and others kept luxurious tables. They dwelt in magnificent halls, and wore costly garments. They were attended by youths of good families as pages, in costly liveries. Even the private monks spurned the sober fare, homely dress, and devout retirement of their predecessors. They kept horses, and were always abroad before the public gaze. They bought their own clothes, chose the finest materials, and even the common dormitory wherein they slept, was now partitioned off into separate chambers. And it may be feared, alas! that many of them erred in weightier matters.

Cleverness and address seemed more common than learning and wisdom.

William, the next abbot, appears to have been a son of Sir Walter Scott of Howpasly.

Robert was abbot in 1510.

James Beaton, nephew of the Archbishop of St. Andrews, was abbot some years after this. Dr Magnus, in a letter informs Cardinal Wolsey, that "the abbots of Melrose and Dunfermline, both brethren and nephews to the archbishop, be slain."

The politic measures of the Scottish government for the good of the country in 1531, are thus noticed by Lindsay—

"The king (James V.) seeing the realm standing in such peace and tranquillity, rejoiced at the same, thinking daily that all things should increase more and more: To that effect, James sent to Denmark, and brought home horses and mares, and put them in parks, that, of their offspring might be gotten to sustain wars in time of need.

"And also he sent to Flanders and France, and brought home artillery, powder, and bullets, with pikes and harness, and other ordinance for war. And also plenished the country with all kinds of craftsmen of other countries; as Frenchmen, Spaniards, Dutchmen, and Englishmen, which were all cunning craftsmen, every man for his own hand. Some were gunners, wrights, carvers, painters, masons, smiths, harnessmakers, tapesters, brondsters, taylors, cunning chirurgeons, apothecaries, with all other kinds of craftsmen that might bring his realm in policy, and his craftsmen apparel his palaces in all manner of operation and necessaries, according to their order, and he gave them large wages and pensions yearly."

Andrew Durie or Drury, was appointed abbot of Melrose, after much competition, by the Pope. In the year 1525, Margaret, the dowager of James IV.,

used her influence with her brother Henry VIII. and
Cardinal Wolsey, to procure the benefice of Melrose
abbey for one of her favourites, she being to receive
an annual income out of the revenues. While Durie
presided, the general chapter of Cisteaux again endeavoured to introduce the ancient discipline. The
faults of the prevailing system, however, were neither
checked by the reproofs of the general chapter, the
complaints of the public, nor the effusions of the ribald
wits who flourished at the Reformation.

The rule was now infringed, if not abrogated altogether, that forbade the brethren to possess any private
property. In the abbey of Melrose, the monks had
pensions allowed them for food and clothing. Each
monk had also a garden for his own particular use
and pleasure. These things were pointed out as
wrong, and Andrew, the abbot, was ordered, upon pain
of deposition, to carry a sweeping reform into effect,
and to punish with excommunication the monks who
dare prove refractory. This led to argument, the
monks petitioned, and the commission assented to their
requests, so that things remained in pretty much the
same state as before.

In 1535, James V. was invested with the administration of the revenues of Melrose abbey. He reproved
the clergy for the looseness of their conduct, but
no actual steps were taken to produce a decided im-

provement. In 1541, the king procured the resignation of abbot Durie, and had his infant natural son,
James Stuart, appointed abbot or commendator of
Melrose. Durie was made bishop of Galloway, had a
retiring pension of a thousand marks granted him
from Melrose, and died in 1558. James V. died anno
1543.

James Stuart, an illegitimate son of King James V.
by Elizabeth Shaw, was appointed abbot or commendator of the abbeys of Melrose and Kelso in 1541;
being then in his infancy. He died in 1558.

After the death of James V. the country was
divided by the factions of the Church and the dissatis-
fied nobles. Mary of Guise, widow of the deceased king,
and Cardinal Beaton were at the head of a powerful
body; and Arran the Regent wavered between two
parties. After subscribing to the proposal made by
Henry VIII., to effect a marriage between the heir-
apparent of England and the young Mary of Scotland,
he joined the cardinal and queen-mother in putting a
stop to the contract. Henry expressed his dissatisfac-
tion in war. An invasion took place, conducted by the
Earl of Hertford. Sir Ralph Evers and Sir Brian
Latoun were employed in making inroads on the
Borders. These two generals, in 1544, laid waste the
whole of Teviotdale, with a degree of barbarism and
ferocity hitherto unfelt before. Towns, towers, and

churches were destroyed; corn wasted, and cattle carried off; and the abbey of Melrose suffered most severely.* In the following spring of 1545, they occupied Jedburgh, and prepared to reduce Teviotdale. As a reward for their services, the successful leaders were promised a feudal grant of whatever they might win from the Scots.

About this period great troubles prevailed in Scotland. The country was divided by faction, Cardinal Beaton and the Romish party on the one hand, and the Protector and Scottish Barons on the other; the former party desiring an alliance with France, while the latter were in favour of one with England. Robert Lindsay of Pitscottie says, " The English knowing this, entered Scotland both by the east and west marches, and utterly spoiled and destroyed all before them, with great slaughter of the inhabitants. So that many were forced to wear the Red Cross and swear allegiance to England. This continued all the summer (1544) till winter came on, at which time, having destroyed Teviotdale and Merse, they took the abbey of Coldinghame, and laid all waste as far as Dunbar. The

---

* Their men-at-arms entered the abbey, and barbarously defaced the tombs of the Douglasses. A long heroic line of the Douglasses was interred on the north-east side the high altar of Melrose abbey. Not a vestige of these tombs is to be seen, however, and there is no doubt but they were broken down and destroyed as history informs us.

Englishmen, with Sir Ralph Ivers and Sir Bryan Latoun, general and lieutenant of the army, grew so proud of the victory, that they accounting the whole lands of Scotland, south of Edinburgh, fully conquered, passed to the court to be rewarded for so great service. Henry VIII., by persuasion of the Duke of Norfolk, condescended to them, that, seeing they had conquered the Merse and Teviotdale, being two most populous and fertile countries in these parts of Britain, and had brought all the inhabitants to the English obedience, (although that conquest had stood the king above thirty thousand pounds sterling), yet he would by charter and infeftment under the great seal of England, give to these two noblemen, those two Sheriffdoms, with the counties adjacent, erected into two Lordships." "For (said the Duke) if indeed they have brought those countries under your obedience, they are worthy so great a reward, and beside, all men shall see how great respect your Majesty hath to valiant spirits, and hereby, ye shall oblige these two noblemen to defend these lands by all means possible." The king, moreover, gave them three thousand men upon his own charge, for a year and day, to assist them in possession of their conquest, besides borderers, who would join with them. These two captains, being glad of their great success, hasted to come and take seisin of their new conquest, and upon the 8th day of March, 1545, came to Jedburgh, with an army of five thousand men, purposing to take seisin of the Merse and Teviotdale, and thereafter to come to Haddington and Edinburgh, if not stopped.

The Earl of Angus seeing no measures taken for resistance, came to the governor, and sharply reproved him, that he, using only the council of the cardinal and priests, suffered the enemy to prevail so far. " If ye continue thus," said Angus, " ye will be shortly thrust out of all Scotland, or else forced to submit yourself as tributary to England. Whereas if you would follow the council of the nobility, we might be able to defend our own, and do the English one ill turn for another; and albeit, you should lie aside, yet I here avow to spend my life on the quarrel, and if they come to take seisin in my lands, I shall bear them witness to it, and perhaps write them an instrument with sharp pens and red ink. And, whereas now, being misguided by the evil council of the Cardinal and Kirkmen, you are in suspicion of me and other of the nobility, yet, if you will follow our council at this time, we shall, God willing, show your grace a real demonstration of the contrary, and take a part ourselves in our own conclusions. Whereas your Kirkmen, when they have brought great trouble on the realm, were never present at the offputting thereof. Go on, therefore, resolutely, and I shall adventure before you in all hazards, for I would rather die with honour in the defence of my country and heritage, than live to see the same brought to bondage."

The Governor, animated by these speeches, with the advice of Angus, resolved to go forward against the enemy, with the small forces which were about them, (the Earl and he both, not exceeding three hundred horse in company,) and sent proclamations to all the nobility and gentry that were near, to follow him.

The English were come that same night to Jed-burgh, and hearing that the Governor was coming to lodge in Melrose with so small a company, they thought all was their own, and came forward in the night to entrap the Governor in his lodgings, yet he being advertised, retired back above the bridge of Melrose, to a place called "The Shiels," and lodged there by the advice of the Earl of Angus, and sent forth heralds with trumpets to advertise the neigh-bouring gentlemen to meet the Governor at Galashiels in all haste. The English missing the Governor, spoiled Melrose, and returned towards Jedburgh. Meanwhile, Norman Lesly, Master of Rothes, and the Lord Lindsay's servants, with the neighbouring barons, the Laird of Lochlevin also, and the gentlemen of the west end of Fife, to the number of twelve score able men, having "ridden all that night, met the governor at Gathen-

side, foreanent Melrose, whereof he was very glad: And
seeing the Englishmen tarrying a little at Libberton's
Cross * to view the Scottish men's array and under-
stand their intent, the Scots marched south-west from
Melrose, round about Ancrum, pretending as if they
minded not to meddle with the English; who marching towards Jedburgh, stayed long at the Sandy-case-
way,† it being so narrow that they could not march
but two abreast. Meanwhile the Laird of Buccleugh
was posting to the Governor, showing him that his
whole followers were coming with all speed, within six
miles. Buccleugh counselled the Governor to send all
the horse back to a hill where the artillery stood, and
to draw themselves into a low place, out of the
Englishmen's sight, whereby they might be persuaded
the Scots had fled, and would follow them without
order, which fell out accordingly. For the English
believing the Scots had fled, pursued them so fast,
that they were all out of breath. The first battle led
by Sir Bryan Latoun and Sir Robert Bouis, had, in
the midst of the battle a thousand spears, and on their

---

* The account given by Lindsay of Pitscottie.

† The term Sandy-case-way is not very intelligible. But it is supposed that the Governor and his adherents bivouacked on the height
above Drygrange, where a temporary ambuscade of thriving timber
would afford ample cover for their horse and the small army that
was with them, and from which elevation they could watch the
ambiguous movements of the English for a considerable distance.

right wing, five hundred hagbutters, and on their left five hundred bows.

" Sir Ralph Ivers led the great battle, containing a thousand spears, a thousand hagbutters, and as many bows. The Scots at the beginning had only three hundred men with the Governor, and two hundred with the Earl of Angus. The English hasted to pursue the flight of the Scots, thinking by one encounter to put an end to the war. But they lighting on the ambush of the Scots, all wearied and out of breath, albeit they were discouraged, yet contemning the fewness of their number, set upon them. The Scots had providentially got advantage both of the wind and sun, being both in the south-west, so that the sunbeams and smoke of the powder took all sight from the English, besides the Scottish men's spears were an ell longer than the English, whereby the English were borne down before they could reach at the Scots, who encountering them most violently, beat back the vanguard upon the great battle, and so disordering both, put them to flight, killing their leaders, Sir Ralph Ivers and Sir Bryan Latoun, and a great number of gentlemen and common soldiers, to the number of five hundred, with the loss of two Scottish men slain recklessly by their own artillery. There were taken a thousand prisoners, whereof eighty were gentlemen.

" The Governor at night returning to his standard,

kneeled down, and gave solemn thanks to God for the unexpected victory, the like whereof had scarcely been read of, that so small a number discomfited so great a host. The chief of the captives, was Howard, the queen's uncle, Hutchinson, Mayor of York, Lord Bowis, Sir John Worthingtou, many of the Herons and Sellies, and other gentlemen of the Borders and knights of great esteem. This battle was foughten in Teviotdale, at Ancrum Muir, the 9th of March, 1545."

After the battle, the Governor, calling for the Earl of Angus, highly commended his valour, resolution, and wisdom, and thanked Sir George Douglas, his brother, for his valiant services, assuring them that the day's success had cleared them from all aspersions of disloyalty, and love to England, laid upon them by their enemies. He thanked the Laird of Buccleugh also for his wise and fortunate counsel. He gave thanks also to the Master of Rothes, Laird of Lochlevin, and the rest of the gentlemen of quality, acknowledging their honourable deservings to their perpetual praise. Thereafter, they rode all together towards Jedburgh, and finding in the fields the dead bodies of Sir Ralph Ivers and Sir Bryan Latoun, he commanded them to be buried, or their corpses to be given to their friends, saying, " This taking of seisin has been no less unfortunate than informal."

This event, however, was fiercely avenged in Sep-

tember of the same year. The Earl of Hertford over-
ran the Merse and Teviotdale with 12,000 men, while
a feeble resistance was made by the Scots. The monastic structures were no longer sacred in the eyes of
the English. What had not been already destroyed
was now burned by the soldiery. Melrose shared in
the general havoc, and from this period the abbey
never resumed its former splendour.

It seems clear, by historical testimony, that on the
night of the 8th of March, 1545, the English army,
then lying at Jedburgh, stole a march to Melrose.
The Scots, being on their guard, retired. The English
collected what booty they could in the monastery and
town of Melrose, and retired again to Jedburgh. The
Scots lay on Gattonside and the hills above Galashiels
and Elwand, under the command of Douglas, Norman
Lesly, the Earl of Rothes, and Walter Scott of Buccleuch. On the morning of the 9th they moved south,
crossed the Leader, and keeping the hill country, made
a feint, gradually marching round towards Ancrum.
The Scots were thus enabled to keep sight of the
English, and the sun had passed the meridian, or ever
the two armies came into contact. The Scots, keeping
their backs north-west, had their country open to
receive them in case of defeat, and it is most probable
the fray began some distance north of Ancrum, and a
favourable position being got by the Scots, their rear-

division came up, and decided the glory of the day rather hastily at length on Ancrum Moor, which is distant about six miles from Melrose.

When near Lilliard's Edge, as it is sometimes called, a heron which rose at the moment, and soared between the two armies, drew from Douglas the following characteristic exclamation: "Oh that I had here my gray goss hawk, that we might all yoke together." The English fell into confusion, and were signally defeated. Thus Douglas got speedy revenge for the insult offered to his family by Evers and Latoun, in desecrating the tombs of the Douglasses in Melrose abbey the year previous.

In September, 1545, in the terrific inroad made by the Earl of Hertford, seven monasteries and friaries, sixteen castles, towers, and peels, five market towns (Jedburgh burnt the previous year), two hundred and forty-three villages, thirteen milns, and three hospitals, were destroyed. At the battle of Ancrum Muir, Sir Ralph Eure (sometimes called Ivers and Evers) was slain by the Laird of Molle, and it is recorded that the English avenged his death in the following barbarous manner in May, 1546, viz.,* "The lord warden of the est Marches (William Lord Eure) having information that the Laird of Moul (Molle), who slew his son, repaired to two toures of his awn, upon the head of

* *Cotton MS.*

Bowbente (Bowmont) in Tivydale, th' one called Moul and th' other Coteiruste, he sent forth the said day at nyght V men of the garrisons of this eestmarches, under the leadinge of his sone Henry Eury, and George Boues, son to Richard Boues, captain of Norhame, who went to the said toueres, and wan and undermyndett them both, and beat them down, and burned the steads and towns thereabouts; the laird of Moul nott being therein, there was one of his brethren and four kynsmen of his, with a dosan of his servandes and frendes, that stode at their defence, and wold not give it over, which were all slayn in the said toueres."*

Ancrum was burnt in the year 1549 by the Earl of Rutland.

Cardinal Guise became Commendator of Melrose abbey upon the death of James Stewart in 1558. This appointment was made by his sister, Mary of Lorrain.   It is doubtful if he ever received any benefit from it, as the property of this and all other religious houses was seized by the Lords of the Congregation in 1559, and in 1560 were annexed to the crown by statute, which provided that the sovereign should not have power to alienate it.   This act was rendered nugatory by subsequent Acts of Parliament, which

* In the Appendix to this book we give a contemporary account of the Earl of Hertford's second expedition to Scotland in September, 1545, which, being the narrative of an eye-witness, is of great historical value.

R

granted portions of this property to individuals favoured by the Court, or on account of public services.

At the Reformation, John Watson, Dean of the Chapter of Melrose, embraced the reformed religion. In 1542 there were one hundred monks at Melrose, who received annually for their consumption sixty bolls of wheat, and three hundred casks of ale. Probably there were also as many lay brethren as monks. For the service of the mass they received eighteen casks of wine, and for the entertainment of strangers thirty bolls of wheat, forty casks of ale, and twenty casks of wine. For the nourishment of the sick, they were allowed four thousand livres Tournois; and the barber, who was also surgeon to the community, received a salary of a hundred livres.[*]

About 1560–67, the Borders were infested with armed banditti, who committed the most lawless depredations, and whom success had made insolent and intolerable. James Stuart, prior of St. Andrews (afterwards the good Regent Moray), was appointed by Queen Mary at this period to be Lord-Lieutenant and Chief Justiciary of the Borders. The military retainers, from no less than eleven counties, were commanded to attend him, and he destroyed many of the strongholds of the freebooters, and executed twenty of the most

* *Scotia Sacra MS.*

notorious offenders.   He sent fifty to Edinburgh, to
undergo the punishment of the law.   Sir James Mel-
vil of Halhill, in his *Memoirs of the Affairs of State*,
says, "He took great pains to steal secret roads upon
the thieves on the Borders, tending much to the quiet-
ing thereof.   He likewise held Justice Ayres in the
In country."

In 1564, one Michael was Commendator of Melrose,
but in 1566 the estates of the abbey were granted by
Queen Mary to the Earl of Bothwell, by whose forfeiture they again reverted to the crown.   The title of
Commendator was conferred the following year upon
James Douglas, second son to Sir William Douglas of
Lochlevin.*   And in 1591, King James VI. granted
to Archibald Douglas, son to the Commendator, a
pension for life of " sex monkis portionis furth of the
abbey of Melrose, and of the superplus of the third
thereof, in consideration of the goid, trew, and thankful service done to his hieness, be his weilbelovit James,
commendator of the said abbey."   James Douglas
took down part of the abbey walls.   With the stones
he built a house for himself, which is still standing,
and called the Priory, and is now occupied by James
Erskine, Esq. of Shieldfield.   It has the date 1590,

---

* This appointment was owing to the affection of the Regent, Earl
of Moray, who was an illegitimate son of James V. by the Commendator's mother.

with his own and his lady's name over one of the
windows.*

In 1599, the lands and baronies, with very few exceptions, were erected into a temporal lordship in
favour of Sir John Ramsay, Viscount Haddington, who
had assisted King James at the time of the Earl of
Gowrie's conspiracy. In 1609, Alexander Ruthven had
a chartered grant of all the lands and baronies which
belonged to the abbey of Melrose, with some exceptions. The estates were subsequently obtained by
that eminent personage, Sir Thomas Hamilton of Priest-
field, raised to the peerage in 1613 by the title of
Lord Binning and Byres, and created Earl of Melrose
also in 1619. By patent, he suppressed his own title,
and was created Earl of Haddington in 1627, that
title having previously become extinct. This distinguished man was successively King's Advocate, Lord
Clerk Register, Secretary of State, Lord President of
the Court of Session, and Keeper of the Privy Seal.
He died in 1637, in his 74th year. In more recent
times, the valuable heritage of the monastery became the property of the Buccleuch family, whose
ancestors had been hereditary bailies under the
abbot of Melrose. Early in the eighteenth century,
the same noble family acquired by purchase the
remainder of the abbey lands included in the lord-

* Mary Ker, Lady of Melros.

ship of Melrose, which still form part of their extensive possessions.

In 1747, when feudal jurisdictions were abolished in Scotland, the Lady Isabella Scott was allowed L.1200 sterling as a compensation for her right to this bailiery.

The unfortunate monks, who at the Reformation saw their community dispersed and their possessions alienated, beheld also their beautiful church in ruins, and their ancient halls and cloisters completely demolished. That extraordinary violence of the populace, who, in 1559 and 1560, destroyed monasteries and religious houses throughout the kingdom, was instigated and encouraged by many who either coveted or had already been enriched by the plunder of the church. Those who had taken possession of the lands and revenues were apprehensive of the most fearful consequences, if the ancient form of religion should be revived. They gave every assistance, therefore, to the destroyer, anxious that their abolition should be as complete as possible.

Large portions of the ruins of Melrose abbey were taken away at various times since the epoch of the Reformation. In 1618, the nave was fitted up as a parish church, and continued in use till 1810.

Various parts of the abbey were taken away to construct a tolbooth, and to repair mills and sluices. Indeed, for a long time, the ruins were looked upon by the inhabitants of the town and district, as a sort of quarry, from which materials were to be obtained for repairing the neighbouring houses.

His Grace the present Duke of Buccleuch, having a strong desire to preserve what remains of these beautiful ruins, has caused additional surveillance to be exercised over the abbey, and many ornamental and exquisitely carved stones have recently, by request and at the sole expense of the noble owner, been recovered from the adjacent kirkyard, and restored to the ruins. In the reign of King William III., the statues which filled the richly-carved niches, and adorned the buttresses and pinnacles of the church, were for the most part standing and entire. In the middle of the 17th century, they were thrown down and demolished, it is said, at the instigation of David Fletcher, then minister of Melrose. That they were wantonly demolished there is no doubt. The humour of demolishing monuments and destroying the inimitable decorative ornaments of ecclesiastical buildings, whose occupants were gone to return no more for ever, might gratify the fanatic, while the wise and sober-minded would lament it. Ignorance might gloat over such spoliation, and a vulgar braggadocio impute to itself some glorious achievement; but it was not only mischievous, but useless, and showed a love of destructiveness as great as could

possibly invest the heart of Alaric himself. Of the
desolation that left the church much as we now witness it, time and the destroyer can only account for.

> "Its fonts and crosses broken lay,
> Its chapels tumble thro' decay;
> And winter's direst blasts assail
> Those turrets high, that breast the gale;
> While glass and painting long have gone,
> And left the windows nak'd and lone.
> Their slender shafts and mullions lie
> On other spots, that meet the eye—
> Near finials, brackets, buttress-strown,
> And many a Gothic arch o'erthrown.
> Its glorious statues, long defac'd
> By heartless Goth—and things that grac'd,
> Its lengthen'd age, and proud decay,
> The mad fanatic tore away."

When the revenues of all the great benefices were
valued in 1561, the rent of Melrose abbey was stated
as follows:—

Scots money, L.1758.

Wheat, 14 chalders, 5 bolls.

Barley, 56   do.   5   do.

Meal, 78   do.   13   do.

Oats, 44   do.   10   do.

Capons, 84 in number.

Poultry, 620   do.

Butter, 105 stones; salt, 8 chalders, out of Preston-
    pans.

Peats, 340 loads; carriages, 500.

Chapter Ninth.

LAST LETTER OF KING ROBERT BRUCE, WRITTEN ANNO
DOM. 1329.

OBERTUS, Dei gratia rex Sco-
torum, David præcordialissimo
filio suo, ac ceteris successoribus
suis salutem, et sic ejus præcepta tenere,
ut cum sua benedictione possint regnare.
Fili karissime, digne censetur videri filius
qui paternos, in bonis, mores imitans, piam ejus nititur
exequi voluntatem, nec proprie sibi sumit nomen
hæredis qui salubribus prædecessoris affectibus non
adhæret. Cupientes, igitur, ut piam affectionem, et sin-
ceram dilectionem quam erga monasterium de Melros, ubi
cor nostrum, ex speciali devotione, disposuimus tumu-
landum, et erga religiosos ibidem Deo servientes, ipsorum
vita sanctissima nos ad hoc excitante, concepimus, tu
cæterique successores nostri, pia sanctitate prosequa-
mini, ut ex vestræ dilectionis affectu, dictis religiosis

post mortem nostram ostenso, ipsi pro nobis, ad oran-
dum ferventius et fortius animentur.

Vobis præcipimus, et quantum possumus instanter
supplicamus, et ex toto corde injungimus, quatenus
assignationibus quas eisdem viris religiosis, pro fabrica
ecclesiæ suæ, de novo fecimus, ac etiam omnibus aliis
donationibus nostris, ipsis libere guadere permittatis
easdem potius si necesse fuerit, augmentantes quam
diminuentes, ipsorum petitiones auribus benevolis ad-
mittentes, ac ipsos contra suos invasores et æmulos, pia
devotione, protogentes, Hanc autem exhortationem,
supplicationem, et præceptum, tu fili, cæterique successores nostri, præstanti animo complere curetis, si
nostram benedictionem habere velitis, una cum benedictione Filii Summi Regis, qui filios, docuit patrum
voluntates, in bono, perficere ; asserens in mundum se
venisse, non ut suam voluntatem faceret, sed paternam.
In testimonium autem nostræ devotionis erga locum
prædictum, sic a nobis dilectum et electum, conceptæ,
præsentum literam religiosis prædictis dimittimus, nostris successoribus, in posterum, ostendendum.   Datum
apud Cardros, undecimo die Maii, anno regni nostri
xxiiij.*

* Çart. Mailros, 104, v.

Robert, by the grace of God, King of Scots, to David his beloved son, and to his successors which shall come after him, wisheth safety and such an obedience to his precepts as may merit his blessing to rest on their future reigns. Dear son, you are aware that he only is worthy to be called a son who, in all just things, imitating his father's example, endeavours with his whole power to obey his wishes ; nor does he rightly merit the name of heir who does not adhere to the salutary desires of his predecessors.

Being desirous, therefore, that you, and the rest of your successors, should continue to entertain with devout respect to our memory that sincere love and pious affection which, being moved thereto by their most holy life, we have conceived towards the monks and monastery of Melrose, in which, according to our special and devout injunctions, our heart is to be buried ; and being the more earnest that this ardour and attachment should be shown by you to these holy men after our decease, in order that they may be thereby animated to pray more fervently and effectually for the welfare of our soul, we therefore direct you (and to this request add our most fervent supplications and injunctions) that you will permit the same holy men to enjoy liberally, and without interruption, the rents which we have assigned to them towards the rebuilding of their church—rather if any change is made, adding to these gifts than abstracting from them, and at all times lending a benevolent ear to their supplications—defending them from their enemies, and all who may invade their rights.   It is our wish, then, that you, my dear son, and others who may be our successors, shall be anxious to retain in your mind these our exhortations and requests, along with the blessing of the Son of God, who taught sons to obey their parents, and declared of himself that he came into the world not to do his own will, but the will of his Father who is in heaven.   In testimony, therefore, of the devotion with which we are animated towards the religious house so highly esteemed and sincerely beloved by us, we have addressed the present letter to these holy men, to be shown hereafter to our successors.   Given at Cardross on the 11th May, in the twenty-fourth year of our reign.*

* Near the close of the thirteenth century, Scotland was under a regency, which continued nine years.   It was during this period that Edward II. so cruelly oppressed Scotland, destroyed the monasteries, and shed innocent blood.   In 1306 Robert the Bruce began to reign. The first few years were overcast with national misery and degradation.   England bitterly persecuted the Scotch.   Robert Bruce was a good, wise, and valiant king.   At the memorable battle of Bannockburn, he vanquished Edward, defeated the entire army of the English, wrought a glorious deliverance for his country, and drove the enemy clean out.   Robert married first, Isabel, daughter of the

Earl of Marr, by whom he had a son and a daughter.   Isabel dying,
he married again.   His second wife's name was also Isabel, daughter
of Haymenus de Bure, Earl of Ulster, in Ireland, who bare unto him
David II. (the subject of the foregoing letter), Margaret, Countess of
Sutherland, and Maud, who died young.   The body of Robert Bruce
was buried in the monastery of Dunfermline, but his heart in Melrose
abbey.

Chapter Tenth.

A SCHEDULE OF THE REVENUES AND POSSESSIONS OF ST.
MARY'S ABBEY, MELROSE, SHOWING HOW ITS LANDS,
CHURCHES, RIGHTS, PROPERTY, PRIVILEGES, AND IM-
MUNITIES, WERE FROM TIME TO TIME ACQUIRED.

ELROSE, ELDUN, DERNWICK.—
These lands were given for ever
to this convent by the founder, David I.,
free from secular impost of any kind.
Also, by the royal munificence, the chapel
of Old Melros, with its rights and pro-
perty ; and to the brotherhood the right of fishing in
the Tweed, on both sides the river, upon his, as well
as their own.*

GATTONSIDE.—North of Tweed, the king afterwards
gave the whole land and wood of Galtownside, the boundary of which ran up the river Leader to a place called

* *Chartulary of Melros.*

Fawhope, where its burn falls into the Leader, thence up the said burn and across the muir to Raeburn, which falls into the Aloent,* and thence down the Aloent into the Tweed.

WEDALE.—The king also gave the right of easements in the lands and forests of Selkirk and Traquair, viz., pasturage and pannage, and wood and timber for building. More especially did the king grant these privileges in that part of the forest called Wedale; bounded on the south-west by the river Gala, on the east by the Leader, and on the north by the lands of the Morvilles, who had great possessions in Lauderdale.†

COLMSLIE.—Malcolm IV. confirmed these grants, and added a portion of land in the lower part of Cumbesley, where the monks might build a place for keeping their cows, and have a fold.‡

BUCKHOLM AND WHITELEE.—Richard Morville, constable of Scotland, gave the convent liberty to have a

---

* The Alwent or Elwand, now called Allen. This romantic stream flows into Tweed, opposite Low-wood, and a little west of Lord Somerville's seat, called the Pavilion, nearly mid-way Melrose and Galashiels. Sir Walter Scott conjured "Glendearg of the Monastery" from this romantic glen and wimpling burn.

† *Chart. Mel.* 31, v.

‡ Leag, a field, Colm, a saint, Colomba, hence Colmslie, or saint's field. There was anciently a Culdee establishment at Colmslie, and the ruins of an old peel may still be seen, which once belonged to the Cairncross family.

place that would hold sixty cows, at Buckholm, on the west-side of the Alwent or Allen, and a convenient dairy house within the enclosures existing there, previous to this grant. Morville also gave them ground in Quhyteley,* within the limits of the forest, where they might have stalls for a hundred cows. Buckholm was eagerly sought by the red deer, large herds of which once covered its towering hill.

BLAINSLIE AND MILKSIDE.—Richard Morville, moreover, gave the monks liberty to plough and sow in the field of Blainsley. He and his wife, Avicia, gave them the chapel of Park, called St. Mary, with the chapelyard, and the whole land of Milchesyde, which is divided from Blainsley by the Mereburn. Richard Morville, in his old age, became an inmate of the monastery, and died there in 1189. His son, William, not only confirmed but enlarged the gifts of his father. Blainslie is now a pleasant village on the right bank of the Leader, and on the main road leading from Lauder to St. Boswell's, and about three miles distant from the former.

ALLANSHAWS.—Alan of Galwey gave the convent the lands of Alwentschaws, in Lauderdale.†

---

* WHITELEE. The monks occupied the open ground, but were forbidden to clear away any more of the forest.

† Allanshaws, from whence the Allen derives its source. The ruins of three Border peels are to be seen in its vale.

SORROWLESSFIELD, (*Doloris valoris.*)*—The exclusive right obtained by the monks to certain parts of territory in Wedale, involved them in serious disputes with their neighbours, who enjoyed rights of forest and pasture in the same territory.   In 1180, King William decided in their favour some dispute of this nature they had with Richard Morville, high constable; and in 1184 the King settled another similar dispute between them and the men of Wedale, belonging to the Bishop of St. Andrews. About 20 years afterwards, the monks accused Patrick, Earl of Dunbar, of having forcibly occupied part of a pasture which was their exclusive property.   Dunbar had great possessions east side of the Leader.   This complaint was sent to Pope Innocent III., who requested the Bishop of St. Andrews and the Archdeacon of Lothian to inquire into the matter.   The Commission proceeded to do so, and summoned the Earl to appear before them to answer the complaint.   Dunbar disregarded the summons, and the Commissioners laid his lands under an interdict.   Upon this the earl submitted.   A representation of the claims of both parties was now sent to the Pope, who, on September 17th, 1207, delegated the Bishop of Moray to decide between them.   By mediation of the bishop, in July, 1208, the matter was finally settled at Selkirk.   The earl gave up to the monks "the whole arable land called Sorouelesfeld, on the west side of Leader, towards the grange of the fore-

---

* The ancient name of Wedale, or Woedale, now Stow.

said monks, as fully as William Soroueles held it."* He also made them a perpetual grant of pasture for 500 sheep and 7 score of cattle, both in wood and plain, in the ground lying between the Leader and the causeway called Malcolmsroad, which goes towards Laudir, from the confines of Cadisley to Fairhope-burne.

It was agreed that neither the monks, nor the earl, or his heirs, should be allowed to have either houses, sheepcotes, enclosures, huts, folds, or any sort of dwelling, within the pasture, and no part was to be ploughed but Sorouelesfeld. The earl's cattle were to return every night to the town of Erslindun (now Earlston), unless hindered by a storm or inundation.

Dunbar gave the monks also right of taking 120 cart-loads of peats every year, from the neighbouring peatery of Scalbedraburch.† His son and successor, Patrick, sixth Earl of Dunbar, went with Louis IX. to Palestine, in 1247, and died at Damietta, in 1248. Previous to his departure, he sold the monks his whole stud of horses, which he had upon his property in

---

* Sorrowlessfield forms now a part of the estate of Cowdenknowes, the charming residence of R. Cotesworth, Esq. There has been much speculation as to the origin of the name, some saying "that the inhabitants of the place went to Flodden field, none of whom ever returned again." It is quite clear, however, that it takes its name from William Sorouells, who held it before the monks of Melrose.

† *Chart. Mel.*

S

Lauderdale, for money to defray his expenses. The price was 120 merks sterling, the twenty being paid to his son Patrick for confirmation of the deed.

ADINGSTON.—At Auldenistun, in the upper part of Lauderdale, the monks of Melrose had an hospital. Leprosy was at this time very prevalent, and they had many sick brethren. Walter, son of Alan, Steward of Scotland, gave them a ploughgate and a-half of land in that village, and another ploughgate and a-half, which Dame Emma de Ednahim held, with pasturage in the forests of Birkenside and Liggardewude,* also liberty to grind at his mill without paying multure.†

LAMMERMUIR.—Earl Waltheof gave the convent pasture in Lammermoor, thus limited: "Scil de Boldrestan per altam viam usque ad Eslingh, et inde deorsum sicut Helingdol cadit in Bothkil, &c."‡ Alan, son of Roland, Grand Constable, gave all his waste on Lambremuir to the convent, in exchange for the land called Keresbarn. King William confirmed the grant of new land Alan gave them in exchange for that William de Moreville bequeathed to them in Cunningham. Earl Patrick gave them fifty-one acres in the south part of Mosiburgierig, in addition to their land in Lambremuir.§

---

* Birchenside and Legerwood.
† *Ibid.* This charter is named "Carta Leprosorum de Moricetun."   ‡ *Ibid.*   § *Ibid.*

REDPATH.—This land, situated between Ercildon and Bemersyde, was given by Thomas Ranulph, Earl of Moray, Lord of Annandale and of Mann. Patrick, Earl of Dunbar and March, as feudal lord, confirmed the same. They had also two oxgangs in Bemersyde.*

GORDON.—Adam of Gordoune gave some land on the south side of Clovindikis, in Gordoune, next the highway that goes to Berwick.† The noble family of Gordon long resided here, and were settled as early as the time of Malcolm Canmore. An old tower in the neighbourhood was once the residence of the zealous covenanter, Pringle of Greenknowe.

HASSINGTON.—William de Alwenton, called also William de Greenlaw, gave the monks three plough-gates of land in the village of Halsintoun, which he got from Sir Robert de Muscamp.‡ In 1428, Patrick Dunbar, Lord of Beil, with other wealthy men, decided a controversy between Dean John Fogo, abbot of Melrose, and Sir Walter Haliburton of that ilk, relative to some lands in Halsington and Moneylaws. It was found the convent had there three ploughlands, two oxgangs, three acres, and also the lands called Bars' Lands.§

HARDLAW and HUNGGERIG, near the vill of Harcarse, in the territory of Fogo, were given by William,

---

* *Harleian MSS.*, 7394.   † *Ibid.*, 79, 7394.   ‡ *Ibid.*   § *Ibid.*

son of Patrick, Earl of Dunbar, for providing a pittance annually for ever, on the feast of the Nativity of the Blessed Virgin. When the convent had possessed this property some years, the abbot, Adam de Maxton, gave it to Nicolas Corbet, brother of the donor,* without consulting any one. He bestowed it on Fogo chapel. When the abbot died, his successor sued for and recovered it back from Richard, rector of Lynton church and the chapel of Fogo.

HORNDEAN.—The lands of Milnecroft, in Horndean, were given them in the reign of Alexander III., by Sir W. de Horndean. Horndean is an ancient village, lying left side of Tweed, and midway between Coldstream and Berwick. It shared most of the events that befel Norham and Ladykirk.†

EDMONSTONE.—Walter, High Steward, son of Alan, gave them four ploughshares at Edmundiston, for the good of the soul of King Malcolm IV.; also, Patrick, Earl of Dunbar, one ploughagate at Edmundiston near Greenlaw. The lady Eve, wife of Robert de Quinci, of Edmonstoun, twenty-five acres which she had bought, lying close to Edmonston Grange, in the time of King William; and in 1490, Robert Laudir of Edrington, engaged to pay to the Abbot Bernard eight chalders

---

* Patrick, fifth Earl of Dunbar, married Christiana Corbet, the daughter and heiress of Walter Corbet of Makerstone.
† *Chart. Mel.*

of victuals yearly, by way of rent, for the lands of Edmundstun Grange. Edrington Castle, four miles from Berwick, was a place of great strength, and figured much in the wars of the Borders.

BERWICK.—The convent had many holdings here. King William gave them the house and land of William Lunnok, in the south corner of Briggate, next the Tweed. Alexander Joceline, a burgess of Peebles, quitted claim to the land and house in the south-east corner of Briggate for 140 marks. Nicholas, the weaver, gave half his land in Briggate to the monks in pure alms. He sold them the other half for 100 marks sterling, and an annual allowance of ten bolls of wheat, one chalder of barley, and half a mark of money to him and his wife for their joint lives. Robert de Berneham sold the convent another parcel of land in the same street. Walter, son of Alan, gave them a croft near the Tweed, and twenty acres in the plain of Berwick. Grim, the son of Guido, the carter of Roxburgh, gave them a toft. Mariota de Monachis, who had been the wife of Nicholas the apothecary, gave the convent all her land in Narewgate, upon the Nesse, below the town of Berwick, with all the buildings thereon. Thomas de Selkirk gave them a tenement upon le Nesse. The monks were to pay forty pence yearly to the Maison Dieu, and nine shillings to his sister's heirs; and his son Peter gave them three marks yearly, for ever, in a burgage in Crossgate. Alexander Fraser gave them lands and houses in Ravennisden Street upon le Nesse. Adam Glasgow, ten acres of arable land called Kiddeslaw, in Bondington; beside, Moyse, the crossbow-maker, gave ten acres without the town, below Hangchester. They also had the land of Snoe for two shillings yearly; the land abutting near the castle foss, for payment of sixpence to the constable of the castle; and, lastly, Robert de Berneham gave them a fishing in Berwick stream.

The famous castle of Berwick, which exists no longer, was erected in the eleventh century. Edward I. imprisoned the Countess of Buchan for four years in it, because she had the honour of placing the crown on the head of Robert Bruce at his coronation. The town of Berwick is of high antiquity, and was a town of note in the twelfth century.

TROLHOPE, IN NORTHUMBERLAND.—For the souls of Richard and John, kings of England, and for his King Henry, Robert Muscamp gave part of his land and pasture, in the territory of Hethpol, called Trolhope, with liberty to cut wood in the forest for building. Hugo de Morwie, Odonello de Forde, and others, are witnesses. The prior and canons of Kirkham* had a right to the tithes of Trolhope, and obtained a Bull from Pope Honorius III., in 1222, commanding the

* Kirkham Priory, near Doncaster.

monks to pay them, yearly, fifty shillings and twenty pence, on St. James's day, in the Church of St. Gregory, at Newton in Glendale.

KILHAM.—Walter de Kilnum, son of Robert de Scottun, gave them eight acres of corn-land in Witelaw-estele, with pasture for twenty-four sheep, twelve oxen, and two horses.

HOUNAM.—John of Hunum, son of Orm, gave them land in Hunum, in the presence of Ingelram, bishop of Glasgow. William, son of John, gave the lands of Raeshaw, in Hunum, to the monks, for which they were to find a chaplain to say mass in a chapel within the boundaries, for the souls of him and his wife, Donancia de Cleresei.* The giver having afterwards repented of this gift, and forcibly taken the lands again, the monks complained of him at Rome, and Innocent III., in 1208, appointed commissioners to investigate the matter, when William confessed he had given it to the monks, and they permitted him to enjoy it his life, so that it became theirs at his death.†

The canons of Jedburgh had care of the church of Hunum, but the monks of Melrose thought they had a right to it ; and in 1237, an agreement was made, whereby the abbot and convent of Melrose renounced all right which they said they had to the church of

---

* _Chart. Mel._ 12.   † _Ibid._

Hunum. For this the canons of Jedburgh exempted them from payment of tithes on the lands within their parish, and agreed to find a chaplain to pray for the souls of William, the son of John and Donancia, his wife, and all the faithful departed in whatever place the Bishop of Glasgow should appoint.

WHITTON.—Robert de Bernolvebi gave twenty acres of land in Witton, called Ravenesfen, before 1199. It run westward from the head of Harehopedene, to the land William de Ridel gave his wife Matilda Corbet as her dowry. Geoffrey, son of Walleve of Lillesclive, gave four ox-gangs of arable land, situated above Ravensfen. Ysabelle, the wife of William de Ridel, gave them an oxgang, lying between Hardlaw and Tockesheles, which William, the parson of Hunum, bought from Geoffrey, the cook, and gave her. Two old border towers are standing at Corbet House and Whitton, the former repaired since the last wars with England, the other in ruins.

GRUBET.—Hucred de Grubbeheued gave them land in Grubbeheued, called Halkale, next the water of Kalne, in Elstaneshaleche, about the year 1181.

CLIFTON.—Walter de Corbet, Laird of Makerston, about the year 1200, gave a tract of land in the muirs of Cliftun, east of Crookhou, and contiguous the land of Hunum, Grubet, Primside, and Molle, partly bounded by Mereburn and Culroueburn. The Bireburn is also mentioned, and the high road that went from Molle to Roxburgh.

PRIMSIDE.—When King William settled the dispute between the convents of Kelso and Melrose respecting the limits of their property on the Eildon Hills, in 1208, the latter had to yield a piece of ground claimed from them by Kelso ; and Kelso, by order of the king, in consideration thereof, gave the convent of Melrose two oxgangs, excepting two acres in Prenwensete, with two acres of meadow, and pasture for four hundred sheep.*

MOLLE.—Anselm of Wittron gave part of his lands of Molle, adjacent the convent lands in Hownam, with a peatery between Mollhope, Berehope, and Herdeshete. As much brushwood out of his wood of Mollhope as a horse could carry to their grange of Hunum, yearly, between Easter and the birth of St. Mary. Walter, son of Alan, gave them some land in Molle in exchange for Freertown, and two hundred marks of money.

ALTONBURNE, in Molle, was given by John de Vesci, in 1279, to William de Sprowstone, his chaplain, sometime vicar of Molle, who granted it to the monks of Melrose. The monks paid tithe of their land in Molle to Kelso.

FAIRNINGTON.—Roger Bernard, in the time of Alexander II., granted them thirteen acres of arable land,

* *Chart. Mel.* 40, v.

and a meadow of eight acres, lying east side of the
land of Symon de Farburne, in Farnindun, below the
high road to Roxburgh.   The monks caused to be cut
a ditch round the meadow, called Estmedow, which they
had bought from Burnard for thirty-five marks.   Burnard granted them a peatery in Farnindun, the boundaries of which were set with large stones, and allowed
them to make a ditch six feet wide around it, outside
the boundary.

MAXTON.—Robert de Besheley, and Cecilia, his wife,
gave the convent, in 1196, a ploughgate of land in
Mackiston, east of Dereshete, between Morrig on the
north, and Lilisyhates and Gretkerigge on the south,
with pasture for a hundred sheep, twenty-two mares
and foals, till they were two years old, common fuel,
and stones from his quarry at Alwerden for building.
Hugh de Normanville, who married Alicia, daughter of
Robert de Berkeley, gave them Kelvessete and Faulau,
on the confines of Ruderfurde, on both sides of the road
from Eckeford to Melrose.   His son John gave them
Lilisyhates, between Grenrig, Derestrete, Farningdun,
and the high road from the vale of Anant to Rokis-
burgh.   He also more than doubled their pasture, and
gave them the land called Jerbrandrig, consisting of
four acres, part of the peat land west side of Ruderfurde
Muir, between Suthside and Arewes.   Thomas, brother
of John de Normanville, gave them a ploughgate, for

which they were bound to pay him, at Roxburgh fair, a pair of gilt spurs, and to the feudal lord a tercelet, or 3s. sterling. Maxton is now a decayed hamlet, but was formerly of nearly the size and importance of Kelso. The shaft of an ancient cross, or relic of Romanism, is still standing there.

LESSUDEN.—Robert I., in 1317, granted the whole of the lands in Lessedwyne to this convent. Laurence de Abernethy gave them the whole land of Makyspoffil about the same time. James Fraser of Ferendrath gave the whole of his land in Cambeston, in 1402, for the annual payment of three pounds. This latter was not to be exacted when the land was laid waste by war.

Lessuden was burnt by the English in 1544 and '45. It was previously a place of considerable strength, and contained sixteen Bastile houses. St. Boswell's is an ancient village, once a place of importance, and is annually, in July, the scene of one of the greatest fairs in the south of Scotland. To the north of the Green stands an elegant hunting establishment, belonging to the Duke of Buccleuch, and in the heart of one of the best hunting suits in Britain.

LILLIESLEAF.—Patrick Ridale, in the time of King William, gave them a portion of the lands of Lillesclive,* with pasture for twelve oxen, ten cows, five

* The boundary ran from the ford of Curlewudburn, on the west side

horses, and a hundred sheep. Margaret de Vesci confirmed this gift. His son Walter added to it Cotemedwe, Mercmedwe, the meadow at the head of Kingesflat, the meadow at Laidholfueslend and Pounemedwe, in Caveris. To this he added another donation, which made the gifts of his family to the convent of Melrose, in Lilliesclive, amount to eleven oxgangs. He confirmed to them the possession of Clerkislande in West Lillesclive, consisting of land in Todholside and Hendestonrig, which they bought from Adam, son of Adam of Durham, for twenty shillings sterling.*

Fourteen peel towers formerly fortified Lilliesleaf, and made the town a centre of great strength in the Border turmoils. The moor was a great meeting-place of the covenanters.

HASSENDEAN.—After some dispute about the right of Hastanden church between King William and Josceline, Bishop of Glasgow, they agreed to devote the property of this church to some charitable purpose. They gave its titles and lands to Melrose, to be expended in founding and maintaining a house of hospitality at Hastan-den, for the reception and entertainment of the way-

---

of Caldlawealong, the road from Selkirk to Jedworth, as far as the Alne; then down the Alne, which divided his lands from those of the Bishop of Glasgow, to the place bounding him and the Abbot of Kelso, and along the same boundary to Curlewudburne, and up said burn to the aforesaid ford. *Chart Mel.*, 43, 44.

* *Chart. Mel.*

faring poor, and the relief of pilgrims journeying to Melrose abbey. A pension of twenty shillings yearly was reserved to the Church of Glasgow. The monks of Melrose had pasturage in the common for two hundred ewes, sixteen oxen, and four cows. The hospital founded by them, where some of them always resided, and performed the duties of Hastanden and Caveris parish, was afterwards called Monks' Tower, and their lands are still called Monks' Croft. Hassendean ceased to be a separate parish in 1682, and was divided between Roberton, Wilton, and Minto. The ruins of its fine old Saxon church, with nearly all its churchyard, near the Teviot, were carried away by a flood in 1796.

CAVERS.—The advowson of the church of Great Cavers was given by William, first Earl of Douglas, in 1358. James, the second Earl, renewed his grant of this church, with the glebe and the chapel, reserving to himself the right of one presentation to the rectory of the said church. Earl William gave Penangushope and Caldecleuch, in the barony of Cavers, for masses to be said, especially for the soul of Sir William Douglas of Lothian, who was buried before St. Bridget's altar in Melrose. Sir Alexander Scott of Hassendean was one of the Border chiefs who fell at the battle of Flodden.

RINGWUDE, upon the Alwent and Teviot, was given

to the monks, by Osulf, in the time of Malcolm
IV.

ETTRICK.—Alexander II. gave to Melrose a large
tract of land in Ettrick Forest. He exempted the
abbey, and four granges lying round it, from forest
laws. In 1415, they got the lands of Winzehop or
Glenkeny, lying south of the rivulet Ternay, between
their land of Midgehope and those of Ettrick and
Dalglese, with twelve acres of meadow, from Robert
Scott, Laird of Rankilburne, in exchange for the lands
of Bellyndeen.* The forest of Ettrick was the famous
hunting ground of the Scoto-Saxon kings. At one
period it contained thousands of deer. In the time of
Robert Bruce, the Douglases got a grant of it as a reward for their public services. James V. converted
large portions of it into sheep walks. Queen Mary
frequented the chase here notwithstanding her domestic troubles. Many places in it bear names derived
from the wild ox and boar, the wolf, red deer, and
palmated stag.

ESKDALE.—Robert de Avenel, in the time of Malcolm
IV., gave the monks his land in Eskdale, consisting of
two parts, to wit, Tumloher and Weidkerroc, between
the Black and the White Eske, extending from their

---

* Bellenden on the banks of the Alemuir Loch, the same neighbourhood. The Scotts of Rankilburn and Mendiestone were the
ancestors of the Buccleuch family.

junction to the forest of Thimei and the mountains.
He reserved to himself the right of hunting the wild
boar, deer, or stag, also a yearly rent of five marks.
One of these he remitted for the maintenance of a light
to burn perpetually before the altar of the Virgin Mary.
On the death of his wife, Sibilla, he remitted the other
four marks to be expended upon four pittances for the
monks, yearly, and at fixed seasons. He entered the
convent in old age, and died there in 1185. His son,
Gervas Avenel, confirmed his father's grant; but Roger,
the son of Gervas, disputed their right, sent his cattle
into their grounds, pulled down their huts, and broke
down their fences. Both parties met in 1235 at Linton,
in the king's presence, when it was decided that the
pastures belonged to the monks; but they were not to
hunt there with packs of hounds, nor bring or allow
others to hunt; not to set traps except for wolves, nor
cut down trees wherein hawks and falcons build their
nests.* Robert I. gave them part of the barony of
Westerker, in Eskdale, forfeited by Lord Soulis.

REINPATRICK.—William de Brus, in the reign of
Alexander II., gave the monks a fishing near the
church of Reinpatrick, in Annandale, an acre of land,
pasturage for four cows and six oxen.

BRANSCATH, AUCHENCRIEF, and DERGAVEL, were
given to the convent by Thomas de Arnnoy.

* *Chart Mel.*, 53.

DUNSCORE.—Affrica, daughter of Edgar, gave a part of her land at Dunscoir, in Nithsdale, for the safety of Alexander II. and his Queen, Joanna, and upon condition that the monks were to have a yearly pittance out of the profits on St. Andrew's day. In 1257, their land in Dunscoir was freed from tithes, and the parish church given to the abbot and convent of Dercongal.

BARMUIR and GODONEC.—Richard Wales gave the monks the lands called Godonec in Galwey, at the head of the burn called Polcarn. He also gave them Barmuir, extending from the mouth of the burn of Hastnewethne up to its source.

TURNBERRY and MAYBOLE.—Duncan, Earl of Carrick, gave two salt works in Tornebiri, with eight acres of corn land and pasture for horses. Duncan, the son of Gilbert, son of Fergus, gave them the lands of Meibothelbeg and Beacchoc. In 1236, Duncan freed them from the annual payment of three marks for the lands of Beacchoc. In 1212, the rector of Maibotil complained that the convent had wronged him of his tithes. Pope Innocent III. appointed a commission to sift the matter, who ordered a payment of ten shillings annually by the monks, for the tithes of Maibothilbech and Largys.

GREENAN.—Roger de Scalbroc gave them a beach fishing at the mouth of the Doon, a salt-work, and some land and tofts in Grenan. In 1196, he gave them the lands of Drumteismene, Alesburc, and Auchnephure.

OCHILTREE.—The patronage of this church was given to the convent in 1316, by Eustachia de Colville, widow of Reginald le Chene.

TARBOLTON.—The patronage of this church was given them by Robert Græme, laird of Welston, before 1369.*

DALSANGAN and BANGOUR.—In 1205 the monks had a dispute about their right to these lands with Peter de Curri, who, afterwards joining the convent, gave them up, by a charter he offered upon the high altar of St. Mary of Melrose.

MAUCHLINE.—Walter, son of Alan, grand steward, joined the convent and died there in 1177. He gave them all the lands of Mauchlyn, a fishing on the water of Ayr, and one of three nets at the mouth of that river. He gave them the pasture of his forest, extending to the mountain of Cairntable, on the limits of upper Clydesdale, and to Glengyle and the boundaries of Douglas and Lesmahago; besides, easements in the wood, a ploughgate they might till, reserving to himself only the birds and beasts of chase in the said forest; for which the monks were to pay five marks annually, nor hunt nor hawk in the forest. The five marks were afterwards remitted. Alexander the

* SIMPSON'S *MS. Collections. Bibl. Harl.* 4707.

T

Steward, freed them from baronial jurisdiction, gave them liberty to buy and sell in any market they chose, and to hold their corn courts at Karentable, Mauchlyn, or Barmoor. For these grants the monks were to have a pittance yearly on St. James's day, out of the profits. The priory at Mauchline was a cell of Melrose. Convicted thieves were to be given up to the steward's bailie, and if manslaughter should take place for the discovery of theft, it should be held justifiable on the part of the abbot, and the goods and chattels of the slain should go to his bailie.

WOLFCLYDE.—Sir David Menyheis, laird of half the barony of Culter in Lanarkshire, gave the whole of his portion, called Wolchclyde, in 1431. After the Reformation, this land came into the possession of Sir William Menzies of Gladstanes.

KINGLEDOORS and HOPECARTON.—In the reign of Robert the Bruce, Simon Fraser gave them the land of South Kingildor, with the chapel of St. Cuthbert, also the lands of Hopcarton, with pasture right in the parish of Drumelzier in Tweeddale.

PEEBLES.—Sir William de Durem gave them all the lands and tenements he had in the town of Peebles. They were to pay what was due to the king. He sold them a burgage in the same town for fourteen marks, which he acknowledged having received. Peebles looms far back in high antiquity, and was the seat of a Culdee establishment in very early times.

PERTH.—Malcolm de Lyn, a burgess of Perth, gave them a land in the South Street, for six shillings yearly.

KINROSS.—Robert I. gave them a toft and croft in the town of Kinros, in the corner beside the road to Perth, and freed them from the annual payment of forty pence due to him for the same.

EDINBURGH.—In 1408, Margaret Bronhill sold the monks a tenement in the south side of the town, which her late brother, Adam Tore, had previously mortgaged to them. In 1428, John Vernour gave a land in the street called Cowgate, to one Richard Lundy, a monk of Melrose, for twenty shillings yearly. He or his heirs were to have the refusal of it, if it were sold. In 1440, William Vernour granted the same to Richard Lundy, then abbot of Melrose, without reserve, for thirteen shillings and fourpence yearly. In 1433, Patrick, abbot of Holyrood, confirmed the monks of Melrose in the possession of their land called Holyroodacre, between the common vennel and another acre they had beside the highway from the Cowgate, for six shillings and eightpence yearly.

LEITH.—In 1414, Robert Logan of Lastalrik, gave the monks of Melrose a tenement in the town of Leyth.

They had also other possessions in Leith, which they acquired by purchase.

PRESTONPANS.—Roland, son of Uctred, gave the convent a salt-work in Preston, with pasture for six cows, six oxen, and a horse. He also gave a toft and croft whereon to build a house, and fuel from his wood of Preston to supply the pans. In 1460, Robert de Hamylton of Fyngalton gave them in his territory of Saltpreston similar grants.

INVERWICK.—Walter, the son of Alan, confirmed to the monks possession of certain lands in the territory of Innerwick, with pasturage in the town common, granted them by Roger, the son of Glay, and others of his vassals.

HEARTSIDE and SPOT.—In the reign of David I., the Earl Gospatric gave them the lands of Hertishead and Spot; and Patrick de Whitsum, a part of his land called Lochaneshalech, also in Spot.

PEATCOX.—Philip de Petcox gave the land lying between Harteshead and the rivulet called Prestumnethburn, with ten acres in the tilled ground of Beleside. He gave them liberty to change the course of Presmunen Burn. This burn was the boundary between him and the monks, and its overflowing often injured the meadows and corn fields.

PAINSHIEL.—John, the son of Michael, of Meckil, gave the whole land of Paneschelys, on condition that three marks of silver be given yearly to the prior, to furnish a pittance for the monks on Trinity Sunday. He gave also the land which Aldred the smith, and his son Oliver, held east side of the brook Fastenei. Henry de Beltun, in 1231, gave the whole of his land called Kingissete, in the territory of Panschelis, lying between Calneburn, Kingeburn, and Witeddre, for the yearly rent of two marks to him and his heirs.

John, of North Berwick, released them of the obligation of the payment to him of thirty shillings for Kingisset.*

YESTER.—John Giffarde made them free of multure at his miln. He also gave them pasture for six cows, sixty sheep, and two horses, and a toft and croft in Yhester.

FISHINGS IN THE TWEED.—David I. gave them right to fish in the Tweed, on both sides, at Melros, Dernwick, Eildun, and Gattonside. Malcolm IV. gave them the fishing at Yhare, called the Selkirk fishing, also seven acres of land, with buildings thereon, and a meadow pasture for eight oxen and eight cows in Wauhop, and timber of the forest for keeping in repair their wear in the said fishery. In 1268, Nicolas Corbet, of

---

* *Chart. Mel.* 77, v. 78. The monks of the Isle of May had some property on the south side of Caleburn, and the place is still called Mayshiel.

Mackerston, granted them all his fisheries adjacent his land of Malcarviston, between the limits of Dalcove and Brokismouth, on condition that the produce of this fishing should be applied faithfully by the sub-cellarer to the proper use of the convent. The monks and lay brethren and their servants might land with their cobells and nets upon any part of his ground, and have free ingress and egress through it, and might even build a house upon it for the convenience of their fishing. In the presence of the king, in the refectory of Melrose, Nicholas Corbet, undertook to be surety for all services due to the king by the monks for the said fisheries. David I. gave them also the fishing of Old Roxburgh, extending to the Brockestrem. Malcolm IV. gave one of the two net-fishings he had in Brockestrem. Robert de Bernham gave them another, which he got from Ralph Hauvil, King Alexander's falconer.

Nes, son of Nes de Walent, gave them in Lyveringham, ten acres of arable land to find the convent in white bread on Easter-day.*

Philip, Count of Flanders, about 1182 gave the monks of this convent a free passage through his dominions, and exempted them from payment of taxes and dues therein.

Alexander II. gave the mouks the privilege, when passing through the country with carriages, of stopping

* *Chart. Mel.*, 105, v. 94.

for one night wherever they chose. They had permission to pasture their beasts on the commons, and
elsewhere, so they kept them out of corn fields and
meadows.*

John, brother of the Steward of Scotland, granted to
the convent at Christmas, 1296, two pounds of wax to
be given on St. James's fair day at Roxburgh, annually, for a wax candle to burn at the tomb of St.
Waltheof.†

SUMMA ANIMALIUM MONASTERII DE MELROS,
TEMPORIBUS ANTIQUIS.‡

Imprimis summa equorum dominicorum .	104
equarum dominicarum .	54
sylvestrium . . .	265
pullorum trium annorum .	39
pollorum 2, annorum utriusque	
sexus, ...	150
stagrorum . . .	270
bovum jugalium . .	1167
vaccarum	3544
taurorum	87
stottorum 4, annorum . .	407

---

* *Chart. Mel.*, 107, v.   † *Harl. MS.*, 4707.

‡ HAY's *MS. Collection of Charters*, vol. i., 471, Advocates' Library, Edinburgh.

stottorum 3, annorum .	.	637
colonidarum .	.	. 1376
stircorum .	.	. 1125
vitulorum .	.	. 11963
ovium .	.	8215
vervecum .	..	. 344
multonum .	.	. 8044
hoggorum .	.	. 5900
ovium tondentium	.	. 22520

With this, as with the previous chapter, and in many other parts of this work, we have tracked with care the steps of the Rev. Dr Morton, author of the *Monastic Annals of Teviotdale*, and have found that work full of research, very painstaking and elaborate in detail. So much so, although possessing great facilities in the way of information, we heartily recommend such of our readers as have a desire to know more upon such matters, to consult his work with perfect confidence.

Statue of St. Peter, with Book, Keys, and Canopy—North Transept.

Seal and Counter Seal of the Abbey.

Chapter Eleventh.

MELROSE ABBEY—THE RUINS.

" No matins now, no vesper sung,
Time mocks at last the human tongue;
The idol and the shrine o'erturns,
The worshipper, that gazing burns;
And with a zealous aim regards,
The laws of pennance, and rewards.
No border strife, or feudal fray,
Stems near these walls in dread array—
Nor lists the warder's wakeful ear,
Pride, glory, ruin, cradle here.
And while we mark their waning bloom,
We sadden as with pensive gloom;
And wish the more that time would spare
These ruins yet, so freshly fair;
That gorgeous, lovely, spell-bound seem,
At once a glory and a dream."

A S we have elsewhere observed, the stone used in the erection of St. Mary's abbey, Melrose, was of a capital description. Time would have dealt gently with it, had not the hand of man been bent on its destruction. So firm and unyielding to any ordinary vicissitude were its parts

combined together, that, independent of the strength
of the cement used at the time, (still flinty and im-
perishably hard), many of the stones in the columns
and supporting walls of the east end are actually
cubed and morticed or grooved into one another, thus
rendering them almost imperishable to the tooth of
time, and the action of sundry atmospheric influences.
It was built as for eternal duration.

As we approach the western entrance, there is an
abrupt termination of the chapels on the south side.
The stones are left as in the order of erection, whole,
not jagged, broken, or mutilated, as if some part had
been removed from those remaining by violence and
war.   We may therefore conclude, that the west
end was so far in course of restoration, but never completed, nor carried beyond the position it now remains
in.   Not a vestige of the two outermost pillars, for the
support of the nave near the west end, can be discovered.
The destruction of the western end from the great
organ screen has been complete. This would be in
September, 1545, when the Earl of Hertford, and the
English troops under him, laid waste the whole of the
Merse and Teviotdale. The commanders of the English forces, under disappointment and difficulty, often
ordered the pulling down of the peel-houses and
fortalices. The tower may have been undermined
from the two pillars eastward, which, in falling, would

bring down the three sides of it also. From that period, more owing to the progress of the Reformation than any other event, it seems probable the abbey was never restored from the state of ruin to which it was then reduced. Still great destruction was entailed upon its sculptures after the year 1545; for it is apparent that the piscinas and altars of the baptistries or chapels, south of the nave, and on both sides of the chancel, which are sixteen in number, have been wantonly mutilated and broken down. Heavy instruments have been in requisition, such as sledge-hammers and crowbars. In some places ornamental stones have been broken or cut clean away, and some have been removed out of the very face of the wall by dint of strength and suitable tools.

Brackets upon Pillars—Flowers.

The key-stones of the roof in the sixth chapel are deserving of particular attention.

In all probability the upper roof of the nave and chancel was composed of wood only, and the side roofs of stone, which may account for the rapid decay of the former. From an examination made of the upper portion of the tower wall in the eighteenth century, by a practical person, who describes them to have been too light to support a spire, there probably never was one, and possibly the tower was left square, and free almost of pinnacle or central ornament, like the cathedral of York at the present day. The roof of the church would be covered with sheet-lead, which was either stript by an enemy, or, after having been set on fire, collected from the ashes beneath. The second expedition of Hertford's was a notable one, for the collecting of lead from the monastic houses, and transporting it over the Borders.

The wall which divides the nave, and now breasts its western extremity, once the lower part of the organ screen, demands attention. Within is a small porch, tastefully decorated with a miniature groined roof, in the centre of which is a sculptured head. A chain of leaves binds the outward moulding, and ascends in a continued series, extending along the wall from the one side to the other. In the eighth chapel of the nave is a very beautiful piscina, ornamented with various

Double Column and Capitol, north side of the Nave.

miniature architectural embellishments. The narrow
north aisle of the nave is most conspicuous for the
neatness of its pointed roof, and the row of massive
pillars from which it springs. Their capitols, repre-

Corbel in the North Aisle.

U

senting leaves, are tastefully chiselled, and have opposite
to them branches of foliage equally well carved, from
which spring the groins of the north side of the roof.
An undivided seat runs along the north side of the
nave, above which are a series of false arches, supported
by peculiarly graceful pedestals.   These arches are less
ornamental than the others.   The western one, in all
likelihood the centre of the range, displays a great deal
of elegant ornament springing from slender pilasters.
There remains no vestige of the roof of the piazza, but
above the false arches there are corbels and corresponding holes, from which the roof had sprung.   Of the
chapter-house, dormitory, and refectory, which lay on
the north side of the church, no vestige remains,
although their foundations are occasionally met with.

In 1839, while certain improvements were being
made on the grounds skirting the house built by the
Commendator Douglas, two large boilers, and other
culinary utensils, were discovered several feet below the
surface of the earth.

The cloister formed a quadrangle on the north-west
side of the church.   This square stretched alongside
the whole of the nave, but now consists of only one
angle.   Seven of the seats in the cloister remain.   These
are covered with false Gothic arches, composed of various members, along the extremity of which a wreath of
flowers, springing from the pilasters at the sides of the

arches, runs upwards to an ornamental frieze. The frieze appertaining to each sedile contains six square compartments, representing beautiful clusters of plants and flowers accurately carved, such as lilies, ferns, house-leeks, palm, holly, grapes, oak leaves, with apples, ash leaves, thistles, fir cones, &c.

Section of the Arcade of the Cloister from the South Wall.

> "Spreading herbs and flow'rets bright,
> Glisten'd with the dew of night;
> Nor herb nor flow'ret glisten'd there,
> But was carved on the cloister arches as fair."
>
> —*Lay of the Last Minstrel.*

Speaking of this part of the venerable pile, Mr Lockhart observes: "There is one cloister in particular, along the whole length of which there runs a cornice of flowers and plants, entirely unrivalled, to my mind, by anything elsewhere extant. I do not say in Gothic architecture merely, but in any architecture whatever. Roses and lilies, and thistles, and ferns, and heaths, in all their varieties, and oak leaves and ash leaves, and a thousand beautiful shapes besides, are chiselled with such inimitable truth, and such grace of nature, that the finest botanist in the world could not desire a better hortus siccus, so far as they go."

In another part of the building, he observes: "There is a human hand holding a garland loosely in its fingers, which, were it cut off and placed among the Elgin marbles, would be kissed by the cognoscenti as one of the finest of them all. It would shame the whole gallery of the Boissere'es."

A footway now closed leads from the cloister to the high road north of the ruins, which is called the Valley Gate. Since the Reformation, it was one of the approaches to the church, and, with a little contrivance would afford a better entrance to the ruins than the present one.

An arched doorway, leading from the cloister at the angle formed by the transept, is exquisitely carved. So beautiful and accurately chiselled is the foliage upon the capitols of the pilasters on each side, that a straw will pass through the interstices between the leaves and stalks. It was through this door the aged monk, in the *Lay of the Last Minstrel,* led William of Deloraine to the grave of Michael Scott, after conducting him through the cloister.

At the distance of fifty feet from the eastern extremity the church is intersected at right angles by the transept. A square tower, nearly a hundred feet high, stood in the centre, the west side of which, raised upon a lofty pointed arch springing from two slender columns, at the eastern extremity of the nave, to the height of eighty-four feet, is still standing. The summit of the tower terminates with a stone ballustrade, the rails of which form quatre-foils, and are ornamented immediately underneath with a frieze of roses in basso relievo.

The two eastern columns which supported the tower, as well as the east, north, and south walls of it, have disappeared altogether, No vicissitude that ever befel the church could have demolished these—neither the agency of time nor fire. That the columns were undermined in 1545, or at the period of the Reformation,

there seems no doubt, and the parts they supported
brought down with them, the materials of which alone
would have sufficed for the erection of any ordinary
dwelling. We are strongly reminded of Antwerp Cathedral by the little turrets of the ruins at the corners
of the tower, which Sir Walter Scott chose to imitate
in the erection of his mansion at Abbotsford.

Two rows of pillars run equidistant from the magnificent supporters of the remnant of the tower, and
with a dead wall on the north, and corresponding pillars
on the south side of the nave, form aisles of which the
original roofs still remain.

Knot on Ceiling of the Nave—Flowers.

The transept has an arcade on the east side of it, next the choir, of the same breadth as the side aisles of the nave. The north transept is roofless, and the angle at the north-east corner of it is gone, and a blank stone wall stretches across this portion, of recent erection, abutting on the garden of the manse.

The original groined vault still covers part of the south transept. The whole east end contained nine windows, six looking to the east, two looking south, and one north. The tracery of the splendid and delicate circular window in the north transept, representing a crown of thorns, we have illustrated in the seventh chapter.

The three pillars on the east side of the north transept are comparatively slender. Their mouldings are of various dimensions, and the foliage of their capitols sharp and natural. Above the capitol of the second pillar, there is an admirable piece of carving. It is a hand grasping a bunch of flowers, and serves as a bracket to the groins of the roof. Venerable-looking heads are placed at the lower extremities of the other groins. Above the arches are two double windows. Those on the outside are divided by perpendicular mullions, and are ornamented with cross bars. The opposite side of the transept is less attractive. Instead of pillars there is a wall, along the under part of which there are traces of a stair leading to a Saxon arched doorway, at some height from the ground. This stair communicated with the refectory or abbot's house, and with the spiral staircase, which still remains on the north side of the building, though in a very dilapidated condition, and which visitors are not permitted to ascend. At the foot of the stair stands a font. The threshold of the door above appears to have been either a tomb-stone or altar-piece, of a date anterior to the rebuilding of the church, from the appearance of figures engraven upon it which are partly built upon. Probably some relic brought away from Old Melrose; for when this part was erected, Old Melrose was desolate and abandoned, or only visited by occasional pilgrims. At the foot of the winding stair, in the year 1730, a secret vault was discovered, concealed by the lowest step, having all the appearance of an armarium. It might have been used as the safe receptacle of the valuable sacred vessels of the church in perilous times.

The dead wall on the west side of the north transept is relieved with four narrow windows, breasting from the interior open balustrade, and one window over the north aisle of the nave; beside which, upon two elevated niches in the wall, below the former, are the statues of St. Peter and St. Paul, the one having a book and keys, and the other a sword. In the north end is a recess in the wall containing fourteen pedestals for small statues. Under this is a door of Saxon architecture opening into a low vaulted chamber, called the wax cellar.

Curious Key-stones of Moulded Ribs of Groined Arches, from the
Wax Cellar.

The choir, or chancel, is built in the form of half a Greek cross, the east end of it, which was probably a chapel in honour of the Virgin Mary, being only half the breadth of the part next the transept.. Four chapels lay disposed north and south of the altar place. Here the greatest architectural skill is displayed, especially in the structure of the eastern window, which is strikingly elegant and beautiful.. It is in the perpendicular style, thirty-seven feet in height and sixteen in breadth, divided by four bars, each only eight inches broad, the upper part interwoven with tracery of a peculiarly light and graceful form. The original beautiful fretted and sculptured stone roof still covers the east end of the chancel. Within the walls are fonts for holy purposes, and recesses for containing the communion vessels. This matchless window has been described by Sir Walter Scott in the following beautiful lines:—

> " The moon on the east oriel shone,
> Thro' slender shafts of shapely stone,
>   By foliaged tracery combin'd,
> Thou would'st have thought some fairy's hand,
> 'Twixt poplars straight the osier wand,
>   In many a freakish knot had twin'd ;
> Then fram'd a spell when the work was done,
> And chang'd the willow wreaths to stone."

Above the entrance of the doorway of the south transept, a passage runs along the whole extent of the wall, below which are placed curiously-carved figures of musicians.

The groins of the roof of the south transept spring on the west side from the figure of a man contorted, and by his countenance indicating the weight of his load, and from an eagle or phœnix much defaced.

Bracket—Figure of a Monk cross-legged.

Strange creatures support the groins of the opposite side. On one of the key stones of this roof are carved three hunting horns, a crosier, and the letters A. H.*

In the small aisle adjoining, there is a beautifully carved piscina, and remains of former altar places.

* These were the arms of the ancient family of Hunter. In 1444, Andrew Hunter was abbot of Melrose; these are probably his armorial bearings. Broadwoodshiel, on Leader Water, near to Blainslie, was the ancient possession of the Hunters.

The capitol of the pillar at the east end of the nave aisle is adorned with Scotch kail or brocoli, wonderfully sharp and exquisitely chiselled.

Piscina in the South-east Chapel or Baptistry.

Having now enumerated the chief features inside this once glorious fabric, let us pass to the exterior by the south door-way, and commence our illustrations from the western extremity of the ruins, in the church-yard, once the open lawn and pleasant garden of the monastery.

The outside of the church is everywhere profusely embellished with niches, having crowns or canopies of the most elegant design; fragile to appearance as the most elaborate carvings in wood, some of them still containing statues, but by far the greater number are empty altogether or disgracefully mutilated.

Beginning from the extreme west of the churchyard, on the first buttress, are the arms of Scotland, supported by unicorns. On one side is the letter I., on the other Q., (Jacobus Quartus) and the date 1505; no doubt put there in the reign of James IV., who, in his pious moments, was an occasional visitor of the church, and one of its lavish donors. Above the royal arms is a pedestal for a statue, on which is inscribed I. H. S., (Jesus hominus salvator). On another pedestal, eastward, are the figures of a mallet (a mell), and a rose, both of modern execution, and either carved ignorantly, or meant as a pun upon the word Melrose. On the adjoining buttress is carved the armorial bearings of the Hunters.

Several stone spouts may be seen from this point stretching out from the eaves, to carry the water from the roof, which are carved in the form of animals, strange

figures, and monsters, with gaping mouths. One of these
on the roof of the nave represents a sow playing on the
bagpipes. The walls are strengthened on the outside
with buttresses, some of which shoot up into elegant

Crockets, with part of Mouldings—Grotesque figures of Monks.

pinnacles; and when the building was entire (of which
we have attempted an illustration), every buttress, and
even every pillar in the interior of the church, shot up
through the roof into a pinnacle, adorned with niches,
and terminating in a sharp crocketed point, springing

from the midst of four miniature crocketed pediments.
Flying buttresses, stretching from pinnacle to pinnacle,
impended over the roof of the chapels in the nave, and
over the roof of all the side aisles.   Some of these, and
many of the pinnacles, remain, and are highly ornamental.

Fox and Geese, exterior west end corner of the South Transept, and
only seen from the Roof.

One of the most beautiful niches is on the side of a
pinnacle over the nave : the canopy represents a temple,
under which is an image of the Virgin Mary bearing the
child Jesus in her arms.   The other is an effigy of St.
Andrew.   In the foremost niche the head of the infant
is demolished.   Tradition says that, in 1649, when the
person employed to destroy the statuary struck at this

statue, a piece of it fell, which hurt his arm, and he was disabled ever afterwards. Is the preservation of the few statues left in the sixty-eight niches still remaining on the different parts of this hoary edifice attributable to this circumstance? If so, superstition proved a useful antidote to blind zeal and destructiveness.

We now approach the south door, once the glory of this part of the church. Through that richly-moulded Gothic portal is the principal entrance. The archway is composed of various members of delicate work, falling behind each other, supported on light pilasters. On each side is a projection of graceful tabernacle work. Several niches above the doorway, decreasing in height as the arch rises, contain mutilated figures. In the centre are the arms of Scotland—a lion rampant within a double tressure. Above this is a half-length effigy of John the Baptist, with his eyes directed upwards, as if looking upon the image of Christ above, and bearing on his bosom a fillet, inscribed—

𝕰𝖈𝖈𝖊 𝖋𝖎𝖑𝖎𝖚𝖘 𝕯𝖊𝖎.*

Above this door is a magnificent window, twenty-four feet in height within the arch, and sixteen feet broad. It is divided by four principal mullions only eight inches thick, terminating in a pointed arch. The tracery remains perfect, and rises in graceful interlacing curves to a wheel of seven compartments. The mouldings of the arch, which is of many members, are bounded by a

---

* Behold the Son of God.

chain of foliage which springs from two well-carved busts, and terminates with a grotesque head immediately above the graceful canopy of a niche that formerly held an image of Christ.

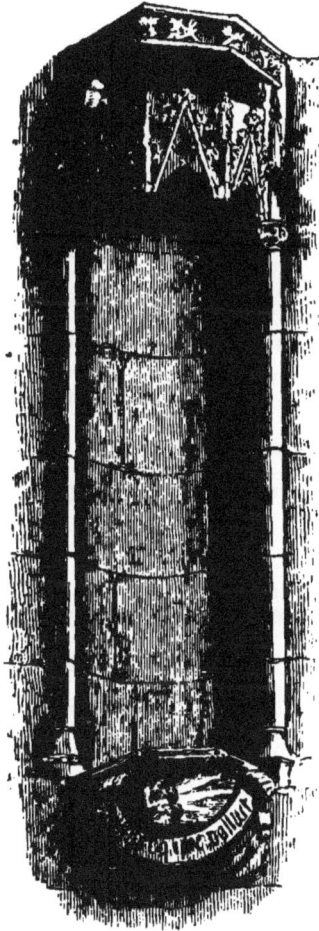

Buttress, Niche, Statue, and Canopy—South front.

X

The figures of the Twelve Apostles adorned the other niches, four of which are on each side the arch, and two within each of the buttresses of the window. The pedestals of the two lowest niches on the buttresses are supported by figures of long-bearded monks.

That on the last buttress is upheld by a venerable monk, bearing a band or scroll, on which is inscribed—

passus : e : q : ipse : boluit.*

On the buttress at the west corner is a figure in monastic costume supporting a pedestal, and holding a scroll, with the inscription—

tu : benit : jes : seq. cessabit : umbra.†

To the west of the last figure, and in the adjoining buttress, is another of a cripple, on the shoulder of a blind man, under which is inscribed the words—

Ante Dei.‡

All the canopies on the south side are delicately carved with tabernacle work, and ornamented with rosettes. The interior of the canopies is formed of ribbed work, terminating in a suspended knot in the centre.

* "Passus, est quia ipse voluit"—He suffered, because He himself willed it.

† "Cum venit Jesus sequitur cessabit umbra"—When Jesus came, the darkness of the world ceased.

‡ See Illustration.

Buttress, Niche, Canopy, and Statue—the Blind carrying the Lame.

At the junction of the south and west members of
the cross, an hexagonal tower rises, pierced with niches,
terminating in a pinnacle, roofed with stone, and highly
ornamented.

The small single-barred windows at the south-east
corner of the building are separated from each other
by double buttresses, pierced with ornamented niches.
The pinnacles and buttresses on this side present a
remarkable and interesting variety of objects, such as
veiled nuns, others richly dressed; musicians, with instruments in their hands, such as the bagpipes, fiddle, and
dulcimer; heads gaping from ear to ear, and others
exhibiting much pleasantness in their countenances.

One of the pedestals is supported by a very expressive and well-chiselled figure of a monk holding a
rosary in his right hand, and his ear in his left, of
which we give an illustration.

On the north side of the ruins, and particularly in
the garden of the manse, the massive, elegant, and well-
executed bases of the buttresses, which support the main
walls, are plainly visible, resting upon the ancient foundations of the building; on the south, they have long
been hidden by the encroachments and upheavings of
the graveyard.

Within a corner, above a small window on the east
of the south window, there is a melancholy-looking
figure, holding his outstretched neck with both hands,

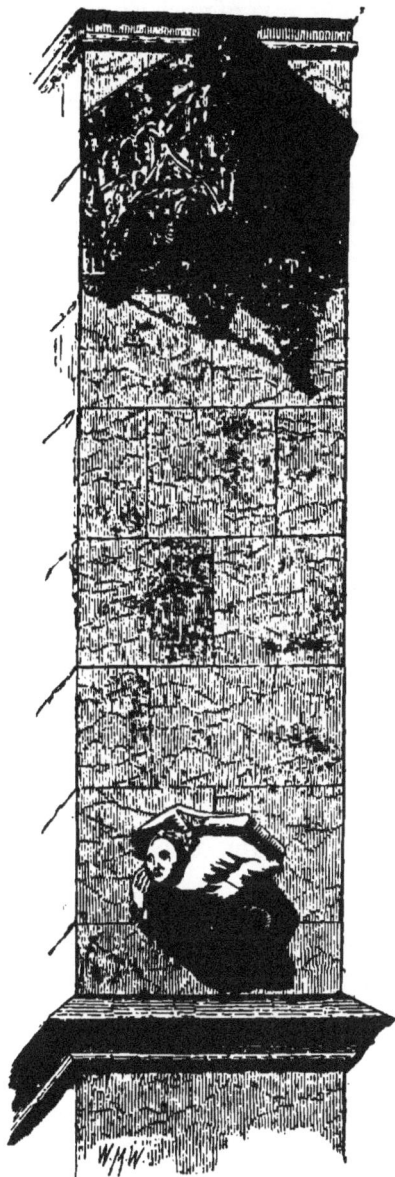

Buttress, Canopy, and Corbel—South front—Monk with Rosary.

and having a knife below his arm, hangs over another figure bearing a ladle.

The window on the south side of the eastern aisle is divided by three upright mullions, seven inches in thickness—the centre mullion dividing and forming small arches ; the others rising to the mouldings of the main arch, are ornamented with Gothic points and cross bars. The opposite window on the north side has been of similar construction: only two of the mullions remain ; the centre bar finishes at the top with a heart of beautiful moulding.

The east end, and its beautiful window, claim particular attention. This window is divided from top to bottom by four perpendicular mullions, formerly intersected near the middle by an elegant cross bar. The traceries are of various figures, chiefly crosses. Around the pointed arch is a range of niches, with mutilated statues in some of them. In one is the figure of an abbot holding a crowned head.

In the centre, above the point of the window, are two figures sitting, which represent David I., and his queen, Matilda.* (Excellent sculptures of these two personages may be seen inside the ruins, both in good preservation, and, compared with the coinage of that period, are striking likenesses.) Over their heads is suspended an open crown, springing from a richly-carved

* See our Illustration of the East Window.

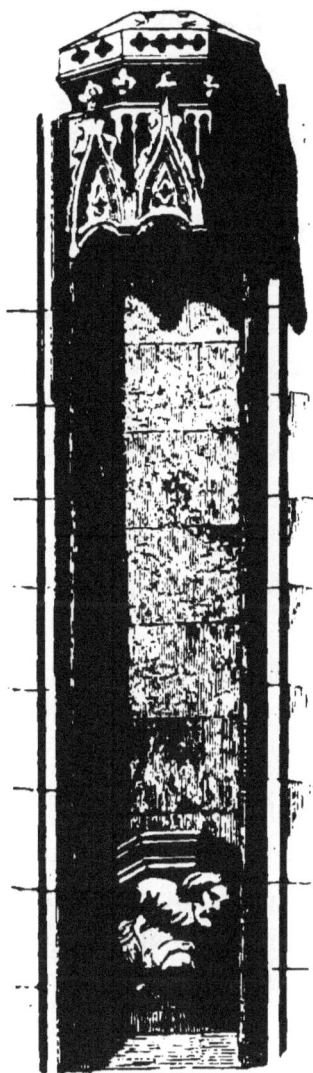

Buttress, Niche, Canopy, and Statue.

chain, which runs along the outside of the delicate mouldings of the window. The king has a globe in his left hand resting upon his knee. Strong double buttresses are seen on each side this window, the summits of which terminate in Gothic pinnacles now sadly defaced. There is a niche in each buttress, with canopies of tabernacle work and grotesquely carved pedestals. Below one of them is carved the figure of a cross-legged man, whose features are expressive of the agony he suffers from his burden. Various figures, of monstrous shape and curious expression, grin from the sloping buttresses and other prominent portions of this part of the building.

Stars and roses decorate at intervals the outer moulding of the angle of the chancel. On the west side of the north transept is the head of a negro, and, pointing off from the buttress, is the figure of an angel conveying some message from the Church. Near the last is a mutilated pedestal and empty niche, graced with one of the most elaborate and exquisite canopies.

A short distance from the abbey, and just beyond the mill-lead, stood once a great bakehouse, containing several storeys of ovens, from which a subterranean passage led to the church. In 1724, a large boiler or brewing pan was found while digging near the site of this building. Since then, foundations of pillars belonging to some erection have been discovered on the north side of the church. This was probably the chapter-house. Adjoining it are the foundations of another building, and the vestiges of an oratory or private chapel.

Near the remains of a house within the precincts of the convent, called Chisholm's tower, numerous English and Roman coins have been found. Relics of antiquity have been dug up in the gardens on the north side of the church. Among these may be mentioned an abbot's ring, with 𝕿. 𝕬. 𝕾. on the one side, and 𝕸. 𝕬. 𝕽. 𝖄. on the other. Also, a counter, inscribed—

Hal. Mary, Star of Heaven, mother of God,

and two silver buckles, on one of which is engraved the words—

Jesus of Nazareth.

Thus have we attempted, how inadequately, to describe the ruins, grand and proud in the moonlight of years, and teeming with beauty and with pensive impressions to the eye and mind of the beholder. Whoever seeks St. Mary's silent aisles may enjoy an hour with antiquity and the spoils of time—

> "And home returning, soothly swear,
> Was never scene so sad and fair."
> Sir Walter Scott.

NOTE.—A good-natured condescension on the part of the public would still add to the interest of these splendid ruins. By giving up the sculptured stones that are to be met with in the walls of houses, stables, and gardens, they would restore to the abbey that which belongs to it, and be entitled to the thanks of the antiquary and curious in such matters.

———

Hertford's second expedition wasted the monasteries of Teviotdale, but a great deal of mischief in detail happened to Melrose abbey shortly before and after that period, such as no army in an enemy's country would ever attempt or spend time to accomplish. With the Reformation, indeed, art lay prostrate, if not for a time exterminated. Sculpture, painting, and architecture, remained idle from fear. If we except St. Paul's, not a single cathedral has been erected since. How different was it with the sister art of poetry. The muse of Britain was, by the genius of Shakspeare and Spenser, placed on an equality with the heathen muses of Greece and Italy. Poetry lost none of its charms and encouragement, but art did ; for Protestants generally had a conscientious aversion to both painting and sculpture. The monks built the noble old abbeys, and being married to the church, laid out great wealth to beautify her. Sculpture and painting have, in a great measure, separated themselves from architecture, more especially the former. We are aware that the use of pictures and images had been grossly abused. A new era dawned. With the inauguration of printing, painting and sculpture seemed no longer applicable to religion, hence their connection ceased. The pages of the New Testament made the Divine will more apparent to men than could be seen through the more showy medium of art. They discovered also that apocryphal saints and miracles had falsely assigned to them positions that true saints and real miracles merited. To kneel and bow to insensible pictures and images they would not. So the first reformers broke and burnt all works of art found in churches, and designated those who countenanced them idolaters. All this was good for salvation, but bad for art. In the year 1538, the images were first commanded to be destroyed, and many fine sculptures perished. Statues were torn from their niches, thrown down and broken, and those fast to the walls had their heads and hands struck off. The Child was torn away from the Virgin. The paintings were cast into heaps and burned. The destruction was indiscriminate, and included saints, martyrs, apostles, conquerors, and kings.

"The command," says Flaxman, "for destroying sacred painting and sculpture, effectually prevented the artist from suffering his mind to rise in the contemplation or execution of any sublime effort, as he dreaded a prison or the stake, and reduced him in future to the miserable ministry of monstrous fashions, or drudging in the lowest mechanism of his profession. This unfortunate check to our national ability for liberal art occurred at a time which offered the most for-tunate and extraordinary assistance to its progress. The lately dis-covered art of printing began to enlighten the European hemisphere with the beams of knowledge in all directions. Copies of the Bible were generally distributed. The philosophy of Plato and Aristotle were understood and well illustrated; mathematics were successfully studied, so was anatomy; linear perspective had been in a great measure already perfected by Paolo Vecello, the Florentine, some time before. These advantages did much towards the formation of Raphael, Michael Angelo, Titian, Leonardo de Vinci, and Correggio, in common with the great scientific and literary luminaries of the same period, such as Bacon, Shakspeare, Spenser, and afterwards John Milton. But the genius of fanaticism and destruction arrested our progress. The iconoclastic spirit continued more or less miti-gated till its great explosion during the civil wars."

In England the crusade preached against painting and sculpture extended only to works of that kind found in the churches, but in Scotland the popular fury was directed against the structures, as well as the images and paintings which they contained. The cathedral of Glasgow alone escaped to tell of the ruin of the rest.

Art lowered its tone, and bent to earthly rather than heavenly things. The interior of palaces blocked out glimpses of paradise, and for glorious landscapes, with angels ascending and descending, art supplied us with cows grazing in meadows, and with boats fishing on the Zuyder Zee.*

True, the works of Rubens and Rembrandt are sublime, but who sees the heavenly halo breathed on them which hovers in ecstacy over those of Michael Angelo, Raphael, and Correggio.

Fuseli says, "Michael Angelo came to nature, but that nature came

* ALLAN CUNNINGHAM.

to Raphael. We stand with awe before the former, but embrace the latter, willing to go wherever he leads us. Raphael was more than any other man the artist of humanity. As painter, sculptor, and architect, Michael Angelo excelled. He was the inventor of epic painting, in that sublime circle of the Sistine chapel, which exhibits the origin, the progress, and the final dispensations of theocracy. He has personified motion in the groups of the cartoon at Pisa, embodied sentiment in the monuments of San Lorenzo, unravelled the features of meditation in the prophets and sibyls of the Sistine chapel, and in the Last Judgment, with every attitude that varies the human body, traced the master-trait of every passion that sways the human breast."

Chapter Twelfth.

MELROSE ABBEY.—THE TOMBS.

" The boast of heraldry, the pomp of pow'r,
And all that beauty, all that worth e'er gave ;
Await alike the inevitable hour,
The paths of glory lead but to the grave."

GRAY.

HE interior of this church has, in former times, been so desecrated by relentless hands, that scarcely a vestige of any memorial remains to point out where the mighty have fallen asleep. The repositories of the dead have been held sacred from remote antiquity by all nations. Where an entire people have been wasted by war and its sad train of calamities, their sepulchres have usually been spared, and their memorials venerated. Not so, however, with the mural tablets and grave-stones of the illustrious dead, that once bare fellowship with these hoary walls, within whose precincts lay enshrined a goodly number of saints and pious ecclesiastics, and a long line of kings, nobles, and border warriors,

> " The cock's shrill echo nor the clarion horn
> No more shall rouse them from their lowly bed."
>
> GRAY.

It had been customary, up to the middle of the thirteenth century, to bury the abbots within the chapterhouse of Melrose. In the year 1240, we are told, " the remains of all the abbots who were buried at the entrance of the chapter-house, except the remains of St. Waltheof, were disinterred, and removed to a place prepared for them in the east side of the same building.* What this building on the east side was, we know not, as not a stone is standing to point out its former position.

On entering the church from the west end, the first division or chapel on the right hand of the nave is occupied as a burial-ground by the ancient family of Bostons, who still possess lands in the neighbouring village of Gattonside, which were held of the church of Melrose by their ancestors, to whom some of the dignitaries of that church were closely related by marriage in later times. On the west wall is the following simple but eloquent and impressive inscription :—

* *Chron. Melros.*

"The dust of many generations of the Bostons of Gattonside, is deposited in this place.

"We give our bodies to this haly abbey to keep."

The next chapel contains the remains of some, that hapless,

"Memory o'er their tombs no trophies raise."

In the third chapel is a tombstone only discovered in 1815, on which is engraved a monastic figure in the attitude of prayer, and an inscription,—

𝕳ic jacet, honorablis bir 𝕮eorge 𝕳alliburton. * * * * * 1 𝕺ctober, 𝕬nno. 𝕯.𝕸., 𝕸𝕯.XXX.𝕍𝕴.

The next division, numbered 4 on the Ground Plan of the church, is the burial-place of the Pringles of Woodhouse and Whytebank, a very ancient family of long local standing and high repute. A number of inscriptions are placed in various parts of this chapel, the most interesting of which are the following:—

"Here lies of guid memorie Dame Margaret Ker, first wyfe . to . James . Pringil . of Wodhous, and . efter . his . deceis . mareit . Sir . David Home, of Wedderburne Knycht. Quha . deceissit . the . 24 . of . Februare . Anno . D . 1589."

Another runs thus:—

"Here lyes ane honorable voman cristin lundie spous to James * * * * * quytbank, scho deceissit 19. July 1602. Lament for syn and styl thou murn for to the clay * * * * * ye man turn."

The fifth chapel forms the burial-place of the Pringles of Galashiels, an honourable and ancient family, known also as the Hope Pringles. The effigy of one of them, the Baron of Smailholm, is seen wrapped in his grave-clothes. Near this figure is an inscription which runs thus:—

" Heir leis ane honourabil man andro Pringil, feuar of Galloschiels quha deceasit ye 28 of February, An. Dom. 1585."

On the wall above is a Latin inscription, to the effect, that another member of the same family died in 1635, and is also interred in the same place. A large marble slab, nearly eight feet by four, lies over another of the tombs, which is the sepulchral inheritance of Hugh Scott, Esq., Laird of Gala. There is little doubt, from the general appearance of this slab, but it has once been the table of an altar-piece of the church. It was inlaid with lead in ornamental characters, the brass plates of which have been taken away. The screws and screw-holes are plainly visible.

In the sixth chapel from the west, is a more modern inscription above the tomb of David Fletcher, a minister of the Established Church of Scotland at Melrose, in ' the seventeenth century. It bears date 1665. This individual ultimately became bishop of Ross.

In the seventh chapel are no traces of tombs.

In the eighth chapel or baptistry, next the chancel of the church, is a most interesting and curious kneeling stone, facing the west, and having deeply carved on its western side, the figures of four horse-shoes,* and, on the east side, in Saxon characters, the words—

"Orate pro anima fratris Petre Aerarii,"

that is, "Pray for the soul of brother Peter the treasurer."

On an elevated stone in the west wall of this chapel is the following inscription:—

Niniani : Ratine
Thome : Pauli : Cuthbt.
te : s : Petre : Retigin.

There is a small door in the west side of the south transept, opening to a stair of seventy-four steps, that winds to the roof, where the clock now is, and leads to narrow galleries, that once communicated with all the other parts of the building. Above the door is a carved shield, bearing compasses and fleurs-de-lis, indicating the profession and native country of the architect or overseer of the building. Though partly obliterated, the inscription reads thus:—

Sa gays ye compass ebyn about
Sa truth and laute do, but doute
Behalde to ye hende q. John Mordo.

"As the compass goes round without deviating from

---

* The horse-shoes are an enigma. In ancient times it was not uncommon to nail them upon the doors of byres and workshops, from the supposition that they kept out evil spirits, witches, and fairies. They were thought to possess a charm capable of counteracting covetousness and evil wishes.

Y

the circumference, so, doubtless, truth and loyalty never deviate. - Look well to the end, or see to the work, quoth John Mordo." This inscription is much older than that which follows, relating to the same individual, although we disagree with Mr Billings as to the age of both.

That John Mordo was at Melrose in the early part of the fourteenth century, we doubt not. He was the " Master of Work," not only of Melrose, but the other places mentioned on the inscribed tablet which follows. In the reign of Henry III., the Pope granted a Bull to some Italian architects to travel over all Europe, to erect chapels; and those architects were masons, and in the accepted sense of that word at the time, these parties were also Free-masons.* They continued to be designated individually "Master of Work" even to Wren's time, who was called by that name, when new St. Paul's was in course of erection. These masons usually held assemblies or lodges in the immediate neighbourhood of the works they superintended. Thus we find there was a lodge at St. Paul's, one at Westminster abbey, one in Holborn, another on Tower-hill, &c. The Romans first introduced masonry into Britain.

The office of Grand-master, which was often held indirectly by the crown, or had the prerogative of it, empowered him who held it to regulate in the frater-

* ASHMOLE'S *Collection.*

nity, what should not come under the cognizance of the law courts.

To him appealed both mason and lord, or the builder and founder, when at variance, in order to prevent law pleas, and, in his absence, they appealed to his deputy or grand-wardens that resided next to the premises.

William St. Clair, baron of Roslin, got a grant of this office from King James II., and he afterwards founded that masterpiece of Gothic architecture, the chapel of Roslin.

John Mordo appears to have had the general superintendence of the erection of Melrose abbey, and the care of all repairs afterwards. He was the patriarch of freemasonry in this part at the time, and a Frenchman by descent. On the south side of this door is another inscription evidently alluding to the same individual, some of the letters are nearly effaced, but may still be deciphered to read thus:—

> John : Morow : sumtym : callit :
> was : ℈ : and : born : in : parysse :
> certainly : and : had : in : keppyng :
> al : mason : werk : of : santan :
> droys : ye : hye : kyrk : of : glas :
> gu : melros : and : paslay : of :
> nyddysdayll : and : of : Galway :
> ✠ pray : to : God : and : Mari : baith :
> and : sweet : sancte : John : to : keep :
> this : haly : kirk : fra : skaith :

This inscription is not older than the fourteenth century

evidently, and may originally have been composed by
John Mordo, but not chiselled on the wall for a long
period afterwards.*

Within the small aisle, on the south side of the
chancel, several years ago, two tombs were discovered
which contained skeletons of great dimensions. On
the stone covering one of the tombs, an inscription ran
thus:—

"Orate : : : anima ivoors de corbirceg."

This person was probably none other than Sir Ralph
Eure or Ivers, the English commander, who fell at the
battle of Ancrum Muir in 1545, and the other, the remains of Sir Bryan Latoun, his lieutenant, who also
fell in the same action. This tomb has been fabulously
called the grave of Michael Scott, the wizard.

Two of the private chapels, right and left of the
chancel, were dedicated to St. Bridget and St. Stephen.
The latter is swept away nearly, the former is still
standing, and there is a statue of St. Bridget in a niche
to the north-east corner of it.

Sir William Douglas of Lothian was buried before
St. Bridget's altar, and William, Earl of Douglas, left
money for masses to be said continually for his soul.†

* In the Appendix we have submitted an able and interesting
paper on this subject, by Dr John Alexander Smith, read before the
R. S. A., Scotland.

† *Chart. Mel.*

The beautiful roof of the chancel, however, covers the tombs of an unknown number of illustrious men. Historians tell us that Alexander II., King of Scotland, was buried here in 1249, near the high altar. On the south side of the chancel is a large slab of polished marble, of a greenish black colour, with numerous petrified skulls embedded in it, which is believed to cover his ashes.

William Douglas, the " dark knight" of Liddesdale, also rests here.   After his murder in Ettrick Forest, his body lay at the church of Lindean for one night, and was removed on the following morning to Melrose, and buried in the chancel of the church.

Many of the tombs of the Douglases studded the north side of the chancel, and its aisles and chapelries. It was these tombs that the English commanders, Sir Ralph Evers and Sir Bryan Latoun, desecrated and dishonoured in 1544, the year prior to the battle of Ancrum Moor, and respecting which the Earl of Angus was so vexed that he vowed vengeance on the desecrators, which he executed in the following year.

Douglas, the hero of Otterbourne, or Chevy Chase, was also buried in this part of the building.

Here likewise was deposited in its final resting-place the heart of Robert Bruce, brought back from Spain by Sir William Keith, after the ineffectual attempt made by James, Lord Douglas, to carry it to Jerusalem.   The latter nobleman fell while fighting under the banner of King Alphonso, against the Saracens, his body was recovered, brought home, and also buried in the midst of his ancestors.

> " Where once the flaming pageant spread,
>   Near the high altar softly tread ;
>   For there the noblest of their race,
>   Sleep, lock'd in death's serene embrace,
>   No sound of dangling sword or spear,
>   Nor foray wakes the warrior's ear ;
>   No breasted fight, nor parlied truce,
>   Beats to the throbless heart of Bruce :—
>   Encompass'd in its narrow urn,
>   The flow'r, the soul of Bannockburn ;
>   Beneath that ugly, shapeless stone,
>   Unhonour'd, nameless, lies alone."

At the end of the north transept, about midway, a circular arched doorway (of Saxon architecture) leads with two steps downward to a dark apartment, traditionally called the wax cellar, where it is supposed the tapers, and other things used in religious worship, were kept. On one stone, partly concealed by the lowest step, there is the following inscription—

✠ 𝕳𝖎𝖈 𝖏𝖆𝖈𝖊𝖙 𝕵𝖔𝖍𝖆𝖓𝖓𝖆 : 𝖉 : 𝕽𝖔𝖘𝖘.

On another is carved a cross and a shield, the latter being that of a knight crusader.

On the north wall of the nave, and just beyond the exquisitely carved doorway that leads from the cloisters, is an elegant inscription, which the late Washington Irvine so justly admired. It runs thus—

Heir lyis the race of ye hous of Zair.

Opposite are seen the graves of the ancient family of Karr, Kerr, Ker, &c., of Kippelaw.

An inscription upon one of the tombs reads thus:—

"Here lyes levtenant collonel Andrew Ker of Kippelaw, who was born at melros the 23 febbuary 1620 years and died at Kippelaw, upon the 3 febbuary 1697, in the 77 year of his age."

There is another inscription to his son, and other members of this ancient and distinguished family, of which the Pringles are lineal descendants.

In the cloister are the remains of seven seats or stalls, beneath the base of which are inscriptions, and the appearance of tombs partially concealed by the mason work. On one of the stones is inscribed, in Saxon characters:—

"Beatrix spouse Rob : : : Fraser," *

and on another the words, "Hic jacet."

When the remains of those interred in the chapter-house were removed, it is probable they were brought

---

* There was one John Fraser, abbot of Melrose, in 1480, who was made bishop of Ross in 1485, and died in 1507. He is described as a good and wise man, and was descended from a family of the same name in Tweeddale. This inscription probably relates to a member of his family.

and deposited at the base of the cloisters. This part of the building was executed in a florid style, with chaste and almost inimitable decorations, consisting of fruit and flowers, and would in beauty and ornament be little inferior to the chapter-house itself.

And as the cloisters formed necessarily one of the earliest portion of all the buildings in connection with the monastery, and as Old Melrose was at this time a desolation, it is more than probable that numbers of coffins, holding the remains of holy and religious men, were brought up and hidden in the foundations on the erection of the new.

It would appear that all along one side of the cloisters there are tombs within the base, and within the line of the perpendicular. These could scarcely be of recent construction, or deposition, and seems, therefore, the more probable that they inherited the position they now occupy at the first restoration of the abbey. We have no account of tombs being recently discovered at Old Melrose, and no description of any in times past, and there is not a vestige of any thing of the kind remaining upon the ancient site, which is in fact wholly obliterated.

The space exterior of the abbey, now, and since the Reformation, used as the parish burial-ground, next claims our attention.

In the minister's portion is the grave of Knox, Milne,

and several others who have from time to time been pastors of the parish.

Upon an old tombstone in the churchyard are the following singularly beautiful lines:—

> " The earth goeth on the earth
>   Glist'ring like gold;
> The earth goes to the earth
>   Sooner than it wold;
> The earth builds on the earth
>   Castles and towers;
> The earth says to the earth
>   All shall be ours."

At the east end of the yard is a tombstone erected to the memory of Thomas Purdie, formerly wood-forester at Abbotsford, who died October 29th, 1829, aged sixty-two years. It bears the following simple but impressive inscription, written by his master:—

> In grateful remembrance
> of
> the faithful
> and attached services
> of
> twenty-two years,
> and in sorrow
> for the loss of a humble
> but sincere friend,
> This stone was erected
> by
> Sir WALTER SCOTT, Bart.,
> of Abbotsford.

There is a very ancient gravestone, with a sword

carvèd upon it, lying a few paces from the east window, but the Saxon characters upon it are too obliterated to be deciphered. We suspect this stone covers no remains, but that it has been brought out of the church, and perpetuates some member or members of the Douglas family. The stone itself is of precisely the same kind as the tombstone we have described in the wax cellar.

Such is the general disposition of the ancient tombs, and family sepulchres, within and without the sacred ruins.

Whether we consider death as the common friend or enemy of mankind, is of little consequence; here the rich and the poor meet together, distinctions cease, the bond become free, and the oppressor bound—truly the grave extinguishes caste.

Here mortality receives its ovation, the weary rest, and the humble believing soul freedom from the chains of earth. The poorest find—

> " There is a calm for those who weep,
> A rest for weary pilgrims found,
> They softly lie and sweetly sleep
>   Low in the ground."
>   JAMES MONTGOMERY.

The three great conflicting creeds of the earth are symbolized in the lotus, the crescent, and the cross. The first, transplanted from the delta of the Nile, covers the boundless plains of Hindostan. After ages of vigour, however, the lotus pines, it sickens under an Indian sky, and the fouler atmosphere of a cognate superstition.

Before the noontide rays of an extending civilization, it will continue to wither till extinguished. The lotus shall die and the crescent wane. Buddhism and Mahommedism shall cease, but the cross shall be in the ascendant. The star of its glory shall neither wane nor grow old; it shall have an universal sovereignty and an undying sway. As in the days of Constantine, it is, and shall be for ever, the only imperishable symbol, the only conquering sign, and those nations and tongues shall only survive the great cycles of futurity that manfully adopt it.

Chapter Thirteenth.

CHARTER GRANTED TO THE FEUARS OF GATTONSIDE
AND WESTHOUSES.

HE author of this history is indebted to Mr Thomas Boston, feuar, Gattonside, for the following ancient Charter, in which six members of his family are honourably mentioned. The original name of this family was Baston, of French descent, sometime spelt Bastoun, but more commonly Boston.

AN ENGLISH TRANSLATION OF A CHARTER GRANTED BY JAMES
DOUGLAS, COMMENDATOR OF MELROSE, AND MARY KERR,
HIS LADY, TO THE FEUARS OF GATTONSIDE AND WEST-
HOUSES, DATED THE LAST DAY OF FEBRUARY, 1590.

JAMES DOUGLAS, Commendator of Melrose and hereditary Superior of the Villages and Lands under Written, greeting, to all who shall see or hear this Charter, Wit ye me with the express consent and assent of my beloved Spouse, Mary Ker, Lady of the Lands under-mentioned, and of the life-rent (vitalis redditus) thereof; having taken diligent consideration and mature deliberation for our real uses and advantage, and my said Spouse, and also for certain sums of money made up in time for us presently thankful and fully paid to us and converted to our use by the persons following, we hold ourselves well content, fully and wholly paid by them, their heirs, executors, and assignees, quietly to be possessed by them for ever, agreeable to the tenor of this our Charter, and for several other great reasons, causes, and considerations moving us to execute the subsequent writing—have sold, and by a clear title of sale, have alienated, and by this our present Charter have confirmed, and likewise do sell, and by clear title of sale do alienate, and by this our present Charter do confirm, To our beloved Thomas Darling, senior, in Westhouses; Patrick Giffin there; Thomas Darling, lawful son of Bartholomew Darling, formerly in Westhouses; John Cairncross, in Gattonside; Bernard Wright there; Bartholomew Frier, in Westhouses; Bernard Boston in Gattonside; Robert Clarke there; Mark Martin in Westhouses; William Gottarson there; John Thomson, junior, in Gattonside; John Cairncross, senior, there; Nicol Boston there; William Blackie there; Thomas Boston, senior, there; Thomas Schuilmuire; John Helliwel there; Thomas Leithen there; Quinty gernis Bagtane there; Adam

Darling, in Westhouses; Isabel Cook in Gattonside; John Myles there; William Mein there; William Brown there; David Wright there; John Donate there; Thomas Gowdie there; William Helliwel, senior, there; Quintine Scot there; William Helliwel, junior, there; Patrick Heliliwel there; Thomas Boston there; John Boston there; John Thomson, senior, there; William Turnbull, in Westhouses; Robert Darling there; John Taitt, in Gattonside; John Wright there; Robert Boston there; George Holme there; John Gilry there; James Wright there; Richard Wright there; William Hog* there; James Leithen there; and to the heirs and assignees respectively, these our whole and entire villages and lands of Gattonside and Westhouses, with the windsheaves thereof included, and each of the aforesaid lands which never used to be separated from the same, with all and each of the parts, pendicles, and pertinents, bounded, limited, and lying in common, as follows, viz., beginning at the Fuird called the Turfford in Tweed mairchand, Wit, the lands of Drygrange, one ye list, and fra them assending up the water of Tweid, one the South syd of the Crumeknow, qu^{lk} pertains to ye said Lands of Gattonsyd to the water of Elwand, qu^r it runns in Tweid, and fra Elwand mou^t assending up the Lamen to ye mon^t of Blakburne, qu^r it enters in Elwand, and fra

---

* A member of this family wrote some very beautiful lines on the Seasons, and attained some celebrity as a writer of pastoral poetry.

there up the said burne called blakburn, to ye syk end called sillersyk, qu^{lk} runnis in Blakburn, and fra then assendand to ye eist as sillersyk gais to the middle of Scabbit rabwit moss, and throw the middle of ye said moss, finallie eist to the heid of the burne callit Faburne, and fra thin decendand ye samen to go neyer fuird of the said burne, callit Lindane-hole, and fra thin assendand sou^t mairchand w^t the Landis of Drygrange, ane ye list, at the hie street gais to the Drycleuthe heid, and frae then dissendand the said cleuthe to and called ye hauthe, yet and fra then descendant as ye auld dyke steid stands to ye foresaid fuird in Tweid callit ye Turffuird. Notwithstanding, reserving to ourselves, our heirs, or assignees and successors, the Mill of Westhouses and Croft of land adjacent thereto, called the Stockilmeadow, and Keudhinch meadow, the lands of Frierslands, of Gattonside, four acres of the lands of Gattonside ground, two acres of land formerly belonging to John Cowper in Westhouses, with two houses, garden, and teind sheaves of the said lands and their pertinents, as they are presently possessed by Robert Ormiston in Westhouses, and also preserving the fishing of the water Tweid, and the lie ferry cobles possessed by the said Robert, and also reserving to ourselves and our foresaids a piece of land occupied by Malecolm Mercer in Darnick, commonly called Boatshiel Croft, and two acres of land belonging to James Scott, in

Selkirk, and presently occupied by Isabella Cook, in
Gattonside, with the teind-sheaves and their pertinents.

Here follow the several grants of land, and quantities
varying from one-half to two acres to the aforesaid
Thomas Darling, &c., lying in Gattonside, the Orchard,
Pendicle and Fremaisters Lands, Smydie Croft, "lying
in the Lordship and Regality of Melrose and within
the Sheriffdom of Roxburgh, as they lye in length and
breadth, in houses, buildings, gardens, crofts, plains,
moors, marches, ways, lakes, ponds, rivulets, meadows,
pastures, hunting, fishing, hawking; peat, turf, coals,
coal-heughs, mindes, mindehills, iron mindes, breweries,
bluidwites, mulierum, merchietis, herezeldis; broom,
whins, woods, groves, twigs both small and big, timber,
stones, limestone, with free isk and entry, and with all
and every liberty, convenience, profit, and for their use
and whosoever belongs to them, as well not named as
named, both above and below ground, far and near of the
aforesaid villages and lands of Gattonside, Westhouses,
and others respectively above written, their heirs and
assignees particularly, in manner following—Pay annually to us, our heirs, assignees or successors aforesaid,
or our factors or chamberlain for the time being, as
followeth, To Wit, the aforesaid Thomas Darling for
his said half acre of land, with the tenement presently
possessed by him, with the teind sheaves of the same
and their pertinents, two firlots of barley of the granary

local measure, Melrose Gurnal met. The aforesaid Patrick Giffin for his acre of land, &c.," and so in the following order, setting forth the equivalents to be paid for the several grants of land specified in this Charter, chiefly grain, but in a few instances money, farm oatmeal, fowls, carriages, peats, capons, &c.

The whole quantity of the barley mentioned extends to fourteen chalders four bolls and three firlots, of the granary local measure of Melrose. The whole quantity of the above-mentioned farm, oatmeal, extends to fifteen bolls, two firlots, and two pecks. The sum of the capons extends to six, the sum of the lie kain fowl extends to fourscore and sixteen, and as many long carriages. The sum of money extends to ten pounds three shillings and four pennies, viz., called the victalia, or feeding at the feast of St. Andrew, and purification of the blessed Virgin Mary, commonly called Candlemas, the said victalia to be brought to our Lordship of Melrose at their own proper expense; and also the heirs of the above-named persons by paying the sum of twenty shillings money the first year of their entry, for confirmation for the aucht ailver cavill upon account of doubling the said feudiformum or feu-duty, and in all times coming to compeer in our Court to be holden in the lordship of Melrose; and likewise they shall be obliged to serve as when we serve the king in the public services, and we and our heirs do warrant, acquit,

Z

and defend the same persons in the same of the services at the hands of the abbot and convent of Melrose for ever.

After entailing some regulations in respect to the non-payment of the feu-duties, &c., the Charter goes on to declare, that, by attorney or notary being present on the part of the feuars, "the delivery of earth and stone of their ground, as use is agreeable, to the tenor of our above written charter, which they respectively have from us, ye with advice, and be justly to be holden without any delay, and this you do by no means omit, for doing of which we command to you and each one of you our said Baillies in that part, constitute our full and irrevocable order, title, and power. In witness of which thing, these presents are subscribed by our hand, our personal seal is appended, together with the proper seal of our said spouse, as a token of her consent, at Melrose, the last day of the month of February the year of our Lord one thousand five hundred and ninety, before these witnesses, Robert Scott and Patrick Cranstone, our writers; Mr John Knox, minister at Melrose, John Scott, notar public, and James Blackie in Gallanbrig, with several others.

JOHN KNOX,   { JAMES, Commendator of Melrose.
Witness.   { MARY KERR, Lady, Melrose.

WALTER CHISHOLM, of that Ilk, Baillie Depute.

N.B.—Some years prior to the granting of this charter, a similar one was granted to many persons in Newstead by the same parties, and they were declared therein exempt from tithes, and all other payments in shape of ministers' money; which privileges they still possess. The same might have happened to Darnick and Gattonside, but immediately after the grant of the charter to Newstead, the Scottish Parliament passed a law, that in all future gifts of land the tithes should not be abrogated, but still pertain as before to the Church.

The rental of Gattonside and Westhouses, payable Martinmas 1717, was L.333, 16s. 3d. Some of the old feuars were then in being. This rental included tenements, gardens, and farm lands. In the rent roll we meet with the names of Bell, Frier, Tait, Boston, Halewell, Lindsay, Thomson, &c.

Darnick Tower.

Chapter Fourteenth.

THE EILDON HILLS, DARNICK, ABBOTSFORD, AND OTHER PLACES OF GENERAL INTEREST IN THE VICINITY OF MELROSE.

" Hail! glorious hills that skirt the horizon's brow,
And peer majestic o'er the vales below!
Long may the purpling heather clothe your breast,
And peaceful summer sunshine on ye rest!
No longer on your stalwart forms are seen
The Roman eagles, nor the beacon's gleam;
Peace o'er the land her loving mantle throws,
And concord's chaplets grace your triple brows.
Still send your amorous looks to bonnie Tweed,
For ye were friends lang syne—old friends indeed!
Oft sought, as landmarks, by the pilgrim's gaze,
Your Alpine summits, and its winding ways,
Oft when the tones of prayer and praise were heard,
What gentle echoes have your bosoms stirr'd;
Look watchful on St. Mary's ruin'd pile,
And to her hapless melancholy smile;
Still breast the seasons, dauntless ever stand,
The proud memorials of this Border land;
While history wanders o'er each classic spot,
Marshal her on, and grace the land of Scott."

LITTLE south of Melrose rises the Eildon hills, once the Trimontium of the Romans, so called from the peculiarity of their form. Properly speaking, the Eildons are only one hill rising from one base, but divided into three peaks. Tradition says that these summits once formed a single cone, which was severed in three by an infernal agent of Michael Scott the wizard. The top of the highest summit is 1364 feet above the sea level. The composition of the rocks of the two northern peaks is felspar, and felspar and porphyry. On the southwest descent of the southern hill the opening of a quarry has laid bare a number of perpendicular pentagonal prisms of beautiful flesh-coloured felspar, each about twenty feet high as exposed, but probably of far greater height, with remarkably acute and distinct angles. Near this locality are traces of stair or trap, rising from the partly broken bed of the strata, and other evidences of a basaltic character; sometimes pieces a foot square, lay exposed jutting out from the surface of the ground, looking towards Bowdenmoor.

At the foot of the southern slope of the Eildons stands Eildon Hall, the newly acquired residence of Lord Walter Scott, son of His Grace the Duke of Buccleuch. Eildon Hall was long the seat of the Honourable Major Baillie. Upon the slopes of the north-eastern hill, and nearest the town of Melrose, is a large, and to all appearance, an artificial tumulus, called the "Bourjo," having a road leading to it, called the Haxalgate. It is traditionally reported to have been the site of a Druidic temple. On the top of the eastern hill, are unmistakable indications of a Roman encampment. Sixteen terraces are traceable on the sides of these hills, which rise one above another like the steps of a stair. Porphyritic trap, with a large proportion of felspar, constitute the chief rocks of the range. There is a view on all sides from these lofty hills of matchless beauty and diversity. First, the abbey and town of Melrose to the north—the joyous valley of the Tweed, and its "lingering looks"—the arcadia of Scotland, and the cradle of romance and song. Southward, on the Northumberland marches, rise "Cheviot's mountains blue," and Flodden on their eastern skirts; and within a short distance the ruins of Dryburgh, Smailholm, and Hume Castle. Thomas the Rhymer's tower, Bemersyde, and "bonny Cowden-knowes," beyond which the eye is carried over tracts of pastoral wildness to the Soutra and Lammermoor hills. Soutra hill is the most westerly of the Lammermoor mountains, and is about 1200 feet above the sea level. Its name signifies the hill with a prospect. Anciently a thriving village stood on the top of the hill, containing a famous cell or hospital belonging to

Melrose, and founded by Malcolm the Fourth about the middle of the twelfth century. All have disappeared but the religious or special road that connected this hospital with Melrose, and was called the Girthgate, which ran from the monastery of Old Melrose through the vale of the Elwand and Lauderdale to Soutra. "I can stand," said Sir Walter Scott, "on the Eildon hill, and point out forty-three places famous in war and verse." From the western peaks are seen the sombre Buckholm hills, the Meiglot, and the black-capped heights above the bustling town of Galashiels, and nearer to us Cauldshiels Loch, Ettrick Forest, Abbotsford, and the foot of Gala Water. The mountains of Selkirk, and the "Dowie Dens of Yarrow," stretching far beyond in fine diversity of form.

The eastern scene is replete with historical incident. Ancrum Muir, or Lilliard's Edge, lies near the stately tapering Waterloo column; south-east stands the colossal statue of Wallace, with the scenery of Kelso and Roxburgh Castle dimly seen.

On the eastern declivity of the Eildons stood the famous Eildon Tree, beneath the shade of which Thomas of Ercildoun is said to have delivered his prophecies. There is a stone, called the Eildon Tree Stone, that still marks the place where the tree flourished.

One of the Rhymer's predictions runs thus:—

> "At Eildon Tree, if you shall be,
> A brig over Tweed you there may see."

Several bridges crossing the Tweed are now to be seen from this spot. On the northern summit of the Eildons there are clear traces of a vast encampment, not less than a mile and a half in circuit, fortified by two fosses around the hill, and in the vicinity there are the remains of no fewer than five camps, with military roads, as well as ditches and earth-works.

The Ettrick Shepherd has imparted an interest to the Eildon hills in one of his wild and beautiful ballads, "The Hunt of Eildon: "—

> " An' round, an' round, and seven times round,
>   An' round about the Eildon tree !
> For there the ground is fairy ground,
>   And the dark green ring is on the lea."

On the summit of the east hill are distinct vestiges of what Mr Milne considers to have been a Roman camp, and on the very top is still to be seen, surrounded with the remains of earthen huts, what may once have been the Prætorium, or General's Quarters. " It has," says Mr Milne, " all the properties of a well-chosen camp, according to the rules Vegetius has given for a camp. It has a large prospect of all the countries lying upon each side of it. It hath many springs of good water near it, the sides of the hill have been covered with wood, and the camp is of that extent, that neither men, beasts, nor baggage, could be pinched for want of room."

In later times, and during the wars of the French

Revolution, and the anticipated attacks of invasion by the first Napoleon, beacons were placed on the summits of these hills, to warn the inhabitants of the surround-ing district of approaching danger.

DARNICK.—Scarcely a mile west from Melrose, and on the Abbotsford road, stands the sequestered village of Darnick, famous in bye-gone days for its three towers or peel-houses.

THE HEITONS OF DARNICK TOWER.—The village of Darnick, containing about 400 inhabitants, attracts the attention of tourists in consequence, chiefly, of its pos-sessing the finest specimen now extant of the ancient Border keeps. This tower, the family property of the Heitons, stood along with two others, both of which are now extinct, and were of inferior dimensions. The names of the proprietors of these smaller towers do not represent any families, the male heirs having died out, though one of the peels is still remembered as Fisher's Tower, and with the proprietors of which the Heitons had intermarried. Antiquaries can find no reason for the clustering of these peels, other than the evident one of their having been erected for mutual defence; though it is not improbable that some other reasons, peculiar to the times, may have contributed, such as that of national security in places more than ordinarily exposed to foreign inroads. In any view, they are an interesting feature of this part of the country, and are always examined with curiosity, as showing the kind of embattled residences in which the gentlemen of former times were obliged to reside, when domestic peace was a blessing, only, as it were, snatched at intervals from continual turmoil. "The barons and gentlemen," says Foster, in his review of Sir Walter Scott's *Border Antiquities*, "had for their residence an inferior kind of fortresses, often heard of in Border history, under the denomination of 'strengths,' constructed upon a limited scale, usually in some situation of natural strength. Having very thick walls, strongly cemented, they could easily repel the attack of any desultory excursion, and the village which almost always adjoined, contained the abodes of the retainers, who, upon the summons of the chieftain, took arms either for the defence of the fortress, or for giving battle in the field." A more graphic description is given by Sir Walter Scott, thus:—"The smaller gentlemen, whether heads of branches of clans, or of distinct families, inhabited dwellings upon a smaller scale, called Peels or Bastle-houses. They were surrounded by an enclosure or barnkin, the walls whereof were according to statute, a yard thick, surrounding a space of at least 60 feet square. Within this outerwork the laird built his tower, with its projecting battlements, and usually secured the entrance by two doors, the outer of grated iron, the innermost of oak, clenched with nails. The apartments were placed directly over each other, accessible only by a narrow turnpike stair, easily blocked up or defended."

This last description is so good a picture of the peel of Darnick as it now stands, that it supersedes any necessity for our describing it. The apartments all over each other and the stair, may still be seen, and in addition to Sir Walter's account, a door at the top leading out to the battlements, which run entirely round, so that in the very last extremity, and when the inmates were actually driven up out of the apartments, they had still not only a refuge, but a position from which to harass whoever remained in the court-yard.

There is no doubt, and indeed there are remaining, traces to show, that Darnick Tower had its full share in the battles and skirmishes of the warlike times. At one period, even so early as 1545, as appears from the curious "Contemporary Account of the Earl of Hertford's Second Expedition to Scotland, and of the ravages committed by the English forces," printed from the MS. in Trinity College Library, Dublin, the tower of Darnick was one of the fortresses cast down and "razed." The present tower was either the old one repaired, (for the word "razed" did not always mean total demolition, an act requiring more time and labour than invaders, in the midst of an angry people, could bestow), or a new one erected on the old site, and probably, as was often the case, with part of the old stones.

The repairing or rebuilding of the present tower was probably accomplished by a principal member of the family, Andrew Heiton, soon after the passing of the act in the reign of Queen Mary, for the improvement of the kingdom by planting and re-building. It was a palpable mistake in the *Border Antiquities* to denominate this tower as belonging to the Fishers, that of the latter being at the time in ruins. The mistake was the more extraordinary, as Sir Walter Scott had made several attempts to purchase this tower from the late Mr Heiton, and, had he succeeded, intended to convert it into an armoury.

This old family of the Heitons, according to a tradition, delivered from father to son, came originally from Normandy, in the company of a family of French knights, about the year 1425, to assist the Scots against the English. They were well received by James I., by whom a grant of land was given them in the vicinity of the village of Darnick, where they had settled. The name is a translation into Saxon-Scotch of the French Hauteville, a word common in Normandy, and serving, according to the usage of the time, as a patronymic derived from the family property or residence. We have an analogous example of the Norman designation in "Heiton," or the "hill," in Roxburghshire—though we doubt if the Normans ever had recourse to so marked an expletive. The property and tower must have been in the family from a period long before the visit of Hertford, but it was after this time that they acquired what was termed their out-field. Andrew Heiton, the then proprietor, was one of those men of substance selected out of the crown vassals, for receiving land under the provisions of the Improving Act, as appears from two charters by Mary, in 1566 and 1567, signed, the one by Lethington, and the other by Bothwell. There is another tradition in the family, that this Andrew Heiton performed a valorous part in defeating Buccleugh's attempt to seize the person of James V., a graphic account of which forms one of the *Border Tales*. The family is at present represented by John Heiton, Esq. of Darnick Tower.* Melrose Abbey has been the burial-place of the Heitons for many generations.

This, like many other of the Border peels, was built or re-built in conformity to an act of Parliament, passed in 1535, "for bigging of strengthis on the Bordouris." Two-thirds of the peels of which there are any remains, were built between the middle of the sixteenth century and the close of it.

The last great clan battle of the Borders was fought here, in 1526, and the place is still called Skirmish

---

* There is a beautiful monogram over the entrance-door to Darnick tower, with the letters 𝔄. 𝔥. on the left, and on the right is the date 1569, with the letters 𝔎. 𝔣. underneath. The crest is a bull's head, with the motto, "Cave taurum."

Field. The struggle lay between Angus and Buccleugh, for possession of the person of James V., which terminated in favour of the former. Buccleugh was wounded, and lost many of his followers; the loss of Angus was considerable, including the heroic Ker of Cessford, who was slain by a servant of Buccleugh.

Lindsay of Pitscottie gives the following somewhat graphic account of this battle. He says: "About this time the king went to the south-land, to the ayres, and held justice in Jedburgh, where there came many plaints to the king of reiff, slaughter, and oppression, but little justice was used but by the purse. For there were among that were of the Earl of Angus's kin, friends and servants, that got justice by favour. Of which the king was nothing content, nor none of the lords that were about him, for they would have had justice equally used to all men without partiality or exception of persons. But, notwithstanding, the Earl of Angus and the rest of the Douglases ruled all which they liked, and no man durst say the contrary. Wherefore the king was heavily displeased, and would fain have been out of their hands, if he might, by any way; and to that effect wrote a quiet letter with his own hand, and sent it secretly to the Laird of Buccleugh, beseeching him, that he would come with his kin and friends, and meet him at Melrose, at his home-passing; and there to take him out of the Douglas's hands, and to put him to liberty, to use himself among the lave of his lords as he thinks expedient."

This letter, we are informed, was sent privately by one of the king's servants, and received thankfully by the "Laird of Buccleugh, who was glad thereof," to be put to such charges and familiarity with his prince, and did great diligence to perform the king's writing, and to bring the matter to pass as the king desired. And to that effect summoned all his kin and friends, and all that would do for him, to ride with him to Melross, when he knew of the king's home-coming, And so he brought in company with him six hundred spears of Liddisdale and Annandale, and countrymen and clans thereabouts, and held themselves quiet while that the king returned out of Jedburgh, and came to Melross, to remain there all that night.

"But when the lords Hume, Cesford, and Farnieherst took their leave from the king, and returned home, there appeared the laird of Buccleugh in sight, and his company with him, in battle array, intending to have fulfilled the king's petition, and therefore came stoutly forwards in the back side of Halidon hill [Eildon hill]. By that the earl of Angus and his brother, George Douglas, with their friends, seeing this enemy coming, marvelled what it meant, until at last they knew the laird of Buccleugh and the company that were with him, when they were the less afraid, and made them manfully to the field contrary them, and said to the king in this manner:—

" ' Sir, yon is Buccleugh and thieves of Annandale with him to molest your grace from the gate. I swear to God they shall either fight or flee, and ye shall tarry here in this knowe, and my brother George with you, with any other company you please, and I shall pass and put yon thieves off the ground, and rid the gate unto your Grace, or else die for it.'

. " The king tarried still as was desired, and George Douglas with him, with sundry other lords, as Lennox, Erskine, and some of the king's own servants, but all the rest passed with Angus to the field against Buccleugh, and joined and countered cruelly, both the said parties in the field of Darnelinver [Darnick], either against other, with uncertain victory. But at last the lord Hume hearing word of that matter, how it stood, returned again to the king in all possible haste, and with him the laird of Cesford and Farnieherst, to the number of four score spears, and set freshly on the left wing of Buccleugh, and his friends, and shortly bore them backwards to the ground, which caused the laird of Buccleugh and the rest of his friends to flee, chased and followed by the laird Cesford and Farnieherst especially, who followed so seriously, till at the foot of a path he was slain by a spear, by one Elliot,

2 A

who was then servant to the laird of Buccleugh.   But
when the laird of Cesford [Ker] was slain, the chase
ceased.   But the earl of Angus returned again [to Mel-
rose] with great merriness and victory, and thanked
God that he saved him from that shame, and passed
with the king to Melross, where they remained all
that night, while in the morn they passed to Edinburgh with the king, who was very sad and dolorous
of the slaughter of the laird of Cesford, and many
other gentlemen and yeomen slain by the laird of
Buccleugh."

Such is the account of this sanguinary conflict given
us by the ancient historian, and the place is known to
this day as Skinner's Hill, or Skirmish Field.   Tradition says, the Laird of Darnick, Heiton, not only saw the
action from his tower (a former one existing on the
present site), but took part in it also.   This tower,
which has two of its rooms decorated with ancient
armour, and other things of interest to the tourist, is
always open to inspection, and will well repay a visit
from the curious.

There was anciently a pottery and tile-works in
Darnick, the property of the monastery of Melrose; and
a bridge spanned the Tweed, from Darnick side to the
west-end of General Duncan's property on the other,
leading by an old road from Melrose over the hills
to Earlston and Lauder.   There was an ancient

ford here also at this part of the river, called the Salter's Fuird.*

BRIDGEND.—About a mile west from Darnick is the small village of Bridgend, a name derived from a bridge erected over the Tweed, to afford a passage to the abbey. It consisted of four stone piers, upon which lay planks of wood. Near the central pillars was a gateway, and over these a room for the toll-keeper. From this bridge, the girthgate was reached, which ran up the valley of Allen or Elwand Water. Near this bridge, at the foot of Allen, stood once a corn mill, known as Westhouses mill, razed by the English, nothing of which remains, except the line of water formed by the wheel-race of the mill. The site of the mill is now a green patch or island, with the Tweed flowing round about it.

A powerful chalybeate spring flows down the rocks at different points, as you ascend the steep acclivities of Allen Water. There is in the sides of the stream a sub-stratum of clay, which is petrified by the water, impregnated with iron, oozing through it, especially after heavy rains. In dry warm weather, chips or fragments drop out, and fall on the bed of the stream,

---

* John Smith, Esq., architect, and A. Currie, Esq., sculptor, are both residents of Darnick. The former family are very old portioners in the village.

where the curious collect them. Some are very interesting, being in singular shapes, such as spectacle-cases, guns, buttons, daisies, and other pleasing diversities of form. The country people call them fairy toys, and the spot about which they are found is named Fairy Dean.

"A bright romance, a greenwood dream,
A vision bards of old have seen."

The girthgate existed long before there was any road by Gala Water, and passed over Soutra and all the intermediate high hills, between Elwand Water and the neighbourhood of Edinburgh. Near Allen Water stood the once considerable village of West-houses, notable also for its peel or tower, which disappeared about fifty years ago. The only relic remaining is a house, once occupied as an inn there, and now serving as the porter's lodge to the Pavilion, a mansion of Lord Somerville's, but for many years the summer residence of H. F. Broadwood, Esq., of London. Near the head of Allen Water may still be seen the remains of three ancient fortalices or towers—the first is that of Langshawmill, the second Colmslie, and the third Hillslop. The latter belonged once to a family named Cairncross, and was inhabited within the last century. The Fairy Dean, at the foot of Allen Water, is a luxuriantly embowered greenwood glade, the Glen-

dearg of the *Monastery* of Sir. Walter Scott, and is
the region of rock and stream his genius described it.
Half a mile due east lies the handsome stone bridge of
Melrose, with a glorious view from its portalled sides
of the silver Tweed adorned, with birchen copse and
shaggy fir — rich opening meadows sloping to its
verdant sides—the sweet retreat of Lowood to the
west, Bruce's Hill, Easter Langlee, and Wester Langlee;
the latter a modern Elizabethan mansion centred in
lovely grounds, the seat of J. R. Dalrymple, Esq.

ABBOTSFORD.—About three miles from Melrose, on
the high road through Darnick, stands the renowned
mansion of Abbotsford, surrounded east and west to
the silver edge of Tweed, with luxuriant woods in
proud array, graced with all that nature can lavish or
art achieve.

Not many years ago, a mean farm-house stood on
part of the site of the present edifice, and a kail-yard
flourished where the embattled court-yard now spreads
itself. Hundreds of acres of plantations and woody
summits, rich in all the harmonizing hues of natural
loveliness, now adorn the classic spot, where was only
seen one long struggling line of stunted firs, dark in
ancestral poverty and barren gloom,

The connection of Sir Walter Scott with Abbotsford
only commenced in 1811. He died there, on the

afternoon of Friday, the 21st of September, 1832. After his death, his eldest son succeeded to the baronetcy, but died in 1847, while on his passage to England from India. The title then became extinct. Walter Scott Lockhart, grandson of the poet, came next into possession. He is since dead, however; and the present owner and occupier is James R. Hope Scott, Esq., a gentleman of large income and enlightened opinion. The mind of Scott was too fervent and poetical for vulgar names. So in proposing to change the face of nature around Abbotsford, which he successfully accomplished, he also changed the names of many places contiguous to it. Thus Cartleyhole became far-famed Abbotsford; Dick's Cleugh, the romantic Rhymer's Glen; and Toftfield, bonnie Huntly-burn. Huntly-burn House is the residence of Lord Henry Kerr.

Abbotsford is, in limited compass, a grand conservatory, containing specimens of all that is rich, rare, curious, and interesting—to be estimated only by the standard of that giant mind, that studied the general arrangement and disposition, inside and out;—who best knew the value—could most truly appreciate what was beautiful, and made the *tout ensemble* of the whole, like his own minstrelsy, "a joy for ever." There is heraldry, ancient armour, sculpture, carving, and painting.

Cabinets of virtu almost beyond price—elegant specimens in natural history—a superb collection of fossils
and specimens in mineralogy and geology—quaint an-
tiques—architectural relics, ornaments, and decorations
—treasures from the east and from the west—trophies
of war and peace—gems of land and sea—combinations
of all that was beautiful in the living and the dead—a
costly and extensive library—one vast labyrinth of objects, enchanting to the mind, as they are dazzling and
overpowering to the eye—viewed as a whole, marvellous
—and as the owner, too, aptly named them collectively,
"a romance in stone and lime," which, however, must
be seen to be rightly admired, and, however studied,
can only be infinitessimally appreciated.

No wonder that Abbotsford is eagerly sought by the
busy tourist—it was the day and life dream of Scott,
and he bequeathed to it a charm, by the scintillations
of his genius, that will impart to it still greater interest
in years to come.

That genius so sublime, that made history pleasing,
and lent the most bewitching fascination to romance—
the light of whose lamp illumined many a distant
hearth in Christendom—made the young glow with
emotion, and the aged warm with delight—whose wick
untimely flickered away, by the wear and tear of brain,
and whose "spirit returned to Him who gave it." The

author of Waverley shall live indelibly in the hearts of
his countrymen, and in the records of those pages the
classical genius of his country is ever illuminating.

> " The minstrel sleeps!—the charm is o'er,
> The bowl beside the fount is broken,
> And we shall hear the harp no more,
> Whose tones to every land hath spoken."
>
> ROBERT GILFILLAN.

Our mission is done, the task we undertook to
accomplish is finished—and if some of our footprints
remain on the minds of those who trust us, our
purpose will be amply and satisfactorily answered.

APPENDIX.

———•———

Milne, page 53 of this book. History of the Parish of Melrose, &c.

A copy of the Rev. Thomas Forrester's "Saytre relating to Public Affairs, 1638–39," has been kindly handed to the writer of this book by James Simson, Esq. It was taken from an old MS., and does not appear ever to have been printed before. Mr Milne, even in his time, had not been able to see a copy of it. This facetious poetry, as Milne properly styles it, appears to have been written by Mr Forrester soon after his deposition in 1638. "Then Mr Thomas Foster's process was given in, containing many grosse and blasphemous poynts, and after the calling of the rolls, the assemblie voted that such a minister as he should be put off in a singular manner, and deposed from the ministrie."—*Records of the Kirk of Scotland.*

Nov. 17, 1631. "Serious people in Scotland were at this time much scandalised by reports from England regarding clergymen who openly preached Arminianism, and others who wrote in favour of a lax observance of the Sabbath. At home the bishops and other leaders of the church were manifestly departing from the old Scottish observances. The house of one Dickson in the Potter-Row, in the suburbs of Edinburgh, was to some of them their place of recreation on the Sabbath afternoons. It was remarked of Spottiswoode and some of the bishops, that they sojourned (travelled) more on that than on any other days; and Mr Thomas Forster, minister of Melrose, having but one hutt of corne in his barne-yard, would needs show his Christian liberty, by causing his servants cart it in upon that holy day. Thus fast were we hastening to destruction."—*Stevenson.*

To show the style and character of Mr Forrester's litany, we quote the following from the First Part:—

1.

" From Glasgow road to which made meeting
Huge troups from all quarters came fleeting
With dogs and guns in forme of warre,
All loyal subjects to debarre.
Wher bishops might not show their faces,
And mushroom elders find their places—
    From such mad freaks of Catharus,
    Almighty God deliver us."

From the Second Part:—

1.

" From Henderson, who doth out-top
The Etnauhs, for he is Pope—
Yet Leekie makes bold to oppose
His Holiness, e'en to his nose.
Leekie a covenanting brother,
Go to, let one Deil ding another.
    From such mad freaks, &c.

3.

" From all who swear themselves meisworn,
From Louthian, Loudone, Lindsay, Lorne,
Princes Rothes and Balmerino,
And devoute Lordlings many moe—
Who lead the dance and rule the roast,'
And forceth us to make the cost.
    From such mad freaks, &c.

5.

" From lay lads in pulpit prattling,
   Twice a-day, rumbling and rattling;
   Priests, Lords, Judges, and Clerks of Towns,
   Proud citizens, poor country clowns—
   Who in all courses disagree,
   And join to cross authoritie.
           From such mad freaks, &c.

10.

" From corner-creeping parlour preachers,
   Of blind disciples, more blind teachers;
   From cisterns that no water hold,
   From Aberdeen's base and false gold,
   From daubers with untempered mortar,
   From Row that spurgold pulpit sporter.
           From such mad freaks, &c.

11.

" From northern Dunbar, Murray's chanter,
   The knave became a covenanter
   To save his life—how may that be,
   The covenant, its a sanctuary
   To felons and to false swearers,
   And all such cheating rogues as he is.
           From such mad freaks, &c.

15.

" From Elliot, Tweeddale's jackanapes,
   In pulpit when it skips and leaps—
   It makes good sport I must confess,
   It's a mad monkey, questionless.
   From Selkirk glory, young and old,
   Selkirke's reproof if truth were told.
           From such mad freaks, &c.

17.

" From covenanting Tamilists,
Amsterdamian Separatists—
Antinomians and Brownists—
Jesuitizing Calvinists—
Murrayinizing Buchannanists—
All monster Misobasilists.
                 These are the mates of Catharus, &c.

19.

" From Sandie Hago and Sandie Gibsone—
Sandie Kinnear, and Sandie Johnstone—
Whose knavery made them covenanters,
To keep their necks out of the halters;
Of falsehood gried, what you'll name,
Of treacherie they think no shame.
              Yet these the mates of Catharus,
              And all the knock-down race of Knoxes,
              From whom good Lord deliver us."

Clergymen and elders referred to in the preceding lines of Mr
Forrester:—

Lothian, William, Earl of, elder, Parish of Dalkeith.
Loudone, John, Earl of, elder, Parish of Irvine.
Lindsey, John, Lord, elder, Parish of Coupar.
Rothes, John, Earl of, elder, Parish of Kirkcaldie.
Balmerino, John, Lord, elder, Parish of Edinburgh.
Guild, William (Aberdeen's false gold), Minister of Aberdeen.
Row, James, Minister at Muthill, Parish of Auchterarder.
Jamieson, William (Selkirk's glory), Minister of Longnewton.
Martin, Robert, Minister, New Kirk of Ettrick.
Knox, John, Minister of Bowden.

Besides many others it is unnecessary to repeat. We have
given sufficient to show the spirit of Mr Forrester and his power
of satire at the time he wrote.

Note 2.

Referring to our brief account in Chapter VIII. of the Marquiss of Hertford's second expedition into Scotland, A.D. 1545, we place before our readers the following most interesting paper upon that subject, as being aptly illustrative :—

A CONTEMPORARY ACCOUNT OF THE EARL OF HERTFORD'S SECOND EXPEDITION TO SCOTLAND, AND OF THE RAVAGES COMMITTED BY THE ENGLISH FORCES IN SEPTEMBER, 1545. FROM A MANUSCRIPT IN TRINITY COLLEGE LIBRARY, DUBLIN. COMMUNICATED BY DAVID LAING, ESQ., F.S.A., TO THE SOCIETY OF ANTIQUARIES, SCOTLAND.

The writer of this journal styles himself " York Herald," and accompanied Lord Hertford in 1545. The Earl of Hertford having assembled his army at Newcastle, on the 5th of September, 1545, advanced rapidly through Northumberland, crossed the Border, and on the 9th of that month encamped before the town and abbey of Kelso.

" The Erle of Harford departhit from Nywcaftell the 5 day of Settember; and all his armey had a day a pointit to mytte att the Stannyngfton[1] vpon Crocke a More,[2] the 8 day of thes present, & all the caryadge and ordenannce and monyffion: and fo the dyd: the faid Erle rod from Nywcafttell to Anwicke a Satherday, and their he reft Sonday; and a Monday to Cheidyngham; and a Tywffeday to the forfaid Ston on Crackamowre, and paft fartr[3] a myll, and their campet; and a Wenefday paft by Warke, and fo a longs the water in iij batelles,[4] and fo paft the furd wt the foreward and the moft part of the battaill and their ordenannce, and the reywaier[5] Twyd roffe fo fuddenley, that hit was 3 or 4 cartf and fom horffes owertrowen[6] by the

---

[1] the Standingstone.
[2] Probably Crookham (muir?), between Ford and Cornhill.
[3] further.   [4] companies, battalions.   [5] the river.   [6] overthrown.

wiollence of the water, and fom ftowff loft and waiett,[1] and this
the rereward and fome of the battaiell campeit on the other fid,
and all o~r~ wittailes wer dier, thes Wenefeday did I YORKE
fomeyn the abbaye of Chelffe [Kelso], and thes day the faid
Abby was batterid and enterid by day, and by mydnyght hit
was wone by the Spanards par force. Scleyn of the Scottes to
the nomer of 40, and thakeyn[2] to the nomer of 5, and efkape by
nyght 13; of the wch 13, 2 was thakyn the nexht day, and a xi
efkape in lywf; a turfeday the campe cam all to the fayd abbey
and town, as well the that wer on the one fyd as the other. The
erle of Comerland had the fourward, and the lord Scrope w^t^ him,
and Sr Robard Bowes, lord wardon of the mydell marches, and
many other knyghts, and the lord Lattemer, and 300 Italians
and Albenefes on horfbac, and ij annconnes[3] of Spanards, and
fome horfhemen of them, and the marfhall; and in this wangard[4]
was the Mr of the ordinnance and his horfhemen, and a 100
hangoners, and in the battaill the Erle of Herford, lord lowtten-
naunt, and my lord Stowrtoun, and Sr Rawf Sadheller, treffuryer
and confelleir, and my lord Newell and his fathers power, and
his brother Thos, and my lord Tho~s~ Greymarke, and the baron
Hilton, the lord Latemer, Sr J. Doon, Sr J. Norris, Sr Piers a
Lighe, Sr Loveras Smyth, Sir J. Brierton, Sr Roger Laffell, Sr
Leonard Beckwithe, Sr Thomas Kolkcrawfft, and iij anngenes of
Spanards, and fome of them a horfbac, and the Clewoies all, and
many knyghts and fquiers mar, and the Ieries[6] men, ij angenes
fometymes in the bataiell and fomtymes in the fowr-ward, and
in the riere-ward the lord Dacers and the lord Connyers, and Sr
John Markam, and Sr Richard Mann, capitain generall of the
rierewards horfhemen, and Sr Robart Conftable, knyght, and
many mor knyghts and efquers. Thes day the wittailles[6] wer
yett fkand and nott plenty, this day the Spanard did fpuiell the
Abbey att their will and euery man; a friday meffur was
thakeyn[7] for to fortifie the faid Abbey, butt hit was or nown

---

[1] wet. [2] taken. [3] ensigns, or companies. [4] vanguard.
[5] Irish. [6] victuals. [7] measures were taken.

thetarmennyt[1] the contrarie, theis day was [*blank*], theis day my
lord commandyt to briek the abbey and thake of the leied,[2] and
outer myen[3] the towres and strong places, and to owaier trowe[4]
all; thea day byng fryday, my Lord rood to Rockefborow [Rox-
burgh] to vis hit[5] for to make a ftrong caftell their, wch is as
ftrong a place to by fourtefied as any is in Scotland by tuyen[6]
ij riveres wch myght by brouwght to com a bowt the faid rocke,
and the wch rever he wold, the on is att his fut and the other
w^tin a stones cast; thes place wrowt well, came to o^r campe
agayn thes day was iiij of the Carres, and ij of the erle of
Angoies is ferwaunts, and iij of the lord Howmes taken and
others, and the[7] of Hum caftell [Hume Castle] had thaken a fon
of Tho^{as} Blanhaffett,[8] and a noter as good as he, and ij mor; and
a Satterday my lord Wardon of the myddell marches, and the
knyght marfhall Sr Henry Knywett, and my lord Newell, all
the horfhemen a most, Engles, Clewoies, and Italians, and
Straliotts, and Spanards, to the nomer of iiij towffent and mor,
and the birynd ij abbeyis, and 30 townes, and corn worth a 1000
li. ft^r, 9 myell Scottes, a myell byeyend Mouroffe [Melrose]; and
a Sonday the abbey of Kelfe was razed, and all put to royen,[9]
howffes, and towres, and ftypeles, and the wittaieles cam, and
cartes loden again w^t the leed[10] of the faid abbey, and my lord
lowttennant did fend ij greit gones[11] to Barwick and Sr Robart
Bowes, and ij other gones to take a caftell ij myll from thes
place, called Dawcowe. 3 Skotts fcleyn, and cartes sent to
Wark loden wt. the leid of the abbey, and wt hym 500 horffes

---

[1] but it was ere noon determined.   [2] take off the lead.

[3] undermine.   [4] overthrow.   [5] see it.

[6] between two   [7] they.

[8] This Thomas Blanhassett was of the ancient Norman family of
Blennerhassetts, who came to England with William the Conqueror,
and after residing in Cumberland for a long period, became staunch
adherents of William of Orange, and settled in Ireland. Blenner-
ville, near Tralee, county of Kerry, has been long the paternal property of their descendants.

[9] ruin.   [10] lead.   [11] great guns.

and an annceyn of Spanards, and the ij angenes of Iryes men, and the towke the faid towre parforce, and returyn agayn to thes campe. Yefterday byng Satterday, whas 3 Scottes men hang in thes campe, and 9 fcleyn[1] in fild be the horfhemen, and the Scottes fclywe 3 Italians that rod owt of the fyght of their fellowes; and on Monday wy departyt from Kelfey abbey that was, to Rockefborowe menes, and their campeit that nyght; and from thens to Bongedwourthe a tywefeday, and birnyng and theiftroyng all that day bod coryn[2] and howfles, and hee[3] and turff, and a weneffeeday burend Jedwourd [Jedburgh] abbey, and the fryers menore, and all the townes ij myell beyond, as Cavaiers [Cavers], and Denam [Denholm], and Mento, and Mantoncrake [Mintocraig], and Bedrowle, and Towres, and Newton, and Langeton, and Haffenden, and the Barne helles [Barnhills], and the Benetts, and Ancram, and many mor, and returnyd to campe that Wenefday to Egelford, and owaier tryw the Moffe nexht mornyng, and birnd Chesford, and outheir mynd[4] the caftell, but hit whas tow tyke[5] and hitt cowd nott by,[6] and fo thes Thurfeday deftruying and birnyng, campeit att Warke that nyght, and their tharid[7] friday and Satheir[day] the campe, bowt[8] all the carthes[9] went for leed to Kelfey, and the horfhmen birnyng and defttruyng all that day, and fo fare as in to wtin half a quarter of a myell of Howme caftell, and maid all the Scottfmen that were a brod to requiell vnto the caftell walles, and ij of theirs thakeyn that day, and by them reportit that their was 10,000 Scottes men a bowtt the faid caftell, and that the erle of Angoies was com their the nyght be for and 10 cartes wt ordenaunce and munycion, wh I thynyk all was nott trywe, bowt fomat hit was,[10] or men birnd fo ner the caftell, that wy kod[11] nott fee the caftell fomtymes nor the caftell ows, and the of the caftell owaier fott ows[12] all many tymes, and a monges ows yett the howrthe non bowt on[13] horfhe, thanks be to

[1] slain.	[5] it was too thick.	[9] carts.
[2] both corn.	[6] it could not be.	[10] but some of it was.
[3] hay.	[7] tarried.	[11] we could.
[4] undermined.	[8] but.	[12] overshot us.
	[13] they hurt none but one.	

God; and thes down, my lord lowthennaunt returneyd to Wark w^t all his iiij thowſſannt horſhemen and no mor, and loſt neur a man all that day, and yt hit was the most dangerows day that wy[1] had in all the days that wy war in Scotteland; the cartes all of o^r campe wer com to Warke lodon wt the abbey of Kelſey is leed, and leyfft nothyng be heynd and cam ſawff hom to the ſaid casſtell of Warke; and a Sonday wy remowid and paſt the water of Tuyd on the eſt marches of Wark, and birnd and deſtrued Egland, and the nonery cald Colſtreme, and ſo to Fogga, and their campeit that nyght, and many a town birnd that day; and a Monday Downes [Dunse] towre and towne owaretrown[2] and birnd, and all the pares wch is L.[3] towns and willaiges by longeyng to the ſaid Downs; and the nexht day to Weſt Nyſbed, w^c was birnd, and owaier trown the caſtell, and many mor, as hit ſhall apier in a nother place of theis bowke the names of all the townes, and thowres, and abbeys, and fryers, and nonerys, and a charter howſſe; and theis down wy campe theis tywſſeday att o^r Lady church [Lady Kirk] w^tin Scotteland; and a Weneſſeday towke moſters of all o^r holle oſt,[4] and o^r armey deſſolwithe w^t o^r ennemys is land; and att nown cam the lord Lattemer to thake heis leywe, as many otheirs did, of my lord Lowtennannt, but my forſaid lord Lowtennannt maid hym knyght in the ſaid campe, and w^t hym 12 mor, that is to ſay, 13 in all, as hit ſhall a pier by their names; and theis down, euery man that was nott goon[5] departed into England, ſome to Norham Caſtell and town, ſome to Sr Thomas Grey of Horton's howſſ, ſome to Banbery, ſome rod farther, and ſome rod all that nyght, and cartes alſo. The Spanards leyfft[6] att Foſter and Horſley is howſſes, and in the wilaigges[7] their abowt; the Clewoyſſes at Norhamſh^r and town and caſtell, the Italians alſo in that fruntyers, and sorteley[8] after, the Italians cam to Nyw

---

[1] we.

[2] overthrown.

[3] parish, which has 50.

[4] musters of all our whole host.

[5] not gone.

[6] left.

[7] villages.

[8] shortly.

caſtell, and of them moſteres thakeyn and ſent to London Ward; and the Albanneſſes alſo; and after them the Cleywoieſes cam to Nyw caſtell, and the[1] wer ſent to Dowram [Durham], and from dens to Bèwerley[2] for to wynter; and after them the horſhemen, Spanards carles the navara was ſend to London; and the futtemen márceid to Nyw caſtell, and their moſtras thaken of them and payd the remaner in Nyw caſtell and in Dowram, and in Biſhope Acqueleand, and theis wy the[3] partid after all theis orthewyd by the lord lowtenant the x day of October, and came to London the 22 day of thes ſame. God ſaue the Kyng and my Lord Prince Edoward. Amen."

According to the Earl of Hertford's despatches, accompanied with plans, which are not preserved, it was intended to convert the abbey of Kelso into a fortified place. But this plan was abandoned; and in his report of their subsequent proceedings, he exultingly informs the English monarch, that so much damage by fire had not been done in Scotland for the last hundred years. I shall merely add, by way of remark, as it is obvious that, during the intermediate period of fourteen years till the Reformation, the injuries which these Ecclesiastical buildings sustained could have only been partially, if at all repaired, it is attributing too much to John Knox and his brethren, to give them the credit for a work of devastation which had previously been done to their hand.

The York Herald, or the writer of this Journal, refers to a list of the places destroyed during this invasion, as elsewhere contained in his book. No such list is now in the volume; but its loss is supplied by the following paper,[4] if the one was not

---

[1] they.   [2] thence to Beverley.   [3] this way they.

[4] From the Collection of State Papers in the reign of Henry VIII., &c., from 1542 to 1570, published by the Rev. Samuel Haynes. London: 1740, folio, p. 52. In the same Collection, pp. 43-51, will be found another similar document, entitled, "Exployts don upon the Scotts, from the beginning of July, anno 36 R. R.

copied from the other, which is preserved among the Burleigh State Papers, and printed by Haynes. It is curious, and may appropriately be here inserted, as furnishing an important contribution of its kind to the topography of Roxburghshire. It is entitled,

THE NAMES OF THE FORTRESSES, ABBEYS, FRERE-HOUSES, MARKET TOWNES, VILLAGES, TOWRES AND PLACES BRENT, RACED, AND CAST DOUNE, BY THE COMMANDMENT OF THERLL OF HERTFORDE, THE KING'S MAJESTIE'S LIEUTENANT GENERALL IN THE NORTHE PARTES, IN THE INVASION INTO THE REALME OF SCOTLAND, BETWEENE THE 8TH OF SEPTEMBER AND THE 23D OF THE SAME 1545, THE 37TH YEARE OF THE KING'S ROYALL MAJESTIE'S MOSTE PROUSPEROUS AND VICTORIOUS REIGNE.

" On the River of Twede.

" First the abbey of Kelfo raced and caft down; the towne of Kelfo brent; the abbey of Melroffe *alias* Mewrofe, Darnyck, Gawtenfide, Danyelton, Overton, Heildon [Eildon], Newton of Heildon, Maxton, Lafeddon [Lessudden], Merton, Beamondfide [Beamerside], Loughefeatte, Batefhele, the abbey of Drybrughe,

---

Henrici 8th." It consists of an abstract of exploits recorded in various letters, from the 2nd July to the 17th November 1544. The sum total is thus given :—

"Towns, Towers, Stedes, Barnekyns, Parishe Churches,

Bastell-Houses,	192
Scotts slain,	403
Prisoners taken,	816
Nolt.	10,386
Shepe,	12,492
Nags and Geldings,	1296
Gayt,	200
Bulls of Corn,	850
Insight geare, &c."	

the town of Drybrughe, the towre of Dawcowe [Dalcove] raced. The towne of Dawcowe, Rotherford, Stockftrother, Newtowne, Trowes, Makerſton, the Manorhill, Charter-houfe, Lugton Lawe [Lunton Law], Stotherike towre raced; Eaſt Meredean, Weſt Meredean, Flowres [Floors], Gallowe Lawe, Broxe Lawe, Broxe mylne, the water-mill of Kelfo. Sum 33.

" On the River of Tiviot.

" The freers nere Kelfo, the Larde Hog's houfe, the barnes of Old Rockefborough towne, the towre of Rockefborough raced, the towre of Ormeſton raced, the towne of Ormeſton, Neyther Nefebett, Over Nefbet, Angeram [Ancrum], Spittell, Bune Jedworth, the two towres of Bune Jedworth raced, the Lard of Bune Jedworth's dwelling-houfe, Over Angeram, Neyther Angeram, Eaſt Barnehill, Mynto Crag, Mynto towne and place, Weſt Mynto, the Cragge End, Whitrick, Heſſington [Hassindean], Bank-heſſington, Over-heſſington, Cotes, Efshebanke, Cavers, Bryeryards, Denhome, Langton [Lanton], Rowcaſtle, Newtowne, Whitchefterhoufe, Tympinton. Sum 36.

" On the Water of Rowle [Rule].

" Rowle Spittel, Bedrowle, Rowlewood. The Wolles, Croffebewghe, Donnerles, Fotton, Weaſt leas. Two Walke mylnes, Tronnyhill, Dupligis. Sum 12.

" On the Ryver of Jedde.

" The abbey of Jedworthe [Jedburgh], the Freers there; the towne of Jedworthe, Hundylee, Bungate; the Banke end, the Neyther mylnes, Houfſtton, Over Craling, the Wells, Neyther Craling, Over Wodden, Nether Wodden. Sum 13.

" On the Ryver of Kealle [Kale, or Kail] in Eaſte Tividale.

" Over-Hownam, Neyther. Hownam, Hownham Kyrke, New Gatefhaughe; the towre of Gatefhaughe, Over Grobet, Neyther Grobet; Grobet mylne, Wydeopen, Crewkedfhawes, Prymfide,

Mylne Rigge, Marbottell, Otterburne, Cesforthe [Cesford], Over Whitton, Neyther Whitton, Hatherlands, Cesforth burne, Cesforth maynes, Mowe-houfe; the Cowe bogge, Lynton, Caverton, Sharpefrige, Throgdon, Pringle ftede, the Mayne-houfe, Eckforde, Moffehoufe, Wefterbarnes, Grymefley [Grahamslaw], Synles, Heyton on the Hill, Newe Hawe, Maffendewe; the Brig end, St Thomas Chapell, Maxwell heughe, Eaft-Woddon, Weft-Woddon, Howden. Sum 45.

"*On the Ryver of* Bowbent [Beaumont] *in* Eaft Tividale.

"Mowe, Mowe Meufles, Clifton Cote, Colerofte, Elfhenghe, Awton burne, Cowe, Woodfide, Owefnopfide, Felterfhawes, Clifton, Haihope, Kirke Yettam [Yetholm], Towne Yettam, Cherytrees, Barears ; the Bogge, Longhoufe, Fowmerden. Sum 19.

"Hecles [Eccles] *Parish in the* Marffe.

"Long Ednam, Little Newton, Newton mylne, Naynethorne, Naynethorne mylne, Over Stytchell, Nether Stichell, Cowngecarle [Queenscairn], Lagers morre, Oxemoure, Kenetfide, Myckell Harle, Lytell Harle, Haffyngton, Haffyngton maynes, Landen [Lambton], Hardacres, Stanefallde; the abbey of Hecles, the towne there ; Newtowne, Hecclefheales, Grafton Rig, Spittle-fheugh, Over Plewland, Nether Plewland, Over Tofts, Nether Tofts, Clerkeleas, Headrigge, Puddingran, Howden, Marfington, and the towre raced; Letam, Belchefter, Boughtrige, New-bigging, Wranghame, Wester Peles ; the Kemes, the Burne-houfe, Thankles, Rowyngfton, Grymeley Rigge, Cowys, Werke, Whinkerstanes, Fowge Rigge, Foge Banke, Sir James Trennate's houfe, Ryfeley, Bettrikfide, Elbank. Sum 57.

"Donce [Dunse] *Parish.*

"Fowge [Fogo] Towne, Sufterpethe, Sufterpethe mylne, Fowge mylne, the Walke mylne there, the Hill, the New Mylne, Slegh-den, Eaftefeld, Hardames, Stanemore Lawe; the Biers, Wode-

hede, Calldeſide, Lowneſdale; the towre of Red Brayes raced,
the towre of Pollerd [Polwarth] raced, Pollerd Towne, Poller-
wood, the Bow-Houſe, Selburne Rigge, Stocke Fote; the towres
and barmekyn of Neſbed [Nisbet] raced; the towre of Neſbed,
Nesſbed Hill, Crongle, Calledrawe, the Brigend, Gretrig, Growell
Dikes; the towre of Dunce raced, Dounce Lawe, Knocke; the
towne of Dounce, Hare Lawe, Borticke, Eaſt Bortick, Parkehed,
Calldeſide, Black Dikes, Byrkenſide, Kaydeſheale, Redheughe,
Manderſton, Nanewarre, Elfoyle, Cromerſteyn, Kawkey Lawe,
Sampſon's Walles; the Brigg End, the Chcck Lawe, Dounce
mylne, the Eaſt Maynes. Sum 52.

"The Caſtell of Wetherburne, Mongouſe Towre, Pele, Rigge,
Kemergeyme, Kemergeyme maynes, Redheughe, Redes houſe,
Godds Maliſone; the Eaſt Mylne, the Kellawe [Kelloe], Edrame;
the Newe Towne, Blackoter Caſtell raced; the Towne of Black-
eter, White Lawe, Eaſt Lawes, Weſt Lawes, Swynton, and
Whitſonne. Sum 20.   Sum Total, 287

        Whereof (it is added) are—

" In Monaſteries and Frearhouſes, ...   7
  In Caſtells, Towres, and Piles (Peels),   .   .   .   16
  In Market Townes, ...   5
  In Villages, ... 243
  In Mylnes, ...   13
  In Spytells and Hoſpitalls, ...   3
                                                       ———
                                                       287 "

NOTE III.

In the *Proceedings of the Society of Antiquaries, Scotland*, the following interesting paper occurs, and elucidates much that we have but briefly noticed in the 11th Chapter:—

"NOTES ON MELROSE ABBEY; ESPECIALLY IN RE-
FERENCE TO INSCRIPTIONS ON THE WALL OF THE
SOUTH TRANSEPT. BY JOHN ALEXANDER SMITH,
M.D., SEC. S.A. SCOT.

"Some time ago I took a careful tracing of the well-known inscribed tablet on the west wall of the south transept of Melrose abbey, which I exhibit to the Society. The whole surface of the stone is gradually crumbling away, so much so, that it may be feared, in the course of a comparatively short time, the wasting process will obliterate the greater part of the inscription, the lowest lines of which are now quite illegible."

[It is with regard to the two inscriptions on the west side of the wall of the south transept that Dr Smith is speaking. Both refer evidently to the same individual, whether his real name was John Morow or Johne Mordo. He was the "master of work" in the fourteenth century, and not only of the abbey of Melrose, but other of the chief abbacies and cathedral churches in Scotland. Dr Smith proceeds to say]:—

"It appears to me strange that the individual mentioned in this inscription, who seems to have been connected with several of our older ecclesiastical edifices, should now be all but unknown. As the first step, therefore, in any attempt to trace his history, it is of importance to ascertain the correct reading of his name, which, with few exceptions, has been carelessly or incorrectly copied, from its first published appearance in Monteith's *Theater of Mortality*, Part II., in 1713, down to the recent valuable work of Mr Billings, on the *Baronial and Ecclesiastical Antiquities of Scotland.*

" Adjoining to the tablet in the wall already referred to, and over the centre of a doorway on the same side of the south transept, there is a sunk panel inclosing a shield, which displays two mason's compasses, partially opened, laid across one another, so as to form a figure somewhat like a saltire, and on each side, and in base, what has been described as a *fleur-de-lis;* forming probably a combined masonic and heraldic blazon. The compass is the badge of a Master Mason, and the three lilies may be those of the shield of France, his native country. On each side of this panel there are the remains of a black letter inscription in relief, which bears marks of having possibly been retouched, although I am inclined to consider the different states of preservation of the letters to be dependent principally on the varying hardness and durability of the stones employed. The explanation given of it in the oldest authority I can find—viz., Monteith's *Theater of Mortality*—including apparently the carving on the shield itself, as if it were symbolic of a sword, is as follows :—

> ' *Above another Door in the said Church.*

> ' Even as the Compass gaes even about,
>   So doth Truth and Lauty, but doubt.
>   Behold to the End of John Murvo.'

It is next published by the Rev. Mr Adam Milne, in his *Description of Melrose Parish*, 1743, in the following terms:—

> ' Sa gayes the compass ev'n about,
>   So truth and laute do but doubt.
>   Behald to the end.   JOHN MURDO.'

The inscription, from the partially wasted surface of the stone, and the unequal spaces between some of the words, is manifestly imperfect, and the explanation given above can scarcely be confirmed now from inspection. I shall, however, only notice the latter part of it, which is cut in the same style of raised lettering on the bevelled edge of the doorway across the top, returning a short way down the left side, and ending with the name MORVO, which runs across the surface of the wall; it is as follows:—BE : HALDE : TO : YE : HENDE : Q : JOHNE : MORVO : not Behold, as it is described, but BE : HALDE : (*i.e.*, let it be held, or holden) TO THE END QUOTH JOHN MORVO ; the conclusion apparently of a devout sentiment of laute or praise, at the termination, shall we say, of the restorations of the building, which he who had the mason work in keeping prays may be held to the end, attesting it by his name. Here the name seems to read MORVO; I took casts of this and of the other name at the commencment of the inscribed tablet; and these which I exhibit have been carefully copied in the subjoined woodcuts :—

[From Inscribed Tablet.]

[From Inscription over Doorway.]

" In the tablet, JOHN : MOROW : is described as having been born in Paris, reminding one of the French name of MOREAU ; yet from the use of the final W (unless we suppose this a subsequent change), we must believe him to have been not French but of foreign extraction. The two names are in all likelihood the same, the latter possibly a monkish change for euphony's sake at the close of the inscription, the second last letter resembling the (b) *v* in *even* of the former part of this inscription, and the last being O; unless indeed we should consider the two last letters to be VV, or to form an imperfect W, and the O to be omitted, as occurs on the inscribed tablet with the name of Glasgow, GLASGW. The name Morow reminds me very much of the local Roxburghshire pronunciation of the Scottish name of Murray, which is exactly similar in sound to Morow; but I know no instance of the name of Murray being spelled like the former.

" We may conjecture that, in addition to this sculptured doorway, inscribed with the old mason's name,—possibly ' In memoriam,' to hand down to later times some information regarding the man who had brought his work so successfully to a conclusion,—the tablet detailing his place of birth and the responsible offices he held, was prepared, and the finished ashlar wall of the transept cut into for its reception; as shown by its being cut a little into the string course which runs below it, as well as by the long narrow stone, unlike the shape of the other courses, which is placed vertically across them on the outside of the tablet at the one end, so as to complete the building of the wall, which had been broken up. This inscription, which has its moulded framing decorated with a series of richly-carved leaves, now almost obliterated, also concludes in devout prayers, in this case for the preservation of the building.

" Mr Billings states that no portion of the present buildings of Melrose abbey appear to be more ancient than the fifteenth century, and he refers, in connexion with the French forms of architecture in this and the other Scottish ecclesiastical buildings, to the tablet now described, which he believes cannot be older than the sixteenth century; he says, " It is not likely that MURDO, . whose name would indicate a Scottish origin, performed any functions beyond repairs and restorations.' Some parts of the present abbey have, with considerable certainty, been ascribed to the latter half of the fourteenth century. The inscribed tablet evidently dates from an earlier period than that fixed on by Mr Billings, for reasons to be afterwards stated; and I cannot but think the sculptured lintel of the old doorway (the details of which he figures incorrectly in his view of the south transept; and to which he does not allude in connection with the mason), tells a tale of ancient, as well as very considerable, renovation of the old abbey. Indeed, the state of apparent imperfection of this inscribed doorway, which may have been assumed from the varying size of the stones with which it is built, is no proof of any comparatively modern repair; as the same thing may be remarked in other parts of the building, where there is not the slightest appearance of any recent restorations having taken place, and was most probably dependent on the difficulty the builders had experienced in getting proper materials, rather than on any comparatively recent patching up of the old walls.

" The planting of the inscribed tablet in what was the finished wall of the transept, I am inclined, as I have already stated, to look upon as an after-thought of rather later date than the sculptured doorway. It is a very difficult matter to attempt to solve the subject of dates; yet, as a step in that direction, I may notice the position which these inscriptions in the transept wall bear to the styles of architecture shown in the adjoining parts of the ruined abbey. We find, then, these inscriptions occupying apparently a central position in the midst of highly-finished masonry of excellent design and workmanship, of the Curvilinear or Decorated style, as shown in the great south window immediately adjoining over the doorway of the transept, with its flowing tracery, and richly-sculptured and canopied niches outside; and the architecture apparently runs into newer styles on each side.

" In conclusion, I may state, that from these inscriptions in the transept wall, and the position which they bear to the rest of the building, I am inclined to believe that, under his ' kepyng the finest and perhaps most ancient part of this southern range of the abbey, instead of mere modern restorations and repairs, had in all probability been executed. It would be interesting, therefore, by a careful examination of the Chartularies of the churches and abbeys mentioned in the inscribed tablet, and other old records such as the Chamberlain's Rolls, to ascer-

tain whether any notices might be gleaned respecting JOHN
MOROW, to whose genius as a master mason, or architect, so
many of our old Scottish buildings may have been indebted
for their architectural order and beauty; and, may we not suppose, that having concluded his various works with Melrose
abbey, some friendly hand had there placed his final stone of
memorial, as a record of his labours."

ERRATA.

Page 233, Andrew Hunter, abbot of Melrose, 1844, *read* 1444.

"   265, foot note, *for* William Sorouells, *read* Soroueles.

"   342, *for* William Hog, *read* William Hoy.

INDEX.

PRINTED BY ANDREW JACK, CLYDE STREET, EDINBURGH.

"A sensible, practical, elegantly-got-up poultry manual, from the refined pen of a lady who thoroughly understands and delights in her subject, is a most welcome addition to the works we already have upon poultry management. Mrs Fergusson Blair has paid such intelligent attention to her favourite pursuit, that she herself has taken, as she tells us in her prettily-written preface, upwards of 460 prizes. . . . We can only recommend our readers to buy Mrs Blair's book, and to judge of its merits for themselves."—*The Field.*

"Farmers declare that poultry-rearing is profitless business; but they would not repeat this if they inspected Mrs Blair's diaries, day-books, and balance-sheets. The said balance-sheet is appended to this volume, and shows a total profit of £26, 17s., but we should conceive that very few poultry-rearers, especially of her own sex, would equal Mrs Blair. Where are the ladies who would become so precise in accounts, in eggs, in chickens, and in ornithological merchandise, even to the selling of feathers and down in the best market? Where, too, is there such concentration of affection and care for a feathered family as to make them feather the Henwife's own nest, at the same time that they feed her own fancies, and her own family? Here we have feminine persistence, Scotch thrift, and fanciful indulgence combined in one lady."—*The Athenæum.*

"This is one of the most genial and instructive little books —thoroughly practical—that we have lately met with. Mrs Blair is completely mistress of her subject."—*The Era.*

"Men who never thought of hen-houses in their lives may read this book with pleasure. Such as are in any way addicted to poultry cannot fail to read it with advantage, whilst, to every one ambitious of the honours of the show-yard, we would recommend the volume as a text-book. They will see that the path to fame is the same in regard to poultry as it is with Mr Webb's southdowns, or Mr Douglass's shorthorns—constant care, perfect cleanliness, food without stint, and that of the best description. As an increaser of the food of the nation, and the provider of a daintier dish, such poultry fanciers as Mrs Blair are benefactors of the public."—*North British Agriculturist.*

"This is a capital book,—one of the most complete of the kind."—*Leeds Times.*

In Small 8vo., with Numerous Illustrations, price 7s. 6d.,

Dairy Stock:

ITS SELECTION, DISEASES, AND PRODUCE.

WITH A DESCRIPTION OF THE BRITTANY BREED.

BY JOHN GAMGEE,

PRINCIPAL OF THE NEW VETERINARY COLLEGE, EDINBURGH.

"In this well written, well illustrated, and in every respect commendable volume, Mr Gamgee has done for Stock-keepers what Lord St. Leonards, in his 'Handy Book on Property Law,' did for the possessors of real and personal estate. . . . The farmer and the amateur stock-keeper may alike read it with profit."—*The Athenæum.*

"Mr Gamgee treats his subject in a philosophical style, and is evidently thoroughly master of the nature of the diseases of cattle."—*British Medical Journal.*

"The work is replete with interest to the Veterinarian, and filled with matters most instructive and valuable to the owners of Dairy stock."—*The Field.*

"Information, varied in kind, and of the most valuable nature, is here presented in a most convenient form, and within the reach of any man—or woman either—who possesses a cow, and wishes to know how to manage her in health or in disease."—*Weekly Agricultural Review.*

"Our readers are constantly making inquiry for a reliable work on the diseases of cattle and their remedies; we confidently recommend to them the above work: indeed, no Stockholder should be without it."—*Irish Farmers' Gazette.*

"Well worthy of perusal by all interested in dairy stock management."—*Dumfries Courier.*

"A handy readable book, free from unnecessary technicality, serviceable to every one who keeps a cow, and interesting even to consumers of dairy produce."—*Caledonian Mercury.*

"To say that a thing is worth its weight in gold is a figurative expression, indicating great value; but the saying might be used literally in reference to this book."—*Perthshire Advertiser.*

"A very handy and excellent manual for breeders and owners of stock."—*Bristol Mercury.*

To be completed in Twenty Parts, price 1s. each,

COPIOUSLY ILLUSTRATED,

Our Domestic Animals

IN HEALTH AND DISEASE.

BY JOHN GAMGEE,

PRINCIPAL OF THE NEW VETERINARY COLLEGE, EDINBURGH ;

AUTHOR OF "DAIRY STOCK," "THE VETERINARIAN'S VADE-MECUM,"

EDITOR OF "THE EDINBURGH VETERINARY REVIEW," ETC., ETC.

"We have recently reviewed in favourite terms, an able book on 'Dairy Stock,' by the distinguished Principal of the New Edinburgh College. We have now to perform a similar office, with relation to a work, the importance of which, both to the man of practice and the theorist, it would be difficult to over-estimate. Happily, we have truly enlightened and scientific men who are possessed of the rare gift of communicating the knowledge which they and their colleagues possess, in a manner so plain as to be intelligible to the meanest capacity. Such a man we have in Professor Gamgee, who is now doing for Veterinary science what Leibig and Johnston have done for agricultural chemistry, and the late Professor Wilson for scientific agriculture. We could expand to a considerable extent on the many excellencies of this—the first instalment of Professor Gamgee's admirable work."— *Weekly Agricultural Review.*

"The ever-active Principal of the New Veterinary College commences, in this shilling number of sixty-four pages, a work which is intended to set forth, within moderate compass, and with a view to the wants of the breeder, grazier, and owner of stock generally, 'the knowledge possessed at the present day on questions relating to the preservation and restoration of the health of our domestic animals.' There is plenty of matter in this number level to the capacity of every ordinarily educated reader, and yet thoroughly informed with the spirit of modern science. It is also, in all respects, well got up, the wood-cuts, paper, and type, being alike excellent, and the price moderate."— *Scotsman.*

"No stock-owner should be without such a work."— *John O'Groat Journal.*

Fairbairn's Crests
OF THE
FAMILIES OF GREAT BRITAIN AND IRELAND.
In two vols., Royal 8vo.   Price L.3, 13s. 6d.

Fine Edition, 2 vols., Royal 4to, India Proof Plates.
Price L.6, 6s.

REVISED BY LAURENCE BUTTERS,

SEAL ENGRAVER IN ORDINARY TO THE QUEEN FOR SCOTLAND.

CONTENTS OF VOLUME I.

1. Index of all the Families of Great Britain and Ireland, with the Description of their Crests and Mottoes.

2. Glossary of Terms used in Heraldry.

3. Alphabetical Index of the Mottoes, with their Translations, and the Names of the Families that bear each.

CONTENTS OF VOLUME II.

1. 146 Plates of Crests, Monograms, Flags, Arms of Principal Cities, &c., &c., beautifully engraved.

2. Key to the Plates, showing the Families that bear each Crest.

" These two magnificent volumes do honour to the Scottish capital, whence they emanate.   They evince an amount of patient research and useful labour, in their own peculiar field, that is creditable to all concerned. . . . The second volume is entirely filled with a series of exquisitely engraved plates of crests, &c., upwards of 2000 in number.   Need we say more in recommendation of so useful and beautiful a reference book."—*The Art Journal.*

Mottoes
OF THE
FAMILIES OF GREAT BRITAIN AND IRELAND.
Price 3s.

This forms a complete Dictionary of the Mottoes used in this country, with correct Translations, and the Names of the Families bearing each attached.

Wade's History of Melrose Abbey.

Just published, price 9s. 6d.,

HISTORY OF ST. MARY'S ABBEY, MELROSE;

ST. CUTHBERT'S CHAPEL AND MONASTERY,

OLD MELROSE;

THE TOWN AND PARISH OF MELROSE;

AND ALL PLACES OF TOPOGRAPHICAL INTEREST IN THE DISTRICT:

COMPRISING

The Monastic Annals of these Abbeys, their Architectural Embellishments, and Antiquarian Remains.

Illustrated with Plates, from Drawings taken on the spot.

BY JAMES A. WADE, DARNICK.

The Work embraces the STREAM OF HISTORY in connection with the DISTRICT OF MELROSE from the SIXTH to the EIGHTEENTH CENTURY; and narrates BATTLES, FORAYS, INVASIONS, STATE of SOCIETY, and AGRICULTURE in these parts; also, ANTIQUITIES, ARCHITECTURE, ECCLESIASTICAL POLITY, BIOGRAPHY of EMINENT CHARACTERS, GENERAL HISTORY and POLITICS.

Jeffrey's History of Roxburghshire.

HISTORY AND ANTIQUITIES

OF

Roxburghshire and Adjacent Districts,

FROM THE MOST REMOTE PERIOD TO THE PRESENT TIME.

BY ALEXANDER JEFFREY, F.R.A.S.

3 Volumes, Post 8vo. Price 25s.

"The information stored up and communicated by Mr Jeffrey is both valuable and interesting, and the style clear, succinct, and readable. Although the book is crowded with facts and information, Mr Jeffrey has successfully avoided the too common temptation of telling us long stories, simply because they are old; his selection has been careful and judicious. To the student of history generally, as well as to those with local ties in the county, the work will prove useful and instructive."—*The Scotsman.*

Price One Shilling,

On the Management of Pit Horses.

By CHARLES HUNTING,

VETERINARY SURGEON TO THE SOUTH HETTON, MURTON, EAST HETTON, AND TRIMDON GRANGE COAL COMPANIES, DURHAM.

Chronological Cards

FOR

EIGHT CENTURIES, FROM A.D. 1000 TO A.D. 1800.

BY A. W. HOPE JOHNSTONE.

Price 4s. in a Case.

These Cards are intended to aid the student in the study of history. Each Century is divided into Quarters, and in each are given the Great Sovereigns, Statesmen of Note, and Eminent Characters that lived, and the Great Events that transpired in that period.

BY THE REV. JOHN PULSFORD.

I.

Quiet Hours.

First Series.　Fifth Edition.　Price 6s.

II.

Quiet Hours.

New Series.　Price 7s. 6d.

" This is a remarkable book. There is a ring in its substance which reminds us of the pith and weight by which not a little of our old English authorship has been characterised. The thought and feeling are truly and deeply Scriptural and Christian. But there is a strength in both which is not a little refreshing in these days of so much formal and conventional authorship. Give it as present, reader, where you wish to induce a Christian thoughtfulness, a reverence of sacred truth, and all things sacred."—*British Quarterly Review.*

www.ingramcontent.com/pod-product-compliance
Lightning Source LLC
Chambersburg PA
CBHW032309280326
41932CB00009B/753